"Efforts to demonstrate academic standards across universities amidst concerns about grade inflation often clash with attempts to use meaningful assessment aligned with learning outcomes. This book fills an important gap in the literature on this topic. It clearly outlines the issues and evaluates current practices such as the use of external examiners. But its greatest strength is detailing a range of strategies for improving existing methods, grounding formal descriptors of achievement, and developing consistency in assessment judgements within and across institutions. I'd highly recommend it, especially to those who think they don't have a problem with academic standards."

Sue Bloxham, *Professor Emerita in Academic Practice, University of Cumbria, UK*

Academic Standards in Higher Education

Academic standards in higher education are important but largely misunderstood. This book examines the notion of academic standards, explaining what they are and why they are important, and identifying the many myths that surround them.

Based on the lessons learnt from the UK-wide Degree Standards Project, which developed, piloted and evaluated a Professional Development Course on degree standards aimed at external examiners, the book offers practical suggestions for ways in which higher education staff can develop a more sophisticated understanding of standards. It discusses the implications of rethinking academic standards for higher education policy and practice, through examples and case studies derived from research evidence, the Degree Standards Project and contributors' own experience and expertise. As a broader approach to assessment literacy, the book aims to develop readers' understanding of academic standards by challenging routine practices and proposing promising alternatives.

Written with a diverse readership in mind, this book is relevant to discipline-based academics, quality officers, academic developers, university leaders and managers, as well as policy makers.

Nicola Reimann is an Associate Professor in Academic Practice in the School of Education and the Centre for Academic Development at Durham University, UK.

Ian Sadler is a Reader and Subject Head in the School of Sport and Exercise Sciences at Liverpool John Moores University, UK.

Jennifer Hill is Head of Learning and Teaching Innovation, and Professor of Higher Education Pedagogies at the University of Gloucestershire, UK.

Academic Standards in Higher Education

Critical Perspectives and Practical Strategies

Edited by
Nicola Reimann, Ian Sadler and
Jennifer Hill

LONDON AND NEW YORK

Designed cover image: © Getty Images

First published 2025
by Routledge
4 Park Square, Milton Park, Abingdon, Oxon OX14 4RN

and by Routledge
605 Third Avenue, New York, NY 10158

Routledge is an imprint of the Taylor & Francis Group, an informa business

© 2025 selection and editorial matter, Nicola Reimann, Ian Sadler and Jennifer Hill; individual chapters, the contributors

The right of Nicola Reimann, Ian Sadler and Jennifer Hill to be identified as the authors of the editorial material, and of the authors for their individual chapters, has been asserted in accordance with sections 77 and 78 of the Copyright, Designs and Patents Act 1988.

All rights reserved. No part of this book may be reprinted or reproduced or utilised in any form or by any electronic, mechanical, or other means, now known or hereafter invented, including photocopying and recording, or in any information storage or retrieval system, without permission in writing from the publishers.

Trademark notice: Product or corporate names may be trademarks or registered trademarks, and are used only for identification and explanation without intent to infringe.

British Library Cataloguing in Publication Data
A catalogue record for this book is available from the British Library

Library of Congress Cataloging-in-Publication Data
Names: Reimann, Nicola, editor. | Sadler, Ian, 1977- editor. | Hill, Jennifer, 1969- editor.
Title: Academic standards in higher education : critical perspectives and practical strategies / edited by Nicola Reimann, Ian Sadler and Jennifer Hill.
Description: Abingdon, Oxon ; New York, NY : Routledge, 2024. | Includes bibliographical references and index. | Identifiers: LCCN 2024018349 (print) | LCCN 2024018350 (ebook) | ISBN 9781032460277 (hardback) | ISBN 9781032460260 (paperback) | ISBN 9781003379768 (ebook)
Subjects: LCSH: Education, Higher–Standards–Great Britain. | Education, Higher–Evaluation–Great Britain. | Educational accountability–Great Britain. | Universities and colleges–Accreditation–Great Britain. | Universities and colleges–Ratings and rankings–Great Britain.
Classification: LCC LB2331.65.G7 A43 2024 (print) | LCC LB2331.65.G7 (ebook) | DDC 378.41–dc23/eng/20240429
LC record available at https://lccn.loc.gov/2024018349
LC ebook record available at https://lccn.loc.gov/2024018350

ISBN: 9781032460277 (hbk)
ISBN: 9781032460260 (pbk)
ISBN: 9781003379768 (ebk)

DOI: 10.4324/9781003379768

Typeset in Galliard
by Taylor & Francis Books

Contents

List of figures   x
List of tables   xi
List of boxes   xii
List of contributors   xiv
Acknowledgements   xvi

1 Introduction   1
IAN SADLER, NICOLA REIMANN AND JENNIFER HILL

PART I
Academic standards context and concepts   9

2 Assuring academic standards: Policy and practice in context   11
CHRIS RUST AND BERRY O'DONOVAN

3 The complexities of academic standards as a contested concept   25
MARGARET PRICE AND BERRY O'DONOVAN

4 Academic standards in a globalised world   37
JON YORKE

PART II
Common responses to the social construction of academic standards   55

5 The role of internal and external moderation for assuring academic standards   57
ANDY LLOYD AND RACHEL FORSYTH

6 External examining: A peer-led system for guarding academic standards 71
MARGARET PRICE

7 Demystifying the role of the external examiner through the lens of assessment literacy 80
EMMA MEDLAND

8 Using social processes to maintain academic standards: Social moderation and calibration 93
NICOLA REIMANN AND IAN SADLER

PART IIIA
Professional development to reduce variation in academic standards 107

9 Strengthening professional development provision for external examiners: The UK Degree Standards Project 109
GEOFF STOAKES AND ERICA J. MORRIS

10 Designing and developing the Professional Development Course for External Examiners 123
ANDY LLOYD AND RACHEL FORSYTH

11 The institutional impact of the Professional Development Course for External Examiners: A case study 136
AMANDA PILL

12 Lessons learnt from the evaluation of the Degree Standards Project 147
JOANNE MOORE

PART IIIB
Practical strategies for reducing variation in academic standards 167

13 Working with rubrics: Codification plus dialogue in developing shared academic standards 169
PETE BOYD AND JENNIFER HILL

14 The need for calibration in the disciplines: A case study from sport and exercise science 186
IAN SADLER AND MATTHEW A. TIMMIS

15 The need for calibration in the disciplines: A case study from geography 202
JENNIFER HILL, HELEN WALKINGTON, BEN PAGE AND STEPHANIE WYSE

16 Making holistic pairwise judgements: Comparative judgement   217
    IAN JONES

17 Taking stock and looking ahead   227
    JENNIFER HILL, NICOLA REIMANN AND IAN SADLER

    Index   239

Figures

4.1	The intersection of globalisation, accountability, quality, learning standards and assessment.	39
5.1	Matrix used to evaluate the effectiveness of the different moderation strategies, as used on the Professional Development Course.	64
5.2	Mean position in which each moderation strategy was placed (based on 200 completed grids).	65
12.1	Numbers participating in professional developments for external examiners by type of delivery and academic year.	153
12.2	All PDC completers by institutional type.	154
14.1	Relevant descriptors for a Level 4 Exercise Physiology Laboratory Report to show the multi-layered nature of reference points and criteria that guide academic standards and marking judgements (using the example of one particular university course, module and assessment task).	189
14.2	Mark variation for three assignments graded prior to a sport and exercise science calibration workshop ($n = 23$).	194
16.1	An illustration of discriminal dispersion (in this example most often B would be chosen over A).	218

Tables

9.1	Modes of delivery for the Professional Development Course.	112
9.2	Stages of the recognition process for new facilitators: Face-to-face and remote delivery.	114
11.1	Timeline of PDC delivery at the University of Gloucestershire.	139
12.1	Perceived change in relation to the PDC learning outcomes based on pre- and post-course survey responses.	157
12.2	Outcomes of the PDC for development of internal academic practice within the institution.	160
13.1	A basic outline for an analytical rubric for use in the UK, with no weighting of assessment criteria.	173
13.2	Exemplar module assessment instructions, including learning outcomes and assessment criteria.	176
13.3	The crucial first step of completing the 'pass' column for an education studies module rubric.	177
14.1	Difference in mark from the mean based on the institution type of the assessor.	194
14.2	Considerations to make explicit in the design of a calibration workshop.	196
14.3	Key reflections on a calibration workshop with example quotes to support.	197
15.1	Common approaches that aim to reduce variation in the judgement of academic standards.	205
15.2	Marks awarded to final year geography coursework essays pre- and post-calibration.	210

Boxes

2.1	The achievement of consistent assessment standards	17
3.1	Codifying standards: Delusions of objectivity and uniformity of interpretation	27
3.2	Assessment criteria: A matter of interpretation	30
4.1	The difficulty of establishing objective standards through codification	40
5.1	Summary of the interplay between quality standards and academic standards and the role of moderation	66
6.1	The importance of peer review in external examining	73
6.2	The need for professionalisation of the external examining system	75
6.3	Stakeholder commitment to the external examiner system	77
7.1	Two pillars of external examining	80
7.2	Assessment literacy is under-conceptualised	82
7.3	External examiner perceptions of assessment literacy	84
7.4	Inconsistent recognition of internal standards	87
7.5	External examiner experience, internal standards, and confidence in the system	88
7.6	The importance of developing a shared language of assessment literacy	89
8.1	Within-module social moderation as a developmental opportunity for staff on casual part-time contracts, Australia	98
8.2	Calibration workshops in accounting, Australia	99
8.3	External peer review of standards in pairs and threes, multiple disciplines, Australia	99
8.4	Characteristics of student work in hospitality, sport, leisure and tourism at different grade levels, UK	100
9.1	The development and delivery of large-scale professional development provision	121
10.1	Key messages in session 1 of the PDC	126
10.2	Key messages in session 2 of the PDC	127
10.3	Key messages in session 3 of the PDC	129
10.4	Key messages in session 4 of the PDC	130

10.5	Key messages in session 5 of the PDC	130
10.6	Key messages in session 6 of the PDC	131
10.7	Key messages in session 7 of the PDC	132
10.8	Key messages in session 8 of the PDC	133
11.1	Opening section of University of Gloucestershire's external examiner report template	142
12.1	Approach to the evaluation of the PDC	150
12.2	Effective design features of the PDC in the UK context	162
13.1	Key questions to ask about your use of rubrics	169
13.2	Six steps in creating an effective rubric	174
13.3	Key points on rubrics	181
15.1	The opportunities and challenges of undertaking calibration in geography	212
16.1	Reflecting upon comparative judgement in your subject area	219
16.2	Your first comparative judgement assessment	223

Contributors

Pete Boyd is Professor Emeritus at the University of Cumbria and Visiting Professor at the University of Hertfordshire, UK.

Rachel Forsyth is an educational developer at Lund University, Sweden.

Jennifer Hill is Head of Learning and Teaching Innovation and Professor of Higher Education Pedagogies at the University of Gloucestershire, UK.

Ian Jones is Reader in Education Assessment and Head of the Department of Mathematics Education at Loughborough University, UK.

Andy Lloyd is Senior Education Developer in the Learning and Teaching Academy at Cardiff University, UK.

Emma Medland is Senior Lecturer in Higher Education and Programme Director of the MA in Higher Education at the Surrey Institute of Education, University of Surrey, UK.

Joanne Moore is a researcher and evaluator specialising in the learning and skills sector in the UK.

Erica J. Morris is Head of Academic Practice at the University of Northampton, UK.

Berry O'Donovan is Professor of Learning and Assessment at the Business School, Oxford Brookes University, UK.

Ben Page is Professor of Human Geography and African Studies at University College London, UK.

Amanda Pill was Director of Quality Enhancement at the University of Gloucestershire, UK, until her retirement in May 2023.

Margaret Price is Professor Emerita of Assessment and Learning in Higher Education at Oxford Brookes University, UK.

Nicola Reimann is Associate Professor in Academic Practice, both in the School of Education and the Centre for Academic Development at Durham University, UK.

Chris Rust is Emeritus Professor of Higher Education and was Associate Dean (Academic Policy) at Oxford Brookes University, UK.

Ian Sadler is Subject Head in the School of Sport and Exercise Sciences and Reader in Sport and Exercise Science Education at Liverpool John Moores University, UK.

Geoff Stoakes is an Associate at AdvanceHE and was formerly Vice Principal at Plymouth Marjon University and Head of Research at the Higher Education Academy, UK.

Matthew A. Timmis is Director of Student Outcomes in the Faculty of Science and Engineering and Associate Professor of Learning and Teaching in Sport and Exercise Science at Anglia Ruskin University, UK.

Helen Walkington is Professor of Higher Education in the School of Law and Social Sciences at Oxford Brookes University, UK.

Stephanie Wyse is formerly of the Royal Geographical Society (with Institute of British Geographers), UK.

Jon Yorke is Associate Deputy Vice Chancellor Academic & Academic Registrar at Curtin University, Australia.

Acknowledgements

Many of the ideas and practices within this book emerged from the work of the AdvanceHE Degree Standards Project (2016–2021). The original team (as of February 2018) who developed the content for the Professional Development Course were:

Professor Sue Bloxham (Consultant), University of Cumbria
Meg House (Senior Administrator), AdvanceHE
Louise Lambourne (Project Manager), AdvanceHE
Andy Lloyd (Consultant), Cardiff University
Dr Teresa McConlogue (Consultant), University College London
Dr Erica Morris (Academic Lead), AdvanceHE
Professor Margaret Price (Consultant), Oxford Brookes University
Dr Nicola Reimann (Consultant), Durham University
Professor Chris Rust (Consultant), Oxford Brookes University
Janine Scheepers (Senior Administrator), AdvanceHE
Dr Geoff Stokes (Head of Special Projects), AdvanceHE

Chapter 1

Introduction

Ian Sadler, Nicola Reimann and Jennifer Hill

Context for academic standards in higher education

Standards are ubiquitous in the modern world, whether that be the practical standard of driving required to pass a driving test or the professional standard required to practise as a doctor. However, these standards are often difficult to communicate and they take time and require multiple points of reference to fully grasp and understand. Academic standards in higher education are no different and to some extent have additional complexity and are even less tangible. They are wrapped up in and vary based on different levels of study, different subjects or (sub) disciplines and the different nature of knowledge, understanding and skills. Despite the complexity of standards, we are often required to make judgements about whether someone meets the standard or not. It is a judgement about level of competence, whether that be the ability to drive a car, treat ill health or have sufficient knowledge, skills and understanding in a particular subject area to be awarded a degree.

The award of a degree qualification is one of the main outcomes of a higher education programme and certifies the achievement of a particular standard. Degree programmes tend to identify different levels of achievement (for instance, UK degrees are classified as first, upper second, lower second, third class, fail or unclassified). What underpins this award are the judgements by the academic staff about the quality of the student performances or assessments that contribute to the final degree. At the core of these judgements are the academic standards that the individuals hold, which Bloxham et al. (2011) have referred to as an individual *standards framework*. This is considered to be one of several important influences upon the decision made about the quality of student work. Based on this centrality, there is little within higher education that is not 'touched' to some extent by the concept of academic standards. It is far reaching and interacts with so many aspects of and people within a university, including those in academic registry and exams offices, colleagues in student support services, quality assurance officers, senior managers, industry and external consultants and of course external examiners.

Higher education systems globally are facing a great deal of external scrutiny, with increased attention placed on issues such as access, affordability, educational quality and graduate employability. With particular reference to this edited

DOI: 10.4324/9781003379768-1

collection, international concern has been expressed about the quality and standards of higher education as it has moved from an elite to a mass system at the same time as experiencing reductions in public funding, increased free market competition and heightened transparency, essentially commodifying educational practice (Sadler, 2017; Baker, 2018; O'Leary & Cui, 2020; Jephcote et al., 2021). Yet within this challenging environment, student attainment, as expressed in degree outcomes, has been rising steadily in many countries. The higher education sector internationally is awarding more first and upper second-class degrees than in the past, despite increasing cohort sizes (Jephcote et al., 2021). Chapter 15, for example, highlights that almost 85% of UK-domiciled, full-time, first-degree graduates in England achieved 'good' (first and upper second class) degrees in 2020–2021, increasing from 67% in 2010–2011 (OfS, 2022). This has raised concern within and beyond the sector as it seems counter intuitive that as more students enter the system there is an apparent rise in the academic achievement (standards) of a broader and more varied intake of students.

Explaining a rise in degree outcomes, studies across higher education institutions have highlighted higher student entry qualifications, developments in curricula, research-informed pedagogy, authentic assessments and improvements in student support as factors that largely account for graduates attaining higher grades (Jephcote et al., 2021). The evidence for grade improvement, however, is often based on individual teacher adaptations, often within particular disciplines and with limited data (Bell & Lygo-Baker, 2019). This has consequently led to allegations by politicians and journalists of grade 'inflation'; the upward shifting of grades without a corresponding increase in learning (Rosovsky & Hartley, 2002) (see Chapter 2). Adding further to this, student success and higher quality work has become a key performance indicator for those academic staff who are making judgements about the standard of student work.

To further exacerbate the issue of grade inflation, there is a pretence within the higher education sector that marking and the award of degrees is reliable. Inconsistency of standards, based on the grades or marks that are used to represent them, has been shown repeatedly in the research literature. Under blind marking conditions empirical studies have shown significant variation in the marks awarded for the same piece of work (for example, Baume et al., 2004; O'Hagan & Wigglesworth, 2015; Rinne, 2024). This research has shown sizable variability in a single assessment item in the same department or university. However, a degree is based upon multiple assessment items over several years and the same award is offered by a large number of different institutions. Therefore the potential for variability in the degree awarded for students at a similar academic standard in terms of their level of knowledge, skills and understanding is extremely large. Universities claim to students, public, professional bodies and funding bodies that the degrees they award are fair, consistent and reliable. However, based on the nature of academic standards and the research on their variability, we would argue that this is unlikely to be the case. Consequently, this book aims to consider ways in which we can achieve greater consistency, which institutional policies and regulations imply exist.

Despite the importance and centrality of academic standards, the assessment in higher education literature over the past two decades has tended to focus more upon assessment for learning (e.g. Sambell et al., 2012) and learning orientated assessment (e.g. Carless, 2007). Although the dual purpose or 'double duty' (Boud, 2000) of assessment has been acknowledged, the main narrative within the assessment literature has been to emphasise the formative/learning duty and to background the summative/certification duty. For example, Gipps (2011) distinguishes between assessment to support learning, assessment for certification and assessment for accountability. The argument made by Gipps is that there has been an emphasis in practice on assessment for certification and accountability and that there needs to be more of a focus on assessment to support learning. As marking and academic standards are associated with the measurement, testing and certification paradigm, which the assessment for learning movement was trying to move away from, this area of assessment has been more neglected from a research and scholarship point of view. This can also be observed in professional development courses for higher education staff, where the assessment related content does not tend to consider issues of marking and standards and the focus is more upon issues of assessment design. The current book aims to make a contribution to the academic standards aspect of assessment. However, it is important to stress that it does not come from a conventional positivist position in terms of reliability and validity of testing standards in an objective manner. Similar to the stance of the assessment for learning movement, we see academic standards from a socio-constructivist perspective in that marks and standards are not separate from the individuals and communities involved in the judgements being made.

Based on this external landscape, the Office for Students (OfS) funded a 5-year UK Degree Standards Project that was delivered by AdvanceHE (AHE). AHE is a member-based charity for the sector that works in the UK and beyond to support and improve higher education for staff, students and society (AHE, 2024). The concept of academic standards was central to the Degree Standards Project. The key mechanism for assuring standards across institutions in the UK is the external examining system. This is a peer-led process whereby an external expert from a similar academic or professional area scrutinises the assessment processes and marks awarded for student work on a specific named award or degree programme. The Project comprised a team of experts in higher education assessment (a) developing a UK-wide Professional Development Course for external examiners and (b) piloting approaches to calibrating the academic standards of individuals within a discipline area. Both the Professional Development Course and the calibration activities took a socio-constructivist approach to reducing the variation in standards through the use of consensus seeking dialogue. This book was conceived to capture much of the thinking and approaches that were developed as part of these project activities and they feature throughout the majority of the chapters. Although external examining and the Degree Standards Project are UK-specific, there are broader lessons for assurance of academic standards in other countries and contexts.

Overview of the structure of the book

The book is structured into three main parts. Part I is made up of chapters that consider theoretical ideas, key concepts, debates and developments relating to academic standards. These chapters provide a *critical perspective* and problematise the notion of academic standards. The second and third parts of the book consider the *practical strategies* for increasing consistency in academic standards. Part II offers some broader responses and insights based on the social construction of academic standards. The theoretical basis and limitations of these strategies are considered. Part III of the book contains chapters that provide overviews of specific projects, events and methods that have been used to attempt to solve some of the issues in relation to academic standards and offer practical advice that busy academics can use in their own local contexts. To support this further, throughout the book we have provide boxes to offer easily accessible ideas from the chapters and these are distinguished as to whether they provide a critical perspective or practical strategy.

Part I: Academic standards context and concepts

Initially, Rust and O'Donovan consider the policy context and the changing nature of higher education (Chapter 2). This includes the changing nature of student participation in higher education and the increased political and managerial scrutiny, all which have brought standards into sharper focus. The understanding of academic standards that practitioners and policy makers have is questioned and how the structures of higher education programmes make sharing of standards difficult. There are some initial insights into what might be done to make academic standards more trustworthy based on previous work.

This context is followed with a definition and conceptualisation of academic standards and their complexity (Chapter 3). Price and O'Donovan argue that due to their nature, greater efforts to make standards explicit through codifying them into criteria, descriptors or guidance create associated problems. How standards are constructed and influenced is foundational to these issues and how it can lead to difficulties for sharing standards and ultimately, inconsistency in marking is foregrounded.

The final contribution in this first part of the book, by Yorke, recognises that the issues with academic standards are a global concern and are critical for international comparability (Chapter 4). Despite the issues raised so far in terms of the problems of defining, measuring and comparing standards, examples from Australia, USA, UK and Brazil are provided to examine how national governments and supranational bodies have attempted to do just this.

Part II: Common responses to the social construction of academic standards

In the next part of the book, Lloyd and Forsyth start by highlighting that within the assessment process there are a range of mechanisms for attempting to ensure consistency in academic standards and the judgements made about student performances (Chapter 5). The role of quality assurance processes and specifically moderation is the first strategy to be considered. As part of this, the growth in and adoption of quality processes are examined and what these strategies may or may not bring for protecting academic standards. The inherent limitations and weaknesses of moderation are also drawn out.

At this point, the role of the external examiner in the UK becomes a central consideration in terms of ways to reduce variation in academic standards. Price provides an overview of how the external examining system is intended for safeguarding standards across institutions (Chapter 6). However, this is critically evaluated in the context of academic standards and the idea of calibration is introduced for the first time. Leading on from this, Medland interrogates the assumed assessment literacy of external examiners and the implications of this for standards (Chapter 7). The development of a shared language to support a more common approach by external examiners is then presented as a potential way forward.

The introduction of calibration is then developed further by Reimann and Sadler (Chapter 8). They interrogate the concept and practice of social moderation and calibration in more detail as a response to the social construction of standards. This chapter provides the theoretical basis for the subject-based case studies in the next part of the book.

Part III: Practical solutions

The final part of the book considers a range of projects, events and methods that offer insights into practical ways forward for reducing variability in standards. This part has two sub-sections. The first is dedicated to professional development activities. As mentioned above, many of the ideas and activities in this book were inspired by the practical solutions proposed by the AdvanceHE Degree Standards Project. The Project work features strongly in this part of the book, both through a focus on the Professional Development Course (PDC) for external examiners and also the associated subject calibration activities, as examples of ways in which the challenges highlighted earlier could be addressed. Stoakes and Morris give an overview of the development of the PDC for external examiners and the challenges of implementation that were encountered (Chapter 9). Next, Lloyd and Forsyth provide an in-depth description of the course itself, the intended outcomes, delivery methods and content (Chapter 10). To conclude this sub-section on professional development, Pill identifies the impact of adopting the PDC within a single higher education institution (Chapter 11) and Moore offers an overview of the broader project evaluation conducted by an independent evaluator (Chapter 12).

The second sub-section and final collection of chapters in the book focuses upon concrete practical strategies for reducing variability in academic standards. Boyd and Hill start with a discussion of the use of assessment rubrics (Chapter 13). Rubrics have become a commonly used method that attempt to make academic standards explicit and increase transparency. Despite this, due to the fundamental nature of academic standards, a number of limitations exist and are explored. The next two chapters return to calibration as a strategy and two case studies on the design and implementation in two different subject areas is provided. Sadler and Timmis describe an event in sport and exercise science (Chapter 14) and Hill et al. consider calibration in the subject of geography (Chapter 15). To conclude Part III, Jones introduces comparative judgement as an alternative approach, which runs counter to trends of more detailed and precise criteria by doing away with rubrics altogether (Chapter 16). Instead, assessors make holistic pairwise judgements of student work and the resultant decisions are statistically modelled to produce a unique score for each piece of work.

To conclude the book, in the final chapter (Chapter 17), Hill et al. identify what the higher education sector can learn from the issues raised across all the chapters in relation to academic standards. This leads to a number of ways forward that includes recommendations for practitioners, policy implications and consideration of what evidence is required in order for us to know more.

Summary

This is a relatively large book that covers a range of different aspects in relation to academic standards. However, there are a number of key and consistent concepts that are repeated across several chapters that you will start to recognise as you read the book. We realise that the book will often not be read as a whole and it is likely that you will dip into chapters individually. Therefore to help summarise and support the recognition of the key ideas in the book we have created the following list for reference:

- Academic standards, defined as levels of student performance/achievement, are central to assessment in higher education and consistency in judging these standards across markers is critical to assuring fair and trustworthy awards.
- Academic standards are multifaceted due to issues such as increased student diversity and participation in higher education, the complex and open-ended nature of assessment tasks encountered, the tacit knowledge markers bring to bear on their judgements, and a growth in managerialism that prioritises increasingly detailed quality assurance codifications.
- Despite governments and institutions attempting to codify and compare academic standards, they cannot be articulated effectively in explicit and commonly understood artefacts such as rubrics. Rather, academic standards are socially situated and interpreted, developing their meaning in use through involvement in academic and professional communities.
- Given the socially constructed nature of academic standards, social processes also need to be employed to address the issue of inconsistency between markers. Markers should ideally share knowledge of standards prior to teaching, discussing examples of student work, and drawing on relevant external reference points, to agree on the rationale for their judgements, thereby becoming calibrated academics.

- Establishing social moderation and calibration internal to institutions, and more widely within subject communities to support external examining in countries where this is carried out, is not without its difficulties. For example, the assessment literacy of staff (including external examiners) needs developing, and institutional and sector-level strategies, polices and approaches need adjusting away from techno-rationalist to social constructivist perspectives, presenting an ongoing challenge for the higher education sector internationally.
- Different contexts over space and time will inevitably lead to a drift in academic standards, but intermittent calibration within subject communities can develop a shared understanding of standards, helping to reassure higher education stakeholders internationally that academic standards are assessed with relative comparability across space and over time.

References

AHE (2024). https://www.advance-he.ac.uk/about-us. *Advance HE website. Accessed January* 2024.

Baker, S. (2018). Is grade inflation a worldwide trend? *Times Higher Education Supplement. 29 June. Accessed* 21 September 2023. https://www.timeshighereducation.com/features/grade-inflation-worldwide-trend.

Baume, D., Yorke, M. & Coffey, M. (2004). What is happening when we assess, and how can we use our understanding of this to improve assessment? *Assessment & Evaluation in Higher Education*, 29(4), 451–477. https://doi.org/10.1080/0260293031000168903 7.

Bell, L. & Lygo-Baker, S. (2019). Student-centred learning: a small-scale study of learning experience in undergraduate translation classes. *The Language Learning Journal*, 47(3), 299–312. https://doi.org/10.1080/09571736.2016.1278030.

Bloxham, S., Boyd, P. & Orr, S. (2011). Mark my words: the role of assessment criteria in UK higher education grading practices. *Studies in Higher Education*, 36(6), 655–670. https://doi.org/10.1080/03075071003777716.

Boud, D. (2000). Sustainable Assessment: Rethinking assessment for the learning society. *Studies in Continuing Education*, 22(2), 151–167. https://doi.org/10.1080/713695728.

Carless, D. (2007). Learning-oriented assessment: conceptual bases and practical implications. *Innovations in Education and Teaching International*, 44(1), 57–66. https://doi.org/10.1080/14703290601081332.

Gipps, C.V. (2011). *Beyond Testing: Towards a theory of educational assessment.* Routledge, London.

Jephcote, C., Medland E. & Lygo-Baker, S. (2021). Grade inflation versus grade improvement: are our students getting more intelligent? *Assessment & Evaluation in Higher Education*, 46(4), 547–571. https://doi.org/10.1080/02602938.2020.1795617.

OfS. (2022). *Analysis of Degree Classifications over Time: Changes in graduate attainment from 2010-11 to 2020-21.* OfS, London.

O'Hagan, S.R. & Wigglesworth, G. (2015). Who's marking my essay? The assessment of non-native-speaker and native-speaker undergraduate essays in an Australian higher education context. *Studies in Higher Education*, 40(9), 1729–1747. https://doi.org/10.1080/03075079.2014.896890.

O'Leary, M. & Cui, V. (2020). Reconceptualising teaching and learning in higher education: challenging neoliberal narratives of teaching excellence through collaborative observation. *Teaching in Higher Education*, 25(2), 141–156. https://doi.org/10.1080/13562517.2018.1543262.

Rinne, I. (2024). Same grade for different reasons, different grades for the same reason? *Assessment & Evaluation in Higher Education*, 49(2), 220–232. https://doi.org/10.1080/02602938.2023.2203883.

Rosovsky, H. & Hartley, M. (2002). *Evaluation and the Academy: Are We Doing the Right Thing? Grade Inflation and Letters of Recommendation*. The American Academy of Arts and Sciences. Cambridge, America.

Sadler, D.R. (2017). Academic achievement standards and quality assurance. *Quality in Higher Education*, 23(2), 81–99. https://doi.org/10.1080/13538322.2017.1356614.

Sambell, K., McDowell, L. & Montgomery, C. (2012). *Assessment for Learning in Higher Education*. Routledge, London.

Part I

Academic standards context and concepts

Chapter 2

Assuring academic standards
Policy and practice in context

Chris Rust and Berry O'Donovan

The international context of higher education

While a deep dive into the purpose of higher education is beyond the scope of this chapter, we do claim, echoing Biesta (2010), that the attainment of knowledge and skills and the accurate certification of the standards of such attainment are centrally important outcomes. Indeed, scholars suggest that globalisation has, since the early 1990s, sparked government interest in the expansion of higher education as a key foundation of international competitiveness emanating from the development of professionals and as a source of knowledge and innovation (Mok, 2016). While we will predominantly focus on developments in the UK, since this is the context in which our own research and practice has been situated, similar trends can be observed elsewhere.

In the UK, increased participation in higher education expanded from around 5% in 1960, peaking at approximately 34% in 1997–1998 (Mayhew et al., 2004, p. 66). This level of participation continues, despite the introduction of student fees, with 2.46 million students entering UK higher education in the academic year 2019–2020, representing over one third of home 18-year-olds (Bolton, 2021). The massification of higher education is a worldwide phenomenon. In 2021, around 35 million undergraduate students were enrolled in degree programmes in China, an exponential increase from 3.4 million in 1990 (Textor, 2022). Diversification of the student body has been slower. Mok (2016) suggests that students from wealthier family backgrounds account for a large proportion of students at China's top-tier universities, and this situation is echoed in the UK's elite universities. However, participation from non-traditional backgrounds has widened in the UK with 22% of 18-year-olds from the areas of lowest higher education participation in England applying to university in 2016 as compared to 12% in 2006 (UUK, 2017).

One impact of these changing demographics is that students can be less familiar with the expectations of university than was previously the case (O'Byrne & Bond, 2014). This has likely been compounded by the global COVID-19 pandemic in which many students experienced what has become termed 'learning loss'. Studies from several countries outlined in a McKinsey Report suggest that school shutdowns across the globe in the second quarter of 2020 put students up to six months behind the academic milestones their cohorts would typically be expected

DOI: 10.4324/9781003379768-3

to reach (Chen et al., 2021). Arguably, students have never been in more need of better support, particularly in terms of clarifying what is being sought in assessment, but at a time when pressure on resources to provide such support is at its highest. The pandemic has brought into sharp contrast the question: is it possible to be fair to students (and this may well be dependent on what one means by 'fairness') and at the same time maintain standards?

Is there evidence for grade inflation?

Against the backdrop of expansion, the UK has 'witnessed several decades of increasing regulation and accountability regarding academic standards' (Bloxham & Boyd, 2012, p. 615), fuelled by concerns in the media about 'dumbing down and grade inflation' (Crossouard, 2010, p. 247). And perhaps these concerns are justified when we look at student achievement data. For example, the number of first-class degrees has risen from 7% in 1994 to 29% in 2019 in the UK, along with master's degrees becoming nearly ten times as common as they were (Lambert, 2019). Lambert (2019) suggests that such an exponential rise in academic achievement could only have three possible causes. Firstly, higher calibre students are now entering university. However, he cautions that this would be a notable achievement as the university students of the past were only the select few. The second is that universities have become much better at teaching, thereby enhancing student achievement. But this would be alongside resource reductions that have resulted in a drop in contact hours and larger classes. Of concern is that Lambert suggests (among many other experts) that the evidence indicates that neither of these is true; it is grade inflation (Lambert, 2019). The Office for Students (OfS) in response to Higher Education Statistics Agency (HESA) statistics in January 2020 commented that 'Grade inflation risks undermining public confidence in higher education for students, graduates and employers alike' (Dandridge, 2020). Indeed, politicians, press and other stakeholders (see Holland, 2022) suggest such inflation has already weakened the value of UK higher education.

Students as consumers and the resulting focus on student expectations

In the UK, the increased scrutiny and regulation of teaching and assessment practices has significantly shaped the policy context with a consequent impact on student expectations. Since 2010, two higher education white papers (focused on England) and the introduction of the Teaching Excellence Framework (TEF) in 2016 have had far-reaching implications for the UK higher education sector. A quasi market-based system that aims to increase competition between institutions and students has been set in motion, particularly with regard to teaching provision and the introduction of student fees. This has 'fundamentally altered the relationship between students and institutions' (UUK, 2017, p. 11). Institutions are focusing on students and their expectations in ways not seen in UK higher education before (UUK, 2017). Students are paying more for their studies and expect a more lucrative return for their money 'whether in academic quality, employability or the facilities offered to them' (Grove, 2015). In the UK the achievement of a first or upper second-class degree has become increasingly important to gain a graduate job (Snowdon, 2012) and this has fuelled a commensurate intensification of student instrumentality in terms of the achievement of high marks and 'good' (first or upper second class) degrees (Dean & Gibbs, 2015).

Consequently, for over a decade, to attract and retain students in an era of 'academic capitalism' (Barnett, 2011, p. 2), universities, both in the UK and internationally, have been compelled to pursue market orientation strategies that place emphasis on meeting these student expectations (Arambewela & Hall, 2013; Mark, 2013). This has fuelled longstanding concerns about standards and quality both in the UK and internationally. According to HEFCE (2009) the quality of English higher education was the subject of much public debate during 2008. There were several criticisms of universities and colleges, including accusations of 'dumbing down', places being awarded to students who are not academically able enough to benefit from higher education, and that institutions admit international students with an insufficient grasp of English. Similar concerns have been voiced in Canada (for example Côté & Allahar, 2011) as well as the US and Australia, as illustrated by the following quotes:

> The quality of student learning at US colleges and universities is inadequate, and in some cases, declining.
> (US Department of Education, 2006, p. 3)

> I regard the 2006–07 data as the best indication yet of the standards of Australian universities ... they're nowhere near the standards required by the profession.
> (Birrell, 2009)

Quality assurance regimes, codification and the impact of student satisfaction

In tandem with this increasingly commercial and consumerist orientation, and arguably in part as a response to it, UK higher education institutions have become increasingly managerial with growing regulation and control through quality frameworks as they strive to compete in a more hostile environment (Harvey, 2005; O'Byrne & Bond, 2014). This has involved the widespread use of quality assurance codifications such as marking schemes, criteria and explicit descriptions of standards with a focus on 'transforming the existing implicit model of academic standards' (Hudson et al., 2015, p. 1310) viewed as unfair and 'subjective, anecdotal, even negligent' (Ecclestone, 2001, p. 301). Such an approach puts more trust in apparently transparent processes that can be monitored (Strathern, 2000) and less in the professional judgement of skilled employees such as academics (Tsoukas, 2003):

> Modernity has come to mistrust intuition, preferring explicitly articulated assertions, it is uncomfortable with ad hoc practices, opting for systematic procedures, it substitutes detached objectivity for personal commitment.
>
> (Tsoukas, 2003, p. 411)

Arguably, nowhere are the tensions between a more consumerist student body and a burgeoning managerialism versus the integrity of knowledge and maintenance of academic standards so intense as in the arena of assessment. Bloxham and Boyd (2007), among others, suggest that, from the student perspective, it is assessment that defines their learning experience, not learning outcomes or activities. This is likely the reason why in student experience surveys, the quality of assessment and feedback practices and processes attracts more critique than any other aspect of the student university experience (O'Donovan et al., 2016). Nowadays, the use of surveys to gauge student perspectives on, and satisfaction with, their higher education experience is ubiquitous across the international HE sector (Bedggood & Donovan, 2012), and the UK is no exception. The UK's National Student Survey (NSS), in which student perspectives on the quality of higher education are made transparent to all stakeholders, is now a potent fixture in course and institutional rankings. Although the survey's design, and thereby its findings, has attracted much criticism particularly in the area of assessment and feedback (MacKay et al., 2019), many stakeholders, such as the UK National Union of Students (NUS), have welcomed the increased influence of student perspectives on their university experience. Indeed, the NUS suggests the NSS has compelled UK higher education institutions to make positive changes to their provision including improvements to assessment and feedback practices (NUS, 2008).

Gibbs (2010, p. 14) agrees that UK institutional and departmental processes and behaviours are driven by student satisfaction data to 'an unprecedented extent'. However, he cautions that measures of student satisfaction are not always good indicators of educational quality and can reflect relatively uninformed views that strongly influence individuals' evaluation of assessment and feedback practice (O'Donovan, 2017). And while students thirst for enhanced clarity on assessment practices, particularly the standards and marking criteria that will be applied to their own work, this has been challenging to provide. In higher education the dominant method for clarifying standards and quality criteria among both staff and students remains explicit transmission (O'Donovan et al., 2008; Hudson et al., 2015). Standards and criteria are articulated and codified in documents, such as assessment guidelines, descriptors, and rubrics, and there remains considerable practitioner belief in the efficacy of these codifications to share understandings of standards and clear criteria (Hudson et al., 2015). However, while sole reliance on explicit articulation is widespread in practice, there has been plenty of research which has shown that such codifications on their own are unlikely to fully communicate standards or criteria (see for instance, Higgins et al., 2001; Rust et al., 2003). Effective practices in sharing understandings of standards (a few of which are briefly referred to later in this chapter, as well as in Chapters 3, 8, 13, 14 and 15) demonstrate the need for active discussion and engagement to interpret such codifications.

Within such a context, academics may feel increasingly disempowered (O'Byrne & Bond, 2014) and increasingly likely to agree to the demands of both managers and students in terms of academic standards (Lambert, 2019). In fact, it has been suggested that as a result of the market driven pressures on both academics and students, what has been described as a 'dis-engagement compact' or 'non-aggression' pact has been struck:

> A non-aggression pact exists between many faculty members and students ... with each side agreeing not to impinge on the other. The glue that keeps the pact intact is grade inflation: easy As for merely acceptable work and Bs for mediocre.
> (Hersh & Merrow, 2005, p. 4)

Or 'academic coddling':

> The desire to attract and satisfy students as though they are mere customers leads to academic coddling, in the form of easy grades and expensive facilities and entertainments.
> (Lewis, 2006, p. 7)

Alongside these assessment issues, the work of academics has become more specialised and fragmented to support a more centralised and performative culture often involving the 'up-skilling' of professional support staff and the 'deskilling' of academic staff (Macfarlane, 2011). This, along with modular degree structures, makes the informal, if slow, harmonisation of standards through the acculturation of new staff and students into disciplinary communities more challenging nowadays and less likely to take place (O'Donovan et al., 2008). Consequently this requires intentional and thoughtful orchestration.

Compounding these issues still further in the UK, many institutions have changed their degree algorithms, the way in which final results are awarded to students, in a way that benefits the students. The Higher Education Academy found that nearly half of the institutions it surveyed in 2015 (98 in total) changed their degree algorithms in the previous five years so as not to disadvantage students in comparison to those in similar institutions (HEFCE, 2015).

Analysis by Allen (2018a, 2018b) has demonstrated how different approaches in discounting and weighting of marks has a sizeable impact on higher education awards. Students with the same marks can receive a different classification depending on the institution they attended (Allen, 2020). Allen (2020) argues this diversity of practice risks inhibiting comparative analysis of degree outcomes and measurement of attainment gaps (see Box 2.1). But even if a common degree algorithm could be agreed and implemented to create a fair and level playing field, this could only be achieved if the individual grade decisions on students' work being fed into the system were comparable across the sector.

European attempts: making learning outcomes more explicit

In Europe, there has been the Bologna Process, named after the university where a declaration was signed by education ministers of 29 European countries in 1999. It is an intergovernmental initiative aimed at creating a European Higher Education Area and the first of the original action lines for the process was the 'adoption of a system of easily readable and comparable degrees'. But the process tries to achieve this through a belief that explicit definitions of learning outcomes can provide comparability.

> By defining the right learning outcomes, standards can be set with regard to the required level of discipline related theoretical and/or experimental knowledge and content, academic and discipline related skills and generic competences. With the exception of the last one these will differ from discipline to discipline. To make programmes more transparent and comparable on a European level, it is necessary to develop learning outcomes and competences for each recognised qualification. These learning outcomes should be identifiable and assessable in the programme that opts for such a qualification. Learning outcomes should not only be defined on the level of formal qualifications such as degrees but also on the level of modules or courses. The inclusion of learning outcomes in the pieces and the total of a curriculum stimulate its consistency. They make explicit what a student should learn.
> (Tuning Educational Structures in Europe, 2003, p. 53)

The flaws with this belief, that explicitness alone can achieve comparability of standards, have already been outlined. And what has been done more widely internationally is discussed in Chapter 4.

In the UK, in 2015, HEFCE instigated the Degree Standards Project, now led by AdvanceHE and managed by the Office for Students on behalf of England and the devolved administrations in Northern Ireland and Wales. The Project focuses on the professionalisation of external examining and the exploration of approaches to the calibration of standards. The UK Degree Standards Project is described in detail in Chapters 9 and 10, exemplified in practice in Chapter 11 and critiqued in Chapter 12. Explicit strategies for reducing variation in academic standards, focusing on calibration, are covered in Chapters 8, 14 and 15.

Academic standards as untrustworthy

Across much of the world, effective and trustworthy higher education assessment practices and policies have become increasingly important to society and government. However, while academic standards have come under mounting scrutiny in light of accusations of grade inflation, how to improve the consistency and comparability of those standards is not really understood by many practitioners and policy makers (Sadler, 2014). Essentially, marking variation, diversity of degree algorithms and quality assurance practices shaped in part by market pressures and limited understanding mean that academic standards are untrustworthy and not comparable across the sector.

On 30 March 2009, the Vice-Chancellors of both Oxford and Oxford Brookes Universities (two different higher education institutions in the same English city), were asked 'Is a 2.1 in history at Oxford Brookes worth the same as a 2.1 in history at Oxford?' Their rambling and convoluted responses were considered so unsatisfactory by the government panel that they were accused of 'obfuscation', and giving an answer that 'would not pass a GCSE essay [a UK school leaver examination]' (Shepherd, 2009). The Committee's final report included the damming conclusion that:

> It is unacceptable for the sector to be in receipt of departmental spending of £15 billion but be unable to answer a straightforward question about the relative standards of the degrees of students, which the taxpayer has paid for.
> (House of Commons Innovation, Universities, Science and Skills Committee, 2009, paragraph 305)

The correct answer to the Committee's question about the relative standards of degrees was in fact a very simple one – we do not know. And we do not know because we do not have the necessary systems in place that would be needed in order for us to know. The Quality Assurance Agency (QAA), established in 1997 in the UK, has conducted regular visits to universities to assess their procedures for monitoring and assuring standards and to make recommendations for improvement. However, it has previously admitted that 'we do not judge the standards themselves' (Richmond, 2018, p. 6). The QAA also acknowledged that there was little evidence that the UK system of 'external examiners', who act as moderators for the marking of assessments at other institutions, is an effective means to safeguard academic standard (Richmond, 2018, p. 6) (See also Chapters 6 and 7).

Early attempts to improve the trustworthiness of standards

Yet, it is not as if we do not know what we would have to do to address comparable standards; in fact, we have known for some time. As far back as 1997, the Higher Education Quality Council (HEQC), the forerunner of the QAA, elucidated a way forward (see Box 2.1).

CRITICAL PERSPECTIVE

Box 2.1 The achievement of consistent assessment standards

Consistent assessment decisions among assessors are the product of interactions over time, the internalisation of exemplars, and of inclusive networks. *Written*

> *instructions, mark schemes and criteria, even when used with scrupulous care, cannot substitute for these.*
>
> (HEQC, 1997a; authors' emphasis)

For this reason:

> HEQC recommended that subject groups and professional networks should develop or extend opportunities to build common understandings and approaches among academic peer groups e.g., maintaining 'expert' panels for validation/accreditation/external examining/assessing; directories of programmes/programme elements in field; relevant programme/award/progression statistics; statistics relating to progression into employment; mechanisms to monitor changes in standards at other educational or occupational levels, and internationally; formal opportunities to discuss and review standards.
>
> (HEQC, 1997b, in Brown, 2009)

But in April 2007 the functions of HEQC were transferred to the newly established QAA and these excellent recommendations were apparently lost or forgotten. HEQC recognised that if we seriously want to be able to make comparisons of standards between institutions and/or between disciplines, and/or between different decades, there is one way this could be achieved (as had been argued previously elsewhere, e.g. Rust, 2009; Rust et al., 2009); through the establishment and development of academic communities of assessment practice. The former chief executive of the Higher Education Academy (Paul Ramsden) in his 2008 report on university teaching submitted to the Secretary of State for Innovation, Universities and Skills tried to resurrect the thrust of what HEQC had proposed a decade before with the idea of establishing what he called 'colleges of peers' to help set common standards:

> Common standards can only be achieved through discussion amongst peers, in appropriate forums, looking at real examples of student work, and discussing each other's assessment decisions. Without the cultivation of such communities of assessment practice, discussions about standards can only be limited to conjecture and opinion – albeit, in some cases, better informed opinion than in others.
>
> (Rust, 2014, p. 242)

A possible way forward: calibration of standards

In Australia, Royce Sadler described the intentional process of discussing standards against exemplars as calibration, and argued that the resulting 'calibrated academics' would be 'able to make grading judgements consistent with those which similarly calibrated colleagues would make but without constant engagement in moderation' (Sadler, 2012, p. 1). The overall aims of calibration are to achieve comparability of standards across institutions and stability of standards over time (Sadler, 2012). One discipline where this has successfully been put into practice in Australia is in accounting education. Called 'Achievement Matters: External Peer Review of Accounting Learning Standards', using assessment tasks and sample student work, this project developed a model of cross-institutional calibration to achieve shared understandings among participants across all the nationally implemented codified accounting learning standards. Following calibration, random samples of student work were anonymously assessed by the calibrated peer reviewers benchmarked against a specific accounting learning standard. The project demonstrated that cross-institutional calibration was both a rich source of professional development around assessment for participating academics from different institutions and improved the consistency of their judgements. Similar improved consistency has been found in the Association of American Colleges and Universities' (AACU) Value project, which also involves calibration:

> VALUE initiative scorers engage in two-day calibration/norming sessions that acquaint scorers with the content and purpose of the specific rubric(s) the scorer will utilize. Most of the time is spent with their colleague scorers in practicing the application of the rubric to examples of student work in order to explore the ways in which, depending on the student's class assignment or disciplinary lens, the dimensions of the learning contained in the rubric are manifested in the work being assessed.
> (Cumming & Maxwell, 1999, in AACU, 2017, p. 15)

Beyond calibration: strategies to protect the value of UK degrees

In 2019, the UK Standing Committee for Quality Assessment (UKSCQA), Universities UK (UUK), Guild HE, and the QAA jointly published a 'statement of intent' regarding degree classification which includes strong support for engagement in subject-specific calibration activities and focused on protecting the value of UK degrees. The statement was founded on common principles that affirmed the responsibility of institutions for the standards of their awarded degrees, the value of the classification system and qualifications based on clear assessment criteria, and the use of common arrangements that protected the value of UK degrees based on shared, consistent and comparable practices. UKSCQA also agreed on four ways to do this:

1. Ensuring assessment and classification criteria stretch and challenge all their students, including meeting and exceeding shared sector qualifications criteria.
2. Reviewing and explaining how their process for calculating final classifications:
    - fully reflect student attainment against learning criteria;
    - protect the integrity of classification boundary conventions;
    - maintain comparability of qualifications in the sector and over time.

3   Enabling staff to protect the value of qualification by:
    - supporting opportunities for academics to work as external examiners, including professional development and subject calibration activities;
    - supporting new, and existing, academics and external examiners to apply institutional assessment criteria and regulations;
    - reviewing and reiterating policies on internal and external moderation to ensure they enable challenge.
4   Reviewing and publishing student outcomes data as part of the ongoing calibration of assessment and classification practice.

(UKSCQA, 2019)

Essentially, the four nations (England, Wales, Scotland and Northern Ireland) agreed that there was a threat to academic standards and committed to protect the value of degrees through shared, consistent and comparable practices for assuring, as far as possible, academic standards in higher education. They endorsed UKSCQA's set of principles and the main strategies to achieve this, but the implementation was to be carried out and monitored via the different national quality assurance/assessment arrangements. Key strategies included, for instance, a detailed Quality Code and conditions of registration for higher education providers (England), a distinctive focus on quality enhancement and enhancement-led reviews (Scotland), and an explicit consideration of external examiners and their professional development (Wales, Northern Ireland).

This concern over grade inflation and commitment to protect the value of degrees was reaffirmed a year later in the review of the 'statement of intent':

> The increase in upper degrees risked eroding the practical usefulness of the classification system for differentiating student and graduate attainment. More problematically, there is a continued risk that public confidence in the value of a degree from UK universities is being undermined by this trend and that instances of genuine student improvement may not be recognized fairly.
>
> (UUK, 2020, p. 4)

Conclusion

The work of unravelling academic standards and how to protect them is important and ongoing. In this chapter we have outlined the different ways in which higher education has attempted to deal with academic standards and accusations of grade inflation, in the context of a rapidly changing policy environment. We have shown that the complexity of academic standards in policy and practice is due to issues such as increased student diversity and participation, students as consumers whose expectations and satisfaction exert a strong influence, and a growth in managerialism and regulation that prioritises the codification of standards instead of valuing and promoting discursive and discipline-based approaches such as calibration. It is high time that this complexity is recognised by policy makers. Without understanding the nature of academic standards and how they can be dependably understood and applied, the value of degrees will continue to attract ministerial concern and national headlines. The following chapters will expand the argument made here by exploring the conceptual and practical challenges, and possible practical solutions that we could only allude to in this chapter.

References

AACU (Association of American Colleges and Universities). (2017). *On Solid Ground: Value Report 2017.* Washington, DC: AACU. www.luminafoundation.org/files/resources/on-solid-ground.pdf.

Allen, D. (2018a). *The Use of Differential Weighting and Discounting in Degree Algorithms and their Impact on Classification Inflation and Equity: A Further Analysis.* Economics Working Paper Series No. 1803. Bristol: University of the West of England. www1.uwe.ac.uk/bl/research/bcef/publications.aspx.

Allen, D. (2018b). *Degree Algorithms, Grade Inflation and Equity: The UK Higher Education Sector.* Economics Working Paper Series No. 1801. Bristol: University of the West of England. www1.uwe.ac.uk/bl/research/bcef/publications.aspx.

Allen, D. (2020) What can be done about degree algorithm variations?https://wonkhe.com/blogs/what-can-be-done-about-degree-algorithm-variations-2/.

Arambewela, R. & Hall, J. (2013). The interactional effects of the internal and external university environment, and the influence of personal values, on satisfaction among international postgraduate students. *Studies in Higher Education*, 38(7), 972–988. https://doi.org/10.1080/03075079.2011.615916.

Barnett, R. (2011). Developing the university in turbulent times. *Educational Developments*, 12(4), 1–5.

Bedggood, R.E. & Donovan, J. (2012). University performance evaluations: what are we really measuring? *Studies in Higher Education*, 37(7), 825–842. https://doi.org/10.1080/03075079.2010.549221.

Biesta, G. (2010). *Good Education in an Age of Measurement: Ethics, Politics, Democracy.* Boulder, CO: Paradigm. https://doi.org/10.4324/9781315634319.

Birrell, B. (2009). Degrees still lure low-skill migrants. *News Com Australia*, 2 October.

Bloxham, S. & Boyd, P. (2007). *Developing Effective Assessment in Higher Education: A Practical Guide.* Milton Keynes: Open University Press.

Bloxham, S. & Boyd, P. (2012). Accountability in grading student work: securing academic standards in a twenty-first century quality assurance context. *British Educational Research Journal*, 38(4), 615–634. www.jstor.org/stable/23263907.

Bolton, P. (2021). Research briefing: higher education student numbers. https://commonslibrary.parliament.uk/research-briefings/cbp-7857/.

Brown, R. (2009). *Comparability of Degree Standards?*Oxford: Higher Education Policy Institute. www.hepi.ac.uk/wp-content/uploads/2014/02/47-Comparability-of-degree-standards.pdf.

Côté, J. & Allahar, A. (2011). *Lowering Higher Education. The Rise of Corporate Universities and the Fall of Liberal Education.* Toronto: University of Toronto Press.

Crossouard, B. (2010). Reforms to higher education assessment reporting: opportunities and challenges. *Teaching in Higher Education*, 15(3), 247–258. https://doi.org/10.1080/13562511003740809.

Chen, L.-K., Dorn, E., Sarakatsannis, J. & Weisinger, A. (2021). Teaching survey: Learning loss is global- and significant. www.mckinsey.com/industries/public-and-social-sector/our-insights/teacher-survey-learning-loss-is-global-and-significant.

Cumming, J.J. & Maxwell G.S. (1999). Contextualising authentic assessment. *Assessment in Education: Principles, Policies, and Practices*, 6(2), 177–194. https://doi.org/10.1080/09695949992865.

Dandridge, N. (2020). Office for Students respond to HESA statistics. www.officeforstudents.org.uk/news-blog-and-events/press-and-media/office-for-students-respond-to-hesa-statistics/.

Dean, A. & Gibbs, P. (2015). Student satisfaction or happiness? A preliminary rethink of what is important in the student experience. *Quality Assurance in Education*, 23(1), 5–19. https://doi.org/10.1108/QAE-10-2013-0044.

Ecclestone, K. (2001). 'I know a 2:1 when I see it': Understanding criteria for degree classification in franchised university programmes. *Journal of Further and Higher Education* 25(3), 301–313. https://doi.org/10.1080/03098770126527.

Gibbs, G. (2010). *Dimensions of Quality*. York: Higher Education Academy.

Grove, J. (2015). 7 Key challenges for UK higher education. *Times Higher Education*, 5 August. www.timeshighereducation.com/features/7-key-challenges-uk-higher-education.

Harvey, L. (2005). A history and critique of quality evaluation in the UK. *Quality Assurance in Higher Education*, 13(4), 263–276. http://dx.doi.org/10.1108/09684880510700608.

Hersh, R.H. & Merrow, J. (2005). *Declining by Degrees*. New York: Palgrave Macmillan.

Higgins, R., Harley, P. & Skelton, A. (2001). Getting the message across: the problem of communicating assessment feedback. *Teaching in Higher Education*, 6(2), 269–274.

HEFCE (Higher Education Funding Council for England). (2009). *Report of the Subcommittee for Teaching, Quality, and the Student Experience. HEFCE's Statutory Responsibility for Quality Assurance 2009/4*. London: HEFCE. https://dera.ioe.ac.uk/137/1/09_40.pdf.

HEFCE (Higher Education Funding Council for England). (2015). *A Review of External Examining Arrangements across the UK: Report to the UK Higher Education Funding Bodies by the Higher Education*. London: HEFCE. https://dera.ioe.ac.uk/23541/1/2015_externalexam.pdf.

HEQC (Higher Education Quality Council). (1997a). *Assessment in Higher Education and the Role of 'Graduateness'*. London: HEQC.

HEQC (Higher Education Quality Council). (1997b). *Graduate Standards Programme Final Report Volume 2*. London: HEQC.

Holland, N. (2002). *Degrees of Inflation? Ensuring the Credibility and Reliability of Higher Education Qualifications*. London: OfS. www.officeforstudents.org.uk/news-blog-and-events/blog/degrees-of-inflation-ensuring-the-credibility-and-reliability-of-higher-education-qualifications/.

House of Commons Innovation, Universities, Science and Skills Committee. (2009). *Students and Universities: Eleventh Report of Session 2008–09 Vol. 1*. London: The Stationery Office.

Hudson, J., Bloxham, S., den Outer, B. & Price, M. (2015). Conceptual acrobatics: talking about assessment standards in the transparency era. *Studies in Higher Education*, 42(7), 1309–1323. https://doi.org/10.1080/03075079.2015.1092130.

Lambert, H. (2019). The great university con: how the British degree lost its value. *The New Statesman*, 21 August.

Lewis, H.R. (2006). *Excellence Without a Soul: How a Great University Forgot Education.* New York: Public Affairs.

Macfarlane, B. (2011). The morphing of academic practice: unbundling and the rise of the para-academic. *Higher Education Quarterly*, 65(1), 59–73. https://doi.org/10.1111/j.1468-2273.2010.00467.x.

MacKay, J.R.D., Hughes, K., Marzetti, H., Lent, N. & Rhind, S.M. (2019). Using National Student Survey (NSS) qualitative data and social identity theory to explore students' experiences of assessment and feedback. *Higher Education Pedagogies*, 4(1), 315–330. https://doi.org/10.1080/23752696.2019.1601500.

Mayhew, K., Deer, C. & Dua, M. (2004). The move to mass higher education in the UK: many questions and some answers. *Oxford Review of Education*, 30(1), 65–82. https://doi.org/10.1080/0305498042000190069.

Mark, E. (2013). Student satisfaction and the customer focus in higher education. *Journal of Higher Education Policy and Management*, 35(1), 2–10. https://doi.org/10.1080/1360080X.2012.727703.

Mok, K.H. (2016). Massification of higher education, graduate employment and social mobility in the Greater China region. *British Journal of Sociology of Education*, 37(1), 51–71. https://doi.org/10.1080/01425692.2015.1111751.

NUS (National Union of Students). (2008). *Mark My Words, Not My Name. The Campaign for Anonymous Marking.* London: NUS. http://samairaanjum.weebly.com/uploads/1/0/5/2/10526755/markmywordsbrief1-1.pdf.

O'Byrne, D. & Bond, C. (2014). Back to the future: the idea of a university revisited. *Journal of Higher Education Policy and Management*, 36(6), 571–584. https://doi.org/10.1080/1360080X.2014.957888.

O'Donovan, B., Price, M. & Rust, C. (2008). Developing student understanding of assessment standards: a nested hierarchy of approaches. *Teaching in Higher Education*, 13 (2), 205–217. https://doi.org/10.1080/13562510801923344.

O'Donovan, B., Rust, C. & Price, M. (2016). A scholarly approach to solving the feedback dilemma in practice. *Assessment & Evaluation in Higher Education*, 41(6), 938–949. https://doi.org/10.1080/02602938.2015.1052774.

O'Donovan, B. (2017). How students' beliefs about knowledge and knowing influence their satisfaction with assessment and feedback. *Higher Education*, 74(4), 617–633. https://doi.org/10.1007/s10734-10016-0068-y.

Richmond, T. (2018). *A Degree of Uncertainty: An Investigation into Grade Inflation in Universities.* London: Reform.

Rust, C. (2009). Assessment standards: a potential role for subject networks. *Journal of Hospitality, Leisure, Sport, and Tourism Education*, 8(1), 124–128.

Rust, C. (2014). The student experience in the US and the UK: two converging pictures of decline? In S. Pickard (ed.), *Higher Education in the UK and the US: Converging University Models in a Global Academic World?*, pp. 225–249. Leiden: Brill.

Rust, C., Carroll, J., Handley, K., O'Donovan, B. & Price, M. (2009). Submission from ASKe to the Innovation, Universities, Science and Skills Select Committee inquiry into Students and Universities. https://publications.parliament.uk/pa/cm200809/cmselect/cmdius/170/170we16.htm.

Rust, C., Price, M. & O'Donovan, B. (2003). Improving students' learning by developing their understanding of assessment criteria and processes. *Assessment and Evaluation in Higher Education*, 28(2), 147–164.

Sadler, D.R. (2012). Assuring academic achievement standards: from moderation to calibration. *Assessment in Education: Principles, Policy & Practice*, 20(1), 5–19. https://doi.org/10.1080/0969594X.2012.714742.

Sadler, D.R. (2014). The futility of attempting to codify academic achievement standards. *Higher Education*, 67(3), 273–288. www.jstor.org/stable/43648653.

Shepherd, J. (2009). Does it matter which Oxford you go to? *The Guardian*, 31 March.

Snowdon, G. (2012). Graduates: Is a 2:1 the best qualification for landing a job? *The Guardian*, 10 February.

Strathern, M. (2000). The tyranny of transparency. *British Educational Research Journal*, 26(3), 309–321. https://doi.org/10.1080/713651562.

Textor, M. (2022). Number of students at colleges and universities in China 2011–2021. www.statista.com/statistics/227028/number-of-students-at-universities-in-china/.

Tsoukas, H. (2003). Do we really understand tacit knowledge? In E. Smith & M. Lyles (eds), *Handbook of Organisational Learning and Knowledge Management*, pp. 410–427. Cambridge, MA: Blackwell.

Tuning Educational Structures in Europe. (2003). Final report phase one. http://tuningacademy.org/wp-content/uploads/2014/02/TuningEUI_Final-Report_EN.pdf.

UUK (Universities UK). (2017). *Report of the Review Group on UK Higher Education Sector Agencies*. London: UUK.

UUK (Universities UK). (2020). *Protecting the Value of UK Degrees: Reviewing Progress One Year On from the Statement of Intent*. London: UUK.

UKSCQA (UK Standing Committee for Quality Assessment). (2019). *Degree Classification: Transparency, Reliability and Fairness – a Statement of Intent*. UK Standing Committee for Quality Assessment.

US Department of Education. (2006). *A Test of Leadership: Charting the Future of US Higher Education*. Washington, DC: US Dept. of Education.

Chapter 3

The complexities of academic standards as a contested concept

Margaret Price and Berry O'Donovan

Introduction

A fundamental responsibility of higher education institutions is the award of qualifications founded on consistent and reliable evaluative judgement of student achievement, and academic standards lie at the heart of these judgements. However, the complex nature of academic standards means that they are challenging to meaningfully explicate and not fully understood by key stakeholders. This chapter examines the complexity of assessment standards. We start by seeking to define academic standards as well as pointing out common misconceptions.

Different theoretical perspectives on the nature of academic standards are then critically appraised before considering assessment standards in action. While the complexity of academic standards poses considerable challenges to establishing something close to a shared understanding, new developments, arising from greater understanding of the nature of academic standards, are identified.

Defining academic standards

Chapter 2 argues that the trustworthiness of assessment practices and policies have become increasingly important to society and government as well as students. As part of this, academic standards have come under mounting scrutiny particularly in light of accusations of inconsistencies and grade inflation. Both the nature of academic standards and how to improve their consistency is not fully understood by many practitioners and policy makers (Sadler, 2014). Here, we start by considering the nature of academic standards and different perspectives on how they are understood.

Many educationalists conflate academic standards with assessment criteria and believe that they are embedded and made explicit in the agreed rules or guidance on the production of an assessed task, such as rubrics, grade descriptors, and learning outcomes (Ajjawi & Bearman, 2018). Indeed, Sadler (2014) suggests that few in higher education attempt to explain, or even question, what is meant by academic standards, perhaps because, as many scholars suggest, standards are both conceptually complex and challenging to define (Coates, 2010; Bloxham,

DOI: 10.4324/9781003379768-4

2012). However, while we acknowledge the blurred line between criteria and standards, we consider assessment criteria, as propounded by Sadler (1989), to be the *attributes* of quality that are being sought (e.g. the use of literature or analysis) and academic standards as the *levels* of performance at which such attributes of quality are enacted. We distinguish between two types of standards, 'sharp standards', which refer to precise, measurable accomplishments, and 'relative standards' that refer to matters of degree. Sharp standards are fixed and can be assessed in exactly the same way by different individuals, as in the case of standard weights or words per minute in typewriting. Relative academic standards are more challenging to share and are commonly used in higher education where complex and open-ended tasks predominate. Precise description of relative standards is difficult because understandings are socially constructed and the level is dependent on context and interpretation. For example, 'highly analytical' could be applied to the work of a PhD student or an undergraduate.

In an attempt to address some of these difficulties the higher education sector has predominantly focused on adjusting and strengthening process measures such as adherence to regulations and policies as well as inputs such as staff qualification or library resources (Boyd & Bloxham, 2014). While useful, this emphasis on input measures, which could also be labelled 'quality standards', has sidestepped fundamental issues with the measurement and sharing of relative academic standards that are the focus of this chapter and book.

The literature on academic standards generally focuses on two influential perspectives as summarised by Bloxham and Boyd (2012). The first is a techno-rational view in which standards are considered to be 'untainted by values, culture or power' (Bloxham & Boyd, 2012, p. 617). This perspective suggests standards can be codified into explicit and stable artefacts, such as assessment criteria or rubrics, that are separate from the knower and are assumed to be uniformly understood by different audiences. The second is a social constructivist perspective wherein standards are socially situated and interpreted. Here, standards reside in the practices of academic and professional communities, underpinned by tacit knowledge that is difficult to articulate and complements explicit knowledge (O'Donovan et al., 2004). In this view, standards are considered to be dynamic and context dependent.

More recently, Ajjawi and Bearman (2018) have promoted an alternative perspective, a sociomaterial framing of standards in which standards are codified into artefacts such as rubrics or marking guides. However, this differs from the techno-rational approach as a uniform interpretation of meaning is not assumed. The artefacts require interpretation by individuals and communities. Ajjawi and Bearman (2018, p. 43) suggest that this 'takes the standard out of the internal cognitive processes of the individual and even beyond the "way things are done around here" of the social'. Here, the value of artefacts (e.g. rubrics) is acknowledged, but their interpretation and enactment is undertaken by people operating in varied and complex social arrangements (Ajjawi & Bearman, 2018). Consequently, while we also recognise the value of rubrics and grade descriptors, particularly for those who have spent time discussing them in their development (see Chapter 13 for a detailed discussion of rubrics), we put forward one further caveat. That is, such artefacts are not only very limited without shared interpretation, but also that their over simplistic use can result in delusions of precision and uniformity (see Box 3.1). While these artefacts may be appealing to novice students and other non-cognoscenti, they can be misleading. This may be a provocative view for many and we pursue this argument in more detail in the next sections.

CRITICAL PERSPECTIVE

Box 3.1 Codifying standards: delusions of objectivity and uniformity of interpretation

Our concern is that consistent and dependable academic standards that can be understood by students, staff and other stakeholders across multiple contexts are often sought by the production of standardised artefacts such as rubrics and grade descriptors. However, assessment tasks, epistemologies, pedagogies and geographies do differ, as do individual and group interpretations. Consequently, such standardised artefacts may confer only a superficial and misleading veneer of consistency, and even bury more deeply held differences that we arguably should be exposing to our students, colleagues and other stakeholders. Essentially, standards are embodied in outputs (i.e. student work) and only fully revealed in a combination of valid assessment tasks, marking criteria and learners' actual performance (Sadler, 2013; Boyd & Bloxham, 2014).

Representing and assuring standards

In practice, the techno-rational view remains the dominant logic of higher education. In an effort to assure academic standards and evaluative judgements, the sector has developed and uses a raft of quality assurance frameworks and practices (Harvey, 2005). What is being sought is that, no matter the context, two pieces of work with the same qualities receive the same grade. As such, reliance on explicit codifications is seen by many as beneficial when viewed from an objectivist perspective. Traditional assessment practices in which standards are largely tacit, and as such undefined, are often considered untrustworthy (Stowell, 2004; Hudson et al., 2016). In an era wherein external control of higher education and the marginalisation of academic voice and control is flourishing (O'Byrne & Bond, 2014), explicit codifications are seen as a way to diminish reliance on individuals' tacit understandings. It is assumed that this enables the effective auditing and accountability of process (Bloxham, 2012; Hudson et al., 2016). Consequently, the explicit codification of marking criteria and standards has become ubiquitous (Handley et al., 2013). Additionally, this type of criterion-referenced evaluative judgement has gained an almost moral ascendancy over norm-referenced evaluative judgement whereby learners' performances are compared against each other and ranked accordingly (Sadler, 2014).

Assessment judgements may represent 'untainted' objective measurement when enacted in contexts involving sharp standards where a learner's work can be reliably evaluated as correct or incorrect against a model answer (i.e. based on factual knowledge and demonstrable techniques). However, it has been argued that this is not the case for high-level and complex work (Sadler, 2014) to which relative academic standards apply. Scholars suggest that the evaluative judgements of complex tasks (i.e. those that embrace divergent responses from students and where two distinctly different assignments could gain the same mark) are always interpretative and socially situated (Shay, 2004; Sadler, 2009, 2014). There is a growing body of work based on social constructivist perspectives, which asserts that standards cannot be established independently from the individuals who are using them in their evaluative judgements (see for instance Shay, 2004, 2005; O'Donovan et al., 2004; Sadler, 2009, 2014; Crossouard, 2010; Bloxham & Boyd, 2012). This represents an ontological shift in how assessment is positioned within the literature (Dawson et al., 2019) whereby the nature of assessment, both the marking of and feedback on complex work, is conceived as a social practice (see for instance, Rust et al., 2005; Orr, 2007; Shay, 2008; Boyd & Bloxham, 2014). This is a strong move away from objectivist assumptions that draw on scientific paradigms and view academic standards as fixed and 'free standing of context' (Orr, 2007, p. 646).

Scholars of assessment practice suggest there are a multiplicity of influences that form the academic standards, which are internalised and used by individual assessors. These influences include: disciplinary knowledge structures and values (Neumann et al., 2002); specialist knowledge (Shay, 2005); socialisation processes (Shay, 2004); and the other social worlds they inhabit (Handley et al., 2013). Accordingly, differences in the evaluative judgements of individual assessors perhaps should be expected (Bloxham, 2012). Drawing on the work of these researchers, academic standards and evaluative judgements, in the words of Shay (2004, p. 323), 'can be understood as context dependent, experience-based and situational judgements'. However, the assurance of standards may be hindered if the prevalence and power of internalised 'teachers' conceptions of quality' (Sadler, 1989, p. 27) or, as Shay puts it, 'assessor's interpretative frameworks' (Shay, 2005, p. 665) are ignored. O'Donovan et al. (2008) suggest that a single-minded techno-rationalist focus on assessment and feedback processes and techniques can undervalue the agency of assessors and the influence of informal participatory practices in relevant assessment communities. These authors challenge whether it is possible to make fully explicit the tacit knowledge involved in assessment decisions. This is particularly so as, despite the sector's best efforts to explicitly codify standards, there is overwhelming evidence that inconsistency in marking exists (Bloxham 2009). Consequently, we argue that sole reliance on the explicit codification of marking criteria and standards is likely to obscure reality, and essentially only confers an illusion of objective consistency or, as Shay describes it, 'a myth of objectivity', (Shay, 2005, p. 676). Building on the work of Bourdieu (1989), Delandshere (2001) asserts assessment practices are generally founded on unacknowledged epistemic assumptions in which knowledge is understood as certain, static and universal, and such assumptions mask the real nature of evaluative judgements:

> The system of beliefs, values and purposes in which the agents involved are participating is rarely discussed. The perspectives taken when stating evaluative judgements are often assumed to be understood and agreed upon, when in fact they are rarely explicit or public, and hence, not open for scrutiny or discussion.
>
> (Delandshere, 2001, p. 121)

Such epistemic assumptions remain both unquestioned and under-researched within assessment practice. As Sadler (2014) suggests, the quality frameworks, processes and techniques we rely on to assure standards may give us a sense of trust in the system, but they do not have the backing of empirical evidence that one might have assumed. This echoes the broader point of an increasing mistrust in professional judgement, already highlighted in Chapter 2. It can be argued that the quest for transparency and accountability in evaluative judgements is as much about the increasing managerial culture of higher education as it is about a quest for reliable and fair measurement and clarity of expectations (Orr, 2007; O'Byrne & Bond, 2014). Indeed, Strathern (2000) suggests that there is a tyranny in transparency that undermines trust in professional judgement. Over-reliance on documentary evidence and auditing processes can not only undermine trust, but can also distort understanding of what is going on within an organisation, concealing as much as revealing the authentic lived experience of stakeholders (Strathern, 2000). However, as Hudson et al. (2016) state, trust is necessary for an expert system to function effectively.

Sharing academic standards in practice

So far in this chapter, the nature of academic standards and assessment criteria has been theorised. This section now turns to the more pragmatic consideration of how relative academic standards may be shared, particularly with students who are eager for clarification on what is expected from them in assessment tasks (O'Donovan et al., 2001).

As stated, explicit codification remains the predominant way of communicating assessment criteria (quality attributes) and academic standards (level of performance) in the higher education sector (O'Donovan et al., 2008; Hudson et al., 2016), but there are many issues that undermine precise communication in practice. Sadler (1987) argues that verbal descriptions of standards are always *context dependent* and somewhat fuzzy, often a matter of degree, and indicative of relative rather than absolute positions. An example of this, using the quality attribute and standard of 'highly analytical', is provided in Box 3.2.

CRITICAL PERSPECTIVE

Box 3.2 Assessment criteria: a matter of interpretation

A student piece of work that is considered 'highly analytical' is likely to depend on both the assessor's interpretation of the meaning of 'analysis' and the relative standard that is considered 'high', the latter being largely dependent on the sociocultural context. Consequently, while a piece of work assessed as 'highly analytical' would be expected to embody a different standard of analysis for work completed by a first year undergraduate than for work at master's level, the verbal description might well remain the same.

The assessment criteria themselves are also subject to multiple interpretations by both individual staff members and students (O'Donovan et al., 2004; Sadler, 2009; Ajjawi & Bearman, 2018). Nevertheless, a common response to these difficulties is to specify written criteria and level descriptors more tightly. However, this can be challenging as relative descriptors benefit from a benchmark or anchor point to share definitive standards (Sadler, 1987) and, in practice, the development of ever more comprehensive and precise anchor definitions can be self-defeating (O'Donovan et al., 2004). The very precision of language and terminology can make explication less understood (O'Donovan et al., 2004), and realising a workable balance between achieving explanatory precision and usefulness can be uneconomic in the long term (Yorke, 2002). Snowdon (2002) asserts there is a cost (in terms of time and resources) to codifying knowledge effectively. This cost comes from the need to create a shared context and it increases in parallel with the diversity of an audience's experience and language.

Sadler (2009) points to other practical problems in the use of the explicit articulation of criteria and standards and criterion-referenced marking. Teachers using a selection of criteria, often embodied in a 'rubric', to mark work, find that their global impression of the work is often different from the sum of their grading of each criterion (see Chapter 13 for further discussion). A piece of work considered 'excellent' by a marker, may not be outstanding in all criteria and vice versa. Sadler (2009) suggests this anomaly is due in part to the predetermined selection of criteria. It may seem during the assessment design process that the most relevant and significant criteria have been comprehensively selected. However, selection means just that, a restricted selection, and can never be completely comprehensive, and there will be many valid criteria that are not selected (Sadler, 2009). Consequently, during the marking process a salient criterion (or more than one), that was not predetermined, can emerge (Sadler, 2009). Even if the pre-set criteria appear appropriate, their boundaries are fuzzy, sometimes merging into each other and it becomes difficult to disentangle them from each other. As Sadler states:

> Criteria which may appear to be distinct in the abstract are often found to overlap, and occasionally even to interfere, with other criteria when an attempt is made to apply them meticulously.
>
> (Sadler, 2014, p. 217)

There is another point of inconsistency and that is in the translation of the qualitative evaluation of the level and quality of a piece of work into a numerical grade awarded. This can be tricky for many reasons, more fully explored in Chapter 13, but one major issue is that numerical marks are not representative of a fixed standard. For example, a mark of 63% in many American college contexts may not indicate an above average standard of achievement, but in the UK, in many subject contexts, it would be indicative of an above average piece of work since marks above 80% and above are very rarely awarded. Such variations in perception of what is average can also occur more locally within nations, institutions or even academic departments. Indeed, many institutions put forward mark profiles for cohorts that are considered acceptable, with averages above or below such profiles prompting investigation and discussion. In a recent calibration workshop in the UK, thirty participants from different subject areas were asked if they had an institutional or departmental expected average, answers ranged from 52% to 66%. Such variation indicates that numerical marks can further confer an illusion of precision and comparability. Essentially, marks are much more than numerical descriptions, they take on meaning depending on their use and how they fit into social and organisational praxis (Spender, 1996). They are portraits of meaning not statistical certainties. The mark that an assessor gives a piece of work is also reflective of the individual's internalised numerical benchmarks, which are borne out of context and experience, leading to statements such as 'I know a 2.1 when I see it'.

While it is difficult to explicitly articulate marking criteria and standards in the abstract (Sadler, 2014), Rust et al. (2003) suggest that the standards and marking criteria can be discerned within exemplar pieces of work. Therefore marking practice and discussion can support assessors (and students) to develop their conceptions of quality (Bloxham, 2012). Active engagement with a spectrum of work can support assessors and students to construct shared conceptions of quality and standards as shown empirically in Rust et al. (2003), and conceptually discussed in O'Donovan et al. (2004). Exemplars make abstract criteria concrete (Sadler, 2014), although they do not constitute standards; standards are embedded within the exemplars and they can support insights into standards (Handley et al., 2013). However, Handley et al. (2013, p. 3) caution that 'exemplars by themselves are insufficient – they need to be interpreted' and consequently, participative activities that support the sharing of interpretations remains of key importance. As noted in Chapter 2, an effective alternative to seeking ever greater precision in explicit codification of assessment criteria and standards is to actively engage participants in discussing and applying the standards to concrete pieces of work, enabling them to engage and develop a shared understanding across their subject community (Price, 2005).

Within a socially constructivist perspective it is the group, not the individual, that makes meaning through participants collectively constructing understandings of their practice (Brown & Duguid, 1991). Through participation and immersion, newcomers share the tacit and implicit understandings embedded in the actions of more experienced members of an assessment community (O'Donovan et al., 2008). This view of sharing common understandings of assessment standards is based on fundamentally different epistemic assumptions that are fundamentally different from a view of knowledge as a reified entity that can be easily exchanged. Here, knowledge of standards is not something a person possesses but a situated, culturally embedded, socially mediated practice (Wegner & Nuckles, 2015). 'Coming to know' is not about acquiring knowledge but a process of becoming part of a community of practice whose members share a joint interest, interact regularly and share a common repertoire of resources including language and discourse (Northedge, 2003). From this epistemic viewpoint, the role of participation and dialogue becomes more significant in a *process* of coming to know what is considered a high quality piece of work or even to come to understand and use feedback (Price et al., 2011). This perspective is a social constructivist approach in which intentional, formalised, activity-based, social learning processes are devised to support a group understanding of quality of standards. Such a process of acculturation can take a considerable period of time (McCune, 2009). However, O'Donovan et al. (2008) suggest that acculturation and enhanced participation in assessment praxis can be speeded through intentional activities and approaches that encourage and support participation and development. Consequently, there is enhanced interest across the higher education sector in intentional 'calibration' activities in which, to reach a shared understanding of standards, academics collaboratively appraise concrete examples of student work and agree on the rationale for their judgements, separately from marking their own students' work. This dialogic process intends to produce 'calibrated academics ... able to make grading judgements consistent with those which similarly calibrated colleagues would make' (Sadler, 2013, p. 5). Detailed discussion of calibration and social moderation can be found in Chapter 8 and calibration in practice is exemplified in practice from two disciplinary communities in Chapters 14 and 15. While there is evidence that engagement in calibration activities results in improved consistency, we are wary of over claiming. The differences between assessment tasks and subject contexts limit the goal of overarching consistency. As Ajjawi and Bearman (2018, p. 44) posit, different contexts over 'space, time, people and materials' will inevitably lead to some adjustments to standards, but with care, not so much so that the 'standard' is no longer recognisable. This can be likened to Wittgenstein's (1953) notion of family resemblance where each enactment of the standard may display similar characteristics but not all 'family members' will necessarily share all features. Ultimately, the realisation of total uniformity in the application of relative academic standards is overly optimistic, but we can hope to move towards a more evidence-based and defendable position.

Conclusion

The complexity of academic standards makes assuring those standards problematic. A plethora of misunderstandings, unfounded assumptions and desire for simple solutions has added to the difficulties of finding a route to collective understandings and common beliefs about academic standards within subject communities. Assumptions within the established techno-rationalist approach have led to delusions of objectivity and beliefs that academic standards can simply be shared through explicit artefacts. However, greater examination and emerging evidence is challenging its dominance. Sociomaterial and social constructivist perspectives are gaining recognition, including acknowledgement that academic standards can only be seen in a combination of valid assessment tasks, material codifications such as marking criteria and the level of performance revealed and judged in actual student outputs. In turn, this is offering new ways to approach the quest for 'consensus', albeit acknowledging the situated circumstances of different assessment events. Attention must be paid to sharing of academic standards throughout the assessment process from task planning, criteria creation through to translation of judgement of the academic standard of student work into a grade. It also has to be acknowledged that approaches such as calibration will inevitably take time and resources and require a commitment by the sector to seek a truly consistent approach to academic standards rather than the mere illusion of objectivity offered by focusing on codifications.

References

Ajjawi, R. & Bearman, M. (2018). Problematizing standards: representation or performance? D. Boud, R. Ajjawi, P. Dawson & J. Tai (eds), *Evaluative Judgment*, pp. 41–50. Abingdon: Routledge. https://doi.org/10.4324/9781315109251.

Bloxham, S. (2009). Marking and moderation in the UK: false assumptions and wasted resources. *Assessment & Evaluation in Higher Education*, 34(2), 209–220. https://doi.org/10.1080/02602930801955978.

Bloxham, S. (2012). 'You can see the quality in front of your eyes': grounding academic standards between rationality and interpretation. *Quality in Higher Education*, 18(2), 185–204. https://doi.org/10.1080/13538322.2012.711071.

Bloxham, S. & Boyd P. (2012). Accountability in grading student work: securing academic standards in a twenty-first century quality assurance context. *British Educational Research Journal*, 38(4), 615–634. https://doi.org/10.1080/01411926.2011.569007.

Bourdieu, P. (1989). *La noblesse d'etat*. Paris: Editions de Minuit.

Boyd, P. & Bloxham, S. (2014). A situative metaphor for teacher learning: the case of university tutors learning to grade student coursework. *British Educational Research Journal*, 40(2), 337–352. https://doi.org/10.1002/berj.3082.

Brown, J.S. & Duguid, P. (1991). Organizational learning and communities-of- practice: toward a unified view of working, learning, and innovation. *Organization Science*, 2(1), 40–57. https://doi.org/10.1287/orsc.2.1.40.

Coates, H. (2010). Defining and monitoring academic standards in Australian higher education, *Higher Education Management and Policy*, 22(1), 41–58. https://doi.org/10.1787/hemp-v22-art2-en.

Crossouard, B. (2010). Reforms to higher education assessment reporting: opportunities and challenges. *Teaching in Higher Education*, 15(3), 247–258. https://doi.org/10.1080/13562511003740809.

Dawson, P., Henderson, M., Mahoney, P., Phillips, M., Ryan, T., Boud, D. & Molloy, E. (2019). What makes for effective feedback: staff and student perspectives, *Assessment & Evaluation in Higher Education*, 44(1), 25–36. https://doi.org/10.1080/02602938.2018.1467877.

Delandshere, G. (2001). Implicit theories, unexamined assumptions and the status quo of educational assessment, *Assessment in Education: Principles, Policy & Practice*, 8(2), 113–133. https://doi.org/10.1080/09695940123828.

Handley, K., den Outer, B. & Price M. (2013). Learning to mark: exemplars, dialogue and participation in assessment communities. *Higher Education Research and Development*, 32(6), 888–900. https://doi.org/10.1080/07294360.2013.806438.

Harvey, L. (2005). A history and critique of quality evaluation in the UK. *Quality Assurance in Higher Education*, 13(4), 263–276. https://doi.org/10.1108/09684880510700608.

Hudson, J., Bloxham, S., den Outer, B. & Price, M. (2016). Conceptual acrobatics: talking about assessment standards in the transparency era. *Studies in Higher Education*, 42(7), 1309–1323. https://doi.org/10.1080/03075079.2015.1092130.

Neumann, R.S., Parry, S. & Becher, T. (2002). Teaching and learning in their disciplinary contexts: a conceptual analysis. *Studies in Higher Education*, 27(4), 405–417. https://doi.org/10.1080/0307507022000011525.

McCune, V. (2009). Final year biosciences students' willingness to engage: teaching-learning environments, authentic learning experiences and identities. *Studies in Higher Education*, 34(3), 347–361. https://doi.org/10.1080/03075070802597127.

Northedge, A. (2003). Enabling participation in academic discourse. *Teaching in Higher Education*, 8(2), 169–180. https://doi.org/10.1080/1356251032000052429.

O'Byrne, D. & Bond, C. (2014). Back to the future: the idea of a university revisited. *Journal of Higher Education Policy and Management*, 36(6), 571–584. https://doi.org/10.1080/1360080X.2014.957888.

O'Donovan, B., Price, M. & Rust, C. (2001). The student experience of the introduction of a common criteria assessment grid across an academic department. *Innovations in Education and Teaching International*, 38(1), 74–85. https://doi.org/10.1080/147032901300002873.

O'Donovan, B., Price, M. & Rust, C. (2004). Know what I mean? Enhancing student understanding of assessment standards and criteria. *Teaching in Higher Education*, 9(3), 325–336. https://doi.org/10.1080/1356251042000216642.

O'Donovan, B., Price, M. & Rust, C. (2008). Developing student understanding of assessment standards: a nested hierarchy of approaches. *Teaching in Higher Education*, 13(2), 205–217. https://doi.org/10.1080/13562510801923344.

Orr, S. (2007). Assessment moderation: constructing the marks and constructing the students. *Assessment and Evaluation in Higher Education*, 32(6), 645–656. https://doi.org/10.1080/02602930601117068.

Price, M. (2005). Assessment standards: the role of communities of practice and the scholarship of assessment. *Assessment and Evaluation in Higher Education*, 30(3), 215–230. https://doi.org/10.1080/02602930500063793.

Price, M., Handley, K., Millar, J. & O'Donovan, B. (2011). Feedback: all that effort, but what is the effect? *Assessment and Evaluation in Higher Education*, 35(3), 277–289. https://doi.org/10.1080/02602930903541007.

Rust, C., Price, M. & O'Donovan, B. (2003). Improving students' learning by developing their understanding of assessment criteria and processes. *Assessment & Evaluation in Higher Education*, 28(2), 147–164. https://doi.org/10.1080/02602930301671.

Rust, C., O'Donovan, B. & Price, M. (2005). A social constructivist assessment process model: how the research literature shows us this could be best practice. *Assessment and Evaluation in Higher Education*, 30(3), 231–240. https://doi.org/10.1080/02602930500063819.

Sadler, D.R. (1987). Specifying and promulgating achievement standards. *Oxford Review of Education*, 13(2), 191–209. https://doi.org/10.1080/0305498870130207.

Sadler, D.R. (1989). Formative assessment and the design of instructional systems. *Instructional Science*, 18(2), 119–144. https://doi.org/10.1007/BF00117714.

Sadler, D.R. (2009). Indeterminacy in the use of preset criteria for assessment and grading in higher education. *Assessment and Evaluation in Higher Education*, 34(2), 159–179. https://doi.org/10.1080/02602930801956059.

Sadler, D.R. (2013). Assuring academic achievement standards: from moderation to calibration. *Assessment in Education: Principles, Policy & Practice*, 20(1), 5–19. https://doi.org/10.1080/0969594X.2012.714742.

Sadler, D.R. (2014). The futility of attempting to codify academic achievement standards. *Higher Education*, 67(3), 273–288. https://doi.org/10.1007/s10734-013-9649-1.

Shay, S. (2004). The assessment of complex performance: a socially situated interpretive act. *Harvard Educational Review*, 74(3), 307–329. https://doi.org/10.17763/haer.74.3.wq16l67103324520.

Shay, S. (2005). The assessment of complex tasks: a double reading. *Studies in Higher Education*, 30(6), 663–679. https://doi.org/10.1007/s10734-013-9649-1.

Shay, S. (2008). Beyond social constructivist perspectives on assessment: the centring of knowledge. *Teaching in Higher Education*, 13(5), 595–605. https://doi.org/10.1080/13562510802334970.

Snowdon, D. (2002). Complex acts of knowing: paradox and descriptive self-awareness. *Journal of Knowledge Management*, 6(2),100–111. https://doi.org/10.1108/13673270210424639.

Spender, J.C. (1996). Organisational knowledge, learning and memory: three concepts in search of a theory. *Journal of Organizational Change Management*, 9, 63–78. https://doi.org/10.1108/09534819610156813.

Stowell, M. (2004). Equity, justice and standards: assessment decision making in higher education. *Assessment and Evaluation in Higher Education*, 29(4), 495–510. https://doi.org/10.1080/02602930310001689055.

Strathern, M. (2000). The tyranny of transparency. *British Educational Research Journal*, 26(3), 309–321. https://doi.org/10.1080/713651562.

Wegner, E. & Nuckles, M. (2015). Knowledge acquisition or participation in communities of practice? Academics' metaphors of teaching and learning at the university. *Studies in Higher Education*, 40(4), 624–643. https://doi.org/10.1080/03075079.2013.842213.

Wittgenstein, L. (1953). *Philosophical Investigations.* Oxford: Blackwell.

Yorke, M. (2002). Subject benchmarking and the assessment of student learning. *Quality Assurance in Education*, 10(3), 155–171. https://doi.org/10.1108/09684880210435921.

Chapter 4

Academic standards in a globalised world

Jon Yorke

Introduction

Institutions and nation states have long sought to advance their positioning in a globalised world. Success in a competitive higher education market is dependent on signals of quality, often rendered 'transparent' through 'objective' comparable data. Public signals of quality are highly influential within globalised higher education (Marginson, 2013, 2022), and those signals relating to academic standards are especially so. While academic standards are central to judgements of quality, they depend on the practices of assessment within institutions. As Chapters 2 and 3 have discussed, a substantial body of literature suggests that while academic standards may be subject to codification, they are ultimately social constructions with validity local to their contextual setting. Such findings have not dissuaded elite policy actors from pursuing the notion that academic standards can be defined, measured, and compared.

Drawing on examples from Australia, USA, UK, and Brazil, this chapter will examine ways in which institutions and nations, and additionally supranational bodies such as the Organisation for Economic Co-operation and Development (OECD), have attempted to codify and compare academic standards. Policy developments in Australia are examined in detail, where the federal government made persistent yet ultimately unsuccessful attempts to draw on academic standards to generate comparative 'measures' to 'prove' academic quality. Eventually, proposed measures were replaced by processes of 'external referencing', an approach which recognises the socially constructed nature of academic standards. The chapter concludes with an outline of contemporary approaches to external referencing in Australia, identifying many characteristics in common with the UK Degree Standards Project (see Chapters 9–12).

Globalisation and the rise of 'objective' comparable data

Borrowing from Rizvi and Lingard (2010), globalisation is taken here to refer to a complex, diffuse and highly intertwined set of processes that, taken together, create social, political, and economic impact across and between nation states. Commentators such as Ball (2012) have argued that neoliberal ideologies, with

DOI: 10.4324/9781003379768-5

their emphasis on economic and market efficiency, have come to exert an increasingly powerful influence, enacted through technologies of accountability that demonstrate that higher education institutions are efficiently and effectively meeting society's expectations.

Market efficiency and competition go hand in hand. Competition inevitably involves comparison, and ratings/rankings draw on various sources of data in their compilation. Some of these rankings are supranational in nature, such as those produced by the OECD who have been identified to be an increasingly powerful policy actor on the world stage (Lewis & Lingard, 2022; Münch & Wieczorek, 2023). The OECD's 'soft' governance by numbers (Grek, 2009) contained within international comparisons have produced intense pressure on national governments to reform policies (Bamberger & Kim, 2022).

Taken together, these increasingly globalised pressures have created a 'relentless drive' (Zajda, 2014, p. 166) on the part of nation states to acquire quantitative comparative data to 'prove' quality to multiple stakeholders (Li et al., 2021). While there are many other good reasons to consider comparative data (equity, safety, input factors, among others), the point being made here is that signals of quality have become particularly influential. Academic institutions are far from immune to these pressures (Carnegie, 2021). However, any judgement of quality, should, of course, involve a consideration of academic standards.

Assessment, academic standards and global stakeholders

Academic standards are enshrined within the multiple judgements that lead to the award of a qualification. Throughout their period of study, students' assessed work is regularly subjected to grading decisions, most of which produce 'codes' (Sadler, 2014), which eventually become aggregated to determine an outcome (pass, fail, degree classification, etc.). Academic standards are therefore inextricably intertwined with assessment and grading practices, and any comparison (local, national, or global) will ultimately depend on these multiple local practices of assessment. The term 'learning standards' is often used (especially in the Australian setting) to refer to academic standards that relate specifically to student learning.

There are many stakeholders with an interest in academic standards, including employers, governments, and, as the preceding discussion has highlighted, this extends to organisations such as the OECD operating at a supranational level. Figure 4.1 draws together these relationships, showing how comparative measures of quality depend on academic (learning) standards and assessment practices, located within contemporary discourses of accountability, and set within an increasingly globalised context.

Academic standards and national/international policy discourses

Over the last thirty years or so, policy discourses at a national and international level have focused on quality and academic standards, and the remainder of this

Figure 4.1 The intersection of globalisation, accountability, quality, learning standards and assessment.
Source: Yorke & Vidovich (2016)

chapter will briefly address developments in the UK, US, Brazil and the OECD before examining the policy evolution in Australia in detail.

United Kingdom: the issue of codification

Given the detailed coverage of the UK setting throughout this book, this section will be brief. The issue of academic standards received a considerable push in the UK with the landmark report titled *Higher Education in the Learning Society* (National Committee of Inquiry into Higher Education, 1997). The UK Quality Assurance Agency subsequently set out to produce subject benchmark *standards*, but by the time of their production in 2000 they had been cast as subject benchmark *statements*. Although these subject benchmarks were intended to convey expectations for graduate capabilities in their discipline, the shift in language from 'standards' to 'statements' conveyed a sense that the process had, from an early stage, failed to 'clearly define explicit standards for all subjects' (Rust et al., 2003, p. 148). As discussed later, this early finding did not dissuade elite policy actors in Australia from doggedly pursuing this agenda.

In retrospect, this difficulty in establishing comparable objective standards is hardly surprising. For example, Knight (2002, p. 280) asserted that 'benchmarks, specifications, criteria and learning outcomes do not and cannot make summative assessment reliable ... it is not possible to know what criteria have been used, what meanings have attached to them and how they have been used'. This critical issue of local meaning is readily apparent in the example contained in Box 4.1.

CRITICAL PERSPECTIVE

Box 4.1 The difficulty of establishing objective standards through codification

A compelling example of the local nature of meaning is given by Rust et al. (2003) within which an assessment 'grid' (rubric) was developed to address external examiners concerns about consistency of standards. When evaluating the project, it was established that the grid had been adopted without any modification or apparent difficulty by markers for both *first year* and *masters* level modules!

Long-standing tensions between various perspectives on the nature of standards are entrenched in the UK literature (e.g. Knight, 2002; Yorke, 2007; Bloxham et al., 2011), and indeed many are examined within this book. For example, some perspectives embrace an assumption that standards are amenable to definition, and that their measurement and comparison is reliable. Ajjawi et al. (2021) see this as the dominant perspective but are quick to identify its shortcomings. Other perspectives see standards as being agreements that emerge from the disciplinary setting, through discussion and negotiation. Sadler's classic definition embraced both possibilities when he referred to standards as being a 'definite degree of academic achievement established by authority, custom, or consensus and used as a fixed reference point for reporting a student's level of attainment' (Sadler, 2012, p. 9). A key question here is 'who owns the standard' – an issue common to the following examples drawn from other countries.

USA: Standardised testing of academic standards

At the turn of the century, a focus on standards and their comparability was also becoming increasingly evident in the USA, when in 2006 the Spellings Commission argued for better indicators and standardised testing across higher education, consistent with the stance taken earlier in schools with the 2002 *No Child Left Behind Act* (Hursh, 2008). In a landmark document titled *A Test of Leadership: Charting the Future of US Higher Education*, the Spellings Commission called for higher education institutions to 'measure student learning using quality assessment from indicators such as, for example, the Collegiate Learning Assessment (CLA)' (US Department of Education, 2006, p. 24). The CLA had been developed in 2002 by the American Council for Aid to Education to evaluate critical thinking, problem solving and written communication, using a standardised test (Hardison & Vilamovska, 2009). However, it is important to note at this point that the CLA was specifically designed to be used for quality enhancement, not quality assurance, and certainly not for large scale comparative purposes.

The reaction to the Commission's proposal to introduce standardised testing of academic standards into American higher education was swift, marked by a flurry of activity by high-level advocacy groups from within the sector to avoid prescription 'from above'. For example, within a year of the Commission's proposal, the American Association of Colleges and Universities embarked on a substantial three-year project to develop detailed standards for 15 graduate-level learning outcomes, labelled 'Valid Assessments of Learning in Undergraduate Education', and known as the VALUE project (American Association of Colleges and Universities, 2023).

An equally swift response came from the American Association of State Colleges and Universities and the Association of Public and Land-grant Universities, who developed the 'Voluntary System of Accountability' (VSA) positioning this as a 'necessary response to the demands of the time' (Jankowski et al., 2012, p. 3). Since inception, the VSA has evolved to permit participating institutions a wider choice of quality instruments than what was offered at the outset, marking what Liu (2017) referred to as a shift from raw accountability towards quality improvement. Despite a visible trend towards ever more complex datasets, Colina and Blanco (2021, p. 140) lamented the 'lack of visibility of academic staff' in institutional quality processes and products, and the questionable impact on student learning. This question of ownership with respect to academic standards is also evident in the Brazilian setting, to which we now turn.

Brazil: a national approach to academic standards in higher education

The long-running example of Brazil's use of data on academic standards to compare institutional quality highlights several issues that are relevant to this discussion. The emergence of standardised testing in Brazilian higher education can be traced back to the mid-1990s, where it arose as a response to calls for increased accountability to deal with perceived quality issues in private institutions. The then Education Minister's approach was to introduce, without consultation, a common exit examination in 1996 for undergraduates across a range of disciplines. The exam was known as the ENC, or Provão ('big test'), and, while it was unpopular with institutions, academics, and students, from the outset 'it received strong support in public opinion and in the press' (Schwartzman, 2010, p. 293).

Until 2000, results from the ENC were used to segregate institutions, which were ranked between 'A' and 'E' in stratified bands (A 12%, B 18%, C 40%, D 18%, E 12%), where the top 12% of institutions were ranked 'A' and so on. This approach side-stepped the need to establish disciplinary-based thresholds, and, while it gave a sense of relative positioning, it did not convey where the institution's courses were in absolute terms. While this is a well-known problem of normative approaches to assessment, it may have been considered a distinct advantage politically, given that it would not be possible to have more than 12% of the sampled courses rated at the lowest level at any one time.

The issues of ranking and league tables are well described and the impact of the ENC was substantial. For example, Salmi (2009) identified that demand for highly ranked courses rose by some 20%, but demand for courses with a poor ENC assessment reduced by 41%. The impact on institutions was differentiated by their relative power; some elite status institutions did not participate in the ENC, and while they were non-compliant there was very little evidence of any action being taken against them (Schwartzman, 2010).

In 2004, the ENC was replaced by ENADE, which also sought to appraise and compare academic standards, but it now represented just one component of a much more complex tripartite system known as SINAES (Pereira et al., 2018). Notable changes within ENADE included a shift from universal coverage of all students to population sampling, with scoring and reporting becoming more complicated. Moreover, a three-year review cycle replaced the previous annual approach.

Over a period of decades, the national examination in Brazil was to evolve from an initially simple reductive rating/ranking to become the more sophisticated and data-rich approach that it is today. Yet, despite the increased sophistication and complexity, fundamental problems persist. The more detailed renditions of data in ENADE were 'received with much less interest' than the predecessor ENC (Schwartzman, 2010, p. 309). The issue of poor motivation and 'soft boycotts' by students choosing not to undertake national assessments remains an issue (Miranda et al., 2019). The persistent effects of game playing are evident; Alves de Oliveria et al. (2022) pointed to the various ways in which institutions have coached their students for the test with preparatory courses and awards for students that completed ENC or the successor ENADE. Ultimately, in the eyes of Pereira et al. (2018), the Brazilian government-owned 'top-down' legislative approach demonstrates that a complex sector is not readily governed by generalised standards.

The OECD: large scale international comparisons in higher education

Before turning to the detailed example of Australia, a brief outline of two significant projects from the Organisation for Economic Co-operation and Development (OECD) is in order. As outlined earlier, supranational bodies such as the OECD have, through publication of comparative data, become major sources of influence in national-level policy discussions.

In 2000, the OECD Programme for International Student Assessment (PISA) was launched, comparing outcomes across schools in participating countries every three years (Organisation for Economic Co-operation and Development, 2023). By 2006, the OECD Education Ministers were considering the possibility of introducing a similar approach within higher education, commissioning a feasibility study in 2008 before launching the Assessment of Higher Education Learning Outcomes (AHELO) project in 2010. Initially referred to as a 'PISA for higher education' (Organisation for Economic Co-operation and Development, 2012, p. 56), the AHELO project sought to develop a 'direct evaluation of student performance at the global level ... valid across diverse cultures, languages and different types of institutions' (Organisation for Economic Co-operation and

Development, 2014, para. 2). Across 15 countries and 150 institutions, work was undertaken to adopt or adapt standardised tests to appraise a suite of generic skills. Both PISA and AHELO in their respective sectors exerted a considerable influence on national governments, who had much to gain from a favourable ranking (and vice versa).

Although PISA continues, the power of AHELO eventually started to wane (Beerkens, 2022) and it was eventually dropped in the light of the equivocal results in piloting and lack of support from high status participants such as the USA and Canada (Kallo, 2021). Large scale comparative studies are politically, financially, and methodologically challenging in higher education (Beerkens, 2018), and to some extent, AHELO rediscovered some of the earlier issues with other test instruments. These would include the Brazilian ENC/ENADE or the summative use of the American CLA where the design of the test instrument was contested, academic staff were relatively uninvolved, and students were reluctant to participate in an additional assessment that had very little direct benefit to them. However, the influences of OECD's extension of global comparisons to higher education in AHELO and the American CLA were far reaching and readily apparent in the Australian setting, to which we now turn.

Australia: the shift from measurement to calibration of academic standards

Australian higher education policy has not been immune to external pressures and 'policy borrowing' (Ozga & Jones, 2006; Alexiadou, 2014). As outlined in later parts of this section, policy influences emanating from the United Kingdom (UK) and the United States of America (USA) are readily identifiable in the Australian setting.

Australian higher education policy has passed through several evolutionary stages over the last three decades, with the first official quality policy being released in the early 1990s (Baldwin, 1991). This early policy saw the distribution of $AUD 76 million for universities that chose to opt in – which of course they all did. The meaning of quality within this document was originally constructed as that of having 'excellent standards', appraised through processes of review. However, the then incoming Minister Beazley added an outcomes component, and the discourse from 1992–1993 became that of 'quality assurance', with increased emphasis on public accountability (Vidovich, 2001).

Towards the turn of the century, the thorny issue of external comparison gained greater prominence when Minister Kemp pointed to the difficulty of comparing Australian standards with other countries (Kemp, 1999). By now, funding that was previously settled on an 'opt in' basis had become conditional funding that was 'at risk' if performance targets were not met. Notably, the language shifted from 'review' to 'audit', with quality to be appraised from 2001 onwards by the newly constituted Australian Universities Quality Agency (AUQA), an independent company. These debates and arguments mirror the complexity of academic standards and the problems of codification discussed in Chapter 3.

It is interesting to note that AUQA had consistently cited the value of benchmarking academic standards in audit reports (Stella & Woodhouse, 2007). Various small-scale projects had been quietly flourishing, supported by the former Australian Learning and Teaching Council and its predecessor, the Carrick Institute. Taking a similar position to the UK Higher Education Quality Council outlined in Chapter 2, these small-scale projects focused on the value of building shared understandings of learning standards within an academic community.

In 2008, Australia saw a landmark policy change, which was to set the scene for several years of turbulence with respect to academic standards and their appraisal. Following the election of the Labor Rudd Government, Education Minister Gillard established a 'Review of Australian Higher Education', chaired by a former Australian Vice-Chancellor. The overarching aim of the review panel was to establish whether the sector was 'meeting the needs of the Australian community and economy' (Bradley et al., 2008, p. 205). Picking up themes of global comparison and competition, the final report (known widely as the 'Bradley Report' after the panel chair) suggested that Australia was falling behind:

> Australia is losing ground. Within the OECD we are now 9th out of 30 in the proportion of our population aged 25 to 34 years with such qualifications, down from 7th a decade ago. Twenty-nine per cent of our 25 to 34 year olds have degree-level qualifications but in other OECD countries targets of up to 50 per cent have already been set. These policy decisions elsewhere place us at a great competitive disadvantage unless immediate action is taken.
>
> (Bradley et al., 2008, p. xi)

The Bradley Report ultimately made 46 recommendations to the Australian Government, including the proposed establishment of new quality assurance arrangements, which would include a set of:

- Indicators and instruments to directly assess and compare learning outcomes; and
- formal statements of academic standards by discipline along with processes for applying those standards.

(Bradley et al., 2008, p. 137)

Most of the Bradley Report's recommendations were accepted in the Australian Government's policy response, titled *Transforming Australia's Higher Education System*. Within this landmark document, far-reaching changes were proposed in a section titled 'A New Era of Quality in Australian Tertiary Education' (Department of Education, Employment and Workplace Relations, 2009a, p. 31). In a flurry of consultation papers that followed, the Australian Government sought to persuade a rather sceptical sector that the lack of clearly defined learning standards was the problem, and, further, that these standards (if defined) could be appraised via a variety of quality indicators. The possibility of Australia adopting standardised testing to appraise academic standards (and fund universities accordingly) was raised, and this was to touch many nerves.

This consultation provoked swift and strongly negative reactions from academics, university groupings, and policy makers. For example, Robson (2009) challenged the underpinning argument that Australia was losing ground, arguing that concerns regarding the quality of Australian graduates were unfounded. Echoing Knight's (2002) concerns, Welsman (2009) warned that the level of detail needed to define/measure academic standards would not achieve the intended purpose – even if the documentation was comprehensive, thereby producing the perverse outcome of bogging down the sector in excessive prescription. Fisher (2009) pointed out that academic standards relied on assessment grading practices, which were far from consistent across the sector.

To progress the attempt to codify academic standards, the Australian Government committed $AUD 2 million to facilitate the Learning and Teaching Academic Standards Project, led by experienced academics ('Discipline Scholars'), drawn from broad disciplinary groupings (Australian Learning and Teaching Council, 2010). In a striking parallel to the UK example outlined earlier in this chapter, the initial deliverable for this group was to identify minimum standards for graduation within that discipline, labelled 'Threshold Learning Outcomes'.

The Australian Government identified future conditional funding that would be distributed to universities from 2012 that met 'institutional targets against sector-wide measures and indicators' (Department of Education, Employment and Workplace Relations, 2009b, p. 5). Although these measures/indicators had not been specified at this stage, several principles for their selection were proposed. Desirable indicators were 'statistically sound and methodologically rigorous ... derived from high quality, objective data sources ... without having a perverse influence on behaviour' (Department of Education, Employment and Workplace Relations, 2009b, p. 6). Whether this admirable and optimistic set of characteristics was even possible was yet to be determined.

The indicators relating to academic standards proved to be most problematic. Although the Australian Government hoped that the Discipline Scholars would eventually create measurable discipline-specific outcomes, the Scholars' Learning and Teaching Academic Standards project had only just commenced. To maintain progress, the Australian Government proposed the interim use of the Graduate Skills Assessment (GSA) as a way of achieving a value-added measure of generic graduate skills.

At this point, it is important to explain that the GSA had been developed much earlier in 1999 by the Australian Council for Educational Research, and it comprised a three-hour assessment consisting of multiple choice (two hours) and written tasks (one hour). Despite being well-established, the GSA was not in wide use, and universities (e.g. Griffith University, n.d.) had pointed to the lack of actionable information provided to universities and employers.

Substantial questions were left unaddressed within the Australian Government's proposal to use the GSA. How would the deployment of the instrument be funded? What incentive would a student have to make a serious attempt on a lengthy examination as an optional additional task separate to their studies? Importantly, by design, the GSA did not cover discipline learning outcomes, which was a serious issue. Moreover, the GSA was also limited in scope with respect to generic learning outcomes such as those in the psychomotor or affective domain, or the ability to work in teams. Was this to be an Australian 'Provão'?

Against a backlash of responses mostly hostile to the proposals, the Australian Government issued a second iteration which dropped the GSA as a measure of learning standards, proposing a new indicator instead; the American Collegiate Learning Assessment (CLA) which was being considered within the OECD's AHELO project. If anything, tensions were only heightened by this policy development (Trounson, 2010). The CLA had been designed for quality improvement, not high-stakes funding – a point made by the founding Council's President upon becoming aware of the intended appropriation for use in the Australian setting (Benjamin, 2010).

A further round of responses, similarly hostile to the second set of proposals, precipitated a third round of policy consultation within which many concessions and changes were made. However, the CLA was still identified as a suitable performance indicator for the quality of learning outcomes, but a clarification was offered that this was to be an Australian version of the American test (Australian Government, 2011). However, what that meant in practice was never very clear.

A year later, all suggestions of using the CLA were dropped. The Australian Government withdrew funding for the development of performance indicators, citing fiscal pressures and observing that sector consultation had shown 'no consensus on the issue of whether it is appropriate to use such indicators for Reward Funding' (Department of Education, Employment and Workplace Relations, 2011, p. 4).

The issue of learning standards and, specifically, their measurement and comparability remained in a state of dispute between the sector and the Australian Government from 2009 to 2013. The Learning and Teaching Academic Standards project completed during this period, producing a set of expectations for graduates in their broad disciplinary groupings. However, criticism was mounted against them for their broad and all-encompassing nature which defied measurement and comparison. For example, Dietrich (2011, para. 17) observed that 'threshold learning standards are so widely drawn almost any criticism can be met with a nod to the outcomes and an assertion they are being complied with'. Perhaps so, but it was also clear that excessive prescription was not the answer either, a position taken by the Australian Technology Network collective of universities who had much earlier argued that 'any useful approach would not be doable and any doable approach would not be useful' (Australian Technology Network, 2009, p. 4). During this period, an alternative approach was put forward by Sadler (2012), who argued that processes of 'calibration' could produce consistent grading judgements without the need for constant and repetitive moderation activities. Like the American VALUE project described earlier, the calibration approaches described by Sadler (2012) would contribute to the assurance of quality, through rich professional development activities and improved shared understandings of academic standards over time, consistent with Knight's (2002) views of academic judgement.

A potential end to the five-year debate was signalled when the newly formed Higher Education Standards Panel put forward a set of consultation documents describing course and learning outcomes (Higher Education Standards Panel, 2013). This draft proposed that the grading of student achievement for selected units within a course of study would be 'referenced' periodically against comparable courses in other Australian institutions. The word 'measure' was nowhere to be seen.

A requirement to undertake 'external referencing' was subsequently enshrined in legislation and described as a periodic (not less than seven yearly) set of review and improvement activities comparing student cohorts against comparable courses of study (Higher Education Standards Framework, 2015). Currently, a comparative consideration of the assessment methods and grading of student achievement in selected units is required for any course undergoing periodic review (Tertiary Education Quality and Standards Agency, 2019).

In a manner reminiscent of the USA example discussed earlier, academic communities and their sector groupings were quick off the mark, and various projects to investigate approaches to external referencing were promptly initiated. However, while the following three projects shared the common purpose of verifying academic standards, they were quite different in the manner of their execution (see, for example Bedford et al., 2016). The Achievement Matters: External Peer Review of Accounting Learning Standards was an early entrant, drawing on Sadler's (2012) conception of calibration, using randomly sampled pieces of student work and a double-blind process to examine consensus on whether the course level learning outcomes were met (Watty et al., 2014). The Australian research-intensive institutions known as the 'Group of Eight' developed the Quality Verification System, a non-blinded process which required reviewers to examine assessed student work and review allocated grades from a stratified random sample across grade bands to verify that course level standards were appropriate, and to determine whether they had been met (Group of Eight, 2018). The Teaching and Learning Standards project also used stratified randomly sampled student work, but reviewers examined 'clean copies' of the assessed work without any knowledge of the previous mark/grade allocated (Krause et al., 2014).

A subsequent initiative sought to build on these approaches. Known as the External Referencing of Standards (ERoS) project, the team developed and tested a collaborative end-to-end calibration process to verify student attainment and academic standards. This sought to encourage academics to engage in a shared conversation about standards, using de-identified student assessments (Sefcik et al., 2018).

In Australia, work continues to embed approaches to external referencing. The Council of Australian University Leaders in Learning and Teaching drew together consolidated guidance relating to external referencing, drawing on previous projects and adapting questions from the ERoS project (Wilson et al., 2019). A Peer

Review Portal has been developed, to organise the process and facilitate partnerships between staff in other institutions. However, given the prominence of external referencing in Australia, it is perhaps surprising, pandemic notwithstanding, that evaluative research on this topic has diminished significantly since the initial work, which is now looking dated. Further, McCubbin et al. (2022) noted that a quarter of sampled universities did not have publicly available documentation on external referencing, and while there are plausible explanations for this (e.g. information stored within the intranet) this is also of potential concern.

At the time of writing, Australia is on the cusp of another turning point in national policy. Under the incoming Minister Clare, a new policy review was launched in November 2022, the first since the Bradley review described earlier. Known as the 'University Accord', and led by former Vice-Chancellor O'Kane, it is positioned to drive 'lasting reform' in the higher education system (Clare, 2022). The issue of funding arrangements that deliver quality is mentioned, although there is no direct reference to academic standards – at least, not yet.

Conclusion

This chapter commenced with a discussion of how public signals of quality depend on academic standards and the local practices of assessment. Herein, the constantly evolving tensions associated with national policies in a variety of settings have been described. In each example, a common interest in academic standards and the 'proof' of comparative quality through the lens of objective data is readily apparent.

Although nation states have considerable autonomy over the policy positions they adopt, those policy trajectories are influenced by a myriad of factors. These factors include comparative pressures that arise within higher education and those that are imported from other sectors (e.g. schools). Furthermore, the timings of key developments in national policy trajectories described in this chapter are remarkably similar, bearing witness to the presence of globalised cross-border influences and intense pressures to conform and perform.

Nevertheless, it is interesting to see how attempts to elucidate academic standards have taken different directions in various national settings. Some have sought to produce ever-more complicated data sets to 'solve the problem of definition' and to offer something to the multiple stakeholders involved. Other approaches, such as the American VALUE project or the various approaches to external referencing in Australia have sought to build consensus and share practice through academic 'calibration' activities that are rich in professional development.

Individual projects may flourish and then fade, but signals of quality will remain influential at a local, national, and global level, and the issue of academic standards will continue to be of ongoing interest to both governments and educational institutions. While the policy position with respect to academic standards and calibration in Australia and other national settings may be in a state of equilibrium, it would be risky to assume that this will endure. Policy positions are only ever interim settlements and external events (such as the emergence of perceived quality issues in Brazil) can rapidly destabilise an otherwise settled position.

References

Ajjawi, R., Bearman, M. & Boud, D. (2021). Performing standards: a critical perspective on the contemporary use of standards in assessment. *Teaching in Higher Education*, 26 (5), 728–741. https://doi.org/10.1080/13562517.2019.1678579.

Alexiadou, N. (2014). Policy learning and Europeanisation in education: the governance of a field and the transfer of knowledge. In A. Nordin & D. Sundberg (Eds.), *Transnational Policy Flows in European Education: The Making and Governing of Knowledge in the Education Policy Field*, pp. 123–140. Oxford: Symposium Books. https://doi.org/10.15730/books.90.

Alves de Oliveira, B.L.C., Soares, F.A., Silva, A.P., Cunha, C.L., Menegaz, J.dC. & da Silva, K.L. (2022). The National Student Performance Examination and the quality of Brazilian higher education in health. *Rev. Latino-Am. Enfermagem*, 30: e3534. https://doi.org/10.1590/1518-8345.5714.3534.

American Association of Colleges and Universities. (2023). Valid Assessment of Learning in Undergraduate Education (VALUE). www.aacu.org/initiatives/value.

Australian Government. (2011). *Advancing quality in higher education information sheet: The Collegiate Learning Assessment*. Canberra, Australia: Australian Government.

Australian Learning and Teaching Council. (2010). Learning and Teaching Academic Standards project: final report. http://web.archive.org/web/20150517165831/www.olt.gov.au/system/files/altc_standards.finalreport.pdf.

Australian Technology Network. (2009). Australian Technology Network of Universities (ATN) response to 'Setting and monitoring academic standards for Australian higher education': a discussion paper. http://pandora.nla.gov.au/pan/127066/20110826-0004/www.auqa.edu.au/qualityenhancement/academicstandards/responses/21b.pdf.

Baldwin, P. (1991). *Higher Education: Quality and Diversity in the 1990s*. Canberra, Australia: Australian Government Publishing Service. https://catalogue.nla.gov.au/Record/2875961.

Ball, S. J. (2012). Performativity, commodification and commitment: an I-spy guide to the neoliberal university. *British Journal of Educational Studies*, 60(1), 17–28. https://doi.org/10.1080/00071005.2011.650940.

Bamberger, A. & Kim, M.J. (2022). The OECD's influence on national higher education policies: internationalisation in Israel and South Korea. *Comparative Education*. https://doi.org/10.1080/03050068.2022.2147635.

Bedford S.B., Czech P., Sefcik L.T., Smith J. & Yorke J. (2016). External referencing of standards – ERoS report: an example of a collaborative end-to-end peer review process for external referencing. Final project report. https://eprints.qut.edu.au/105591/1/105591.pdf.

Beerkens, M. (2018). Evidence-based policy and higher education quality assurance: progress, pitfalls and promise. *European Journal of Higher Education*, 8:3, 272–287. https://doi.org/10.1080/21568235.2018.1475248.

Beerkens, M. (2022). An evolution of performance data in higher education governance: a path towards a 'big data' era? *Quality in Higher Education*, 28(1), 29–49. https://doi.org/10.1080/13538322.2021.1951451.

Benjamin, R. (2010). No substitute for hard evidence. *The Australian*, 8 December. www.theaustralian.com.au/news/no-substitute-for-hard-evidence/news-story/4e10745b4383d746216a7e9ecc05b46e.

Bloxham, S., Boyd, P. & Orr, S. (2011). Mark my words: the role of assessment criteria in UK higher education grading practices. *Studies in Higher Education*, 36(6), 655–670. https://doi.org/10.1080/03075071003777716.

Bradley, D., Noonan, P., Nugent, H. & Scales, B. (2008). *Review of Australian Higher Education: Final report*. Canberra, Australia: Department of Education, Employment and Workplace Relations. http://hdl.voced.edu.au/10707/44384.

Carnegie, G. (2021). When university missions and visions are reduced to numbers. *Campus Morning Mail*, 31 October. https://campusmorningmail.com.au/news/when-university-missions-and-visions-are-reduced-to-numbers.

Clare, J. (2022). Universities accord. Media release, 16 November. https://ministers.education.gov.au/clare/universities-accord.

Colina, F.E. & Blanco, G.L. (2021). Accountability compliance, and student learning as competing rationales for assessment: a case study of us tuning in practice. *Tertiary Education and Management*, 27, 129–142. https://doi.org/10.1007/s11233-021-09069-1.

Department of Education, Employment and Workplace Relations. (2009a). Transforming Australia's higher education system. http://hdl.voced.edu.au/10707/131634.

Department of Education, Employment and Workplace Relations. (2009b). An indicator framework for higher education performance funding: discussion paper. http://nla.gov.au/nla.arc-113401.

Department of Education, Employment and Workplace Relations. (2011). Development of performance measurement instruments in higher education: discussion paper. http://hdl.voced.edu.au/10707/215222.

Dietrich, J. (2011). Law threshold lowers the bar. *The Australian*, 30 March. www.theaustralian.com.au/news/law-threshold-lowers-the-bar/news-story/27181626fa4d22be4cec1968cb3e3d30.

Fisher, R. (2009). Untitled letter to AUQA. http://pandora.nla.gov.au/pan/127066/20110826-0004/www.auqa.edu.au/qualityenhancement/academicstandards/responses/6.pdf.

Foley, B. & Goldstein, H. (2012). Measuring success: league tables in the public sector. www.britac.ac.uk/policy/Measuring-success.cfm.

Grek, S. (2009). Governing by numbers: the PISA 'effect' in Europe. *Journal of Education Policy*, 24(1), 23–37. https://doi.org/10.1080/02680930802412669.

Griffith University. (n.d.). An indicator framework for higher education performance funding. Response by Griffith University. https://webarchive.nla.gov.au/awa/20140212135429/http://industry.gov.au/highereducation/Policy/Documents/Griffith.pdf.

Group of Eight. (2018). Group of Eight quality verification system. www.adelaide.edu.au/learning/quality-assurance/benchmarking/go8-quality-verification-system.

Hardison, C.M. & Vilamovska, A-M. (2009). The collegiate learning assessment: setting standards for performance at a college or university. www.rand.org/content/dam/rand/pubs/technical_reports/2009/RAND_TR663.pdf.

Higher Education Standards Framework. (2015). Higher Education Standards Framework (Threshold Standards) 2015. www.legislation.gov.au/Details/F2015L01639.

Higher Education Standards Panel. (2013). HES draft standards for learning outcomes (coursework) – March 2013. www.education.gov.au/higher-education-standards-panel-hesp/resources/hes-draft-standards-learning-outcomes-coursework-march-2013.

Hursh, D. (2008). *High-Stakes Testing and the Decline of Teaching and Learning: The Real Crisis in Education.* Lanham, MD: Rowman & Littlefield.

Jankowski, N., Ikenberry, S., Kinzie, J., Kuh, G., Shenoy, G. & Baker, G. (2012). *Transparency and Accountability: An Evaluation of the VSA College Portrait Pilot.* Champaign, IL: National Institute for Learning Outcomes Assessment, University of Illinois. www.learningoutcomesassessment.org/wp-content/uploads/2019/02/VSA_Report.pdf.

Kallo, J. (2021). The epistemic culture of the OECD and its agenda for higher education. *Journal of Education Policy*, 36(6), 779–800, https://doi.org/10.1080/02680939.2020.1745897.

Kemp, D. (1999). *Quality assured: a new Australian quality assurance framework for university education.* Workshop on the New Quality Assurance Framework, Canberra, Australia.

Knight, P. (2002). Summative assessment in higher education: practices in disarray. *Studies in Higher Education*, 27(3), 275–286. https://doi.org/10.1080/03075070220000662.

Krause, K-L., Scott, G., Aubin, K., Alexander, H., Angelo, T., Campbell, S., Carroll, M., Deane, E., Nulty, D., Pattison, P., Probert, B., Sachs, J., Solomonides, I. & Vaughan, S. (2014). Assuring learning and teaching standards through inter-institutional peer review and moderation: final report of the project. www.westernsydney.edu.au/__data/assets/pdf_file/0007/576916/External_Report_2014_Web_3.pdf.

Lewis, S. & Lingard, R.L. (2022). PISA for sale? Creating profitable policy spaces through the OECD's PISA for Schools. In C. Lubienski, M. Yemini & C. Maxwell (eds), *The Rise of External Actors in Education: Shifting Boundaries Globally and Locally*, pp. 91–112. Policy Press. https://doi.org/10.2307/j.ctv2p7j5d6.11.

Li, G., Shcheglova, I., Bhuradia, A., Li, Y., Loyalka, P., Zhou, O., Hu, S., Yu, N., Ma, L., Guo, F. & Chirikov, I. (2021). Large-scale international assessments of learning outcomes: balancing the interests of multiple stakeholders. *Journal of Higher Education Policy and Management*, 43(2), 198–213. https://doi.org/10.1080/1360080X.2020.1767327.

Liu, O.L. (2017). Ten years after the Spellings commission: From accountability to internal improvement. *Educational Measurement: Issues and Practice*, 36(2), 34–41. https://doi.org/10.1111/emip.12139.

Marginson, S. (2013). Australia and world university rankings. In S. Marginson (ed.), *Tertiary Education Policy in Australia*, pp. 139–149. Melbourne, Australia: Centre for the Study of Higher Education. https://melbourne-cshe.unimelb.edu.au/__data/assets/pdf_file/0009/2306484/Tert_Edu_Policy_Aus_2013.pdf.

Marginson, S. (2014). University rankings and social science. *European Journal of Education*, 49(1), 45–59. https://doi.org/10.1111/ejed.12061.

Marginson, S. (2022). What is global higher education? *Oxford Review of Education*, 48(4), 492–517. https://doi.org/10.1080/03054985.2022.2061438.

McCubbin, A., Hammer, S. & Ayriss, P. (2022). Learning and teaching benchmarking in Australian universities: the current state of play. *Journal of Higher Education Policy and Management*, 44(1), 3–20. https://doi.org/10.1080/1360080X.2021.1934244.

Miranda, G.J., Leal, E.A., Ferreira, M.A. & Barbosa de Miranda, A. (2019). Enade: are the students motivated to take the test? *Revista de Educação e Pesquisa em Contabilidade*, 13(1), 12–27. https://doi.org/10.17524/repec.v13i1.1720.

Münch, R. & Wieczorek, O. (2023). Improving schooling through effective governance? The United States, Canada, South Korea, and Singapore in the struggle for PISA scores. *Comparative Education*, 59(1), 59–76. https://doi.org/10.1080/03050068.2022.2138176.

National Committee of Inquiry into Higher Education. (1997). *Higher Education in the Learning Society*. Norwich: HMSO. www.educationengland.org.uk/documents/dearing1997/dearing1997.html.

Organisation for Economic Co-operation and Development. (2012). AHELO feasibility study report: Volume 1 – design and implementation. www.oecd.org/edu/skills-beyond-school/AHELOFSReportVolume1.pdf.

Organisation for Economic Co-operation and Development. (2014). Testing student and university performance globally: OECD's AHELO. www.oecd.org/education/skills-beyond-school/testingstudentanduniversityperformancegloballyoecdsahelo.htm.

Organisation for Economic Co-operation and Development. (2023). Programme for International Student Assessment (PISA). www.oecd.org/pisa/.

Ozga, J. & Jones, R. (2006). Travelling and embedded policy: the case of knowledge transfer. *Journal of Education Policy*, 21(1), 1–17. https://doi.org/10.1080/02680930500391462.

Pereira, C.A., Araujo, J.F.F.E. & Machado-Taylor, M. de L. (2018). The Brazilian higher education evaluation model: 'SINAES' sui generis? *International Journal of Educational Development*, 61, 5–15. https://doi.org/10.1016/j.ijedudev.2017.11.007.

Rizvi, F. & Lingard, B. (2010). *Globalizing education policy*. Abingdon: Routledge. https://doi.org/10.4324/9780203867396.

Robson, A. (2009). Untitled letter to AUQA. http://pandora.nla.gov.au/pan/127066/20110826-0004/www.auqa.edu.au/qualityenhancement/academicstandards/responses/5.pdf.

Rust, C., Price, M. & O'Donovan, B. (2003). Improving students' learning by developing their understanding of assessment criteria and processes. *Assessment & Evaluation in Higher Education*, 28(2), 147–164. https://doi.org/10.1080/02602930301671.

Sadler, D.R. (2012). Assuring academic achievement standards: from moderation to calibration. *Assessment in Education: Principles, Policy & Practice*, 20(1), 5–19. https://doi.org/10.1080/0969594X.2012.714742.

Sadler, D.R. (2014). The futility of attempting to codify academic achievement standards. *Higher Education*, 67(3), 273–288. https://doi.org/10.1007/s10734-013-9649-1.

Salmi, J. (2009). The growing accountability agenda: progress or mixed blessing? *Higher Education Management and Policy*, 21(1), 101–122. https://doi.org/10.1787/hemp-v21-art7-en.

Schwartzman, S. (2010). The national assessment of courses in Brazil. In D.D. Dill & M. Beerkens (eds), *Public Policy for Academic Quality: Analyses of Innovative Policy Instruments*, pp. 293–312. London: Springer. https://doi.org/10.1007/978-90-481-3754-1.

Sefcik, L., Bedford, S., Czech, P., Smith, J. & Yorke, J. (2018). Embedding external referencing of standards into higher education: Collaborative relationships are the key. *Assessment & Evaluation in Higher Education*, 43(1), 45–57. https://doi.org/10.1080/02602938.2017.1278584.

Stella, A. & Woodhouse, D. (2007). Benchmarking in Australian higher education: a thematic analysis of AUQA audit reports. http://pandora.nla.gov.au/pan/127066/20110826-0004/www.auqa.edu.au/files/publications/benchmarking_final_text_website.pdf.

Tertiary Education Quality and Standards Agency. (2019). Guidance note: external referencing (including benchmarking). www.teqsa.gov.au/latest-news/publications/guidance-note-external-referencing-including-benchmarking.

Trounson, A. (2010). No end to row over standards. *The Australian*, 1 December. www.theaustralian.com.au/higher-education/no-end-to-row-over-standards/story-e6frgcjx-1225963552564.

US Department of Education. (2006). A test of leadership: charting the future of US higher education. http://hdl.voced.edu.au/10707/253086.

Vidovich, L. (2001). That chameleon 'quality': the multiple and contradictory discourses of 'quality' policy in Australian higher education. *Discourse*, 22(2), 249–261. https://doi.org/10.1080/01596300120072400.

Watty, K., Freeman, M., Howieson, B., Hancock, P., O'Connell, B., de Lange, P. & Abraham, A. (2014). Social moderation, assessment and assuring standards for accounting graduates. *Assessment & Evaluation in Higher Education*, 39(4), 461–478. https://doi.org/10.1080/02602938.2013.848336.

Welsman, S. (2009). Academic achievement standards paper – comments. http://pandora.nla.gov.au/pan/127066/20110826-0004/www.auqa.edu.au/qualityenhancement/academicstandards/responses/3.pdf.

Wilson, G., Bedford, S. B. & Readman, K. (2019). External peer review of assessment: a guide to supporting the external referencing of academic standards. https://researchdirect.westernsydney.edu.au/islandora/object/uws:53024.

Yorke, D.M. (2007). *Grading Student Achievement in Higher Education: Signals and Shortcomings*. New York: Routledge. https://doi.org/10.4324/9780203939413.

Yorke, J. & Vidovich, L. (2016). *Learning Standards and the Assessment of Quality in Higher Education: Contested Policy Trajectories*. Cham: Springer. https://doi.org/10.1007/978-3-319-32924-6.

Zajda, J. (2014). Globalisation and neo-liberalism as educational policy in Australia. In D. Turner & H. Yolcu (eds), *Neoliberal Education Reforms: A Critical Analysis*, pp. 164–183. Hoboken, NJ: Taylor & Francis. https://doi.org/10.4324/9780203067758.

Part II

Common responses to the social construction of academic standards

Chapter 5

The role of internal and external moderation for assuring academic standards

Andy Lloyd and Rachel Forsyth

Introduction

Standards are deeply embedded in quality assurance discourse and policy. This is why this chapter starts with a brief overview of quality assurance in university education over time and the way in which it has influenced debates and guided current practices that purport to assure academic standards. The chapter's authors have long-standing careers in supporting academics and institutions to develop high quality teaching-learning environments, predominantly in the UK, including the Professional Development Course for External Examiners (see Chapters 9–12). This provides the broad context for our reflections. We then focus on two key practices that are extensively used to assure standards in UK higher education: external and internal moderation. Based on a critical review of current moderation practices, a case is made for approaches that take place prior to marking and that foster community, peer observation and dialogue.

Quality assurance in university education

Historically, the responsibility for quality and standards in UK higher education has rested with individual universities. The relatively small number of degree awarding institutions, the regular exchange of scholars between them, the homogeneity of students and the public reputation of universities provided sufficient stability for the system to continue relatively unchanged for centuries. However, with increases in participation, changes in funding and a significant increase in the number of degree awarding institutions in the UK (see Chapter 2) came more public and regulatory interest in standards. From the mid-1980s the UK government took on oversight of standards and set out a trajectory for the creation of principles as well as dedicated bodies to ensure accountability and efficiency in publicly funded universities (Harvey, 2005). By the mid-1990s 'British institutions were faced with five external processes: subject-based teaching quality assessment, institutional audit, the research assessment exercise, professional and regulatory body accreditation, and external examining' (Harvey, 2005, p. 268). The UK Quality Assurance Agency was established in 1997 to provide a

DOI: 10.4324/9781003379768-7

single approach to quality assurance in all British universities (i.e. those in England, Wales, and Scotland). Oversight of research and of professional and regulatory body accreditation remained separate.

In the context of a discussion of quality assurance, it is important to make a distinction between academic standards and quality standards. Academic standards underpin judgments made about student achievement and the quality of their work, whereas quality standards relate to inputs, e.g. resources and processes used to ensure the quality of education provided (AdvanceHE, 2018, p. 31). The first nationwide systems overseeing academic quality in the UK involved the review of individual subject areas within institutions. The focus was on inputs such as teaching rather than outputs (i.e. the academic standards visible in student work). The assessment of teaching included classroom observations carried out by peers from other universities, which only provided a snapshot of the teaching environment and were therefore neither useful as a marker of overall teaching quality nor of academic standards. The system of subject-based review of quality was controversial, and there was thought to be little evidence that it raised standards of teaching. Critics also suggested that teaching quality scores were shaped by influences beyond teaching, since existing hierarchies of institutions tended to be confirmed (Drennan & Beck 2001, cited in Greatbatch & Holland, 2016), and scores did not necessarily represent staff experiences on the ground (Harvey, 2005). The subject-based quality assessment was subsequently dropped from the QAA portfolio in 2001 (Greatbatch & Holland, 2016).

The next quality assurance development relevant to standards was the introduction of national frameworks that outlined individual aspects of standards derived from the research literature. These national frameworks predominantly provided criteria for quality standards, such as the provision of learning outcomes, attention to feedback on assessments, the safety of examinations, and so on, in order to guide institutional procedures. In the UK, this took form in the UK Quality Code. In its first version, the purposes of the code (QAA, 2015) were described as follows, with 'academic standards' notably occurring first:

- 'safeguarding' academic standards;
- assuring the academic quality of learning opportunities;
- promoting continuous and systematic improvement (enhancement); and
- ensuring that information about programmes is fit for purpose, accessible and trustworthy.

This initial version was extensive and comprised three separate parts, each containing several chapters. It was quite prescriptive, and many UK universities used it to create detailed instructions for the provision of information about degree programmes and for their design, teaching, assessment, and evaluation. In a later version, the purposes were less clearly defined, stating that the Code would 'fulfil its role as the cornerstone for quality in UK higher education, protecting the public and student interest, and championing UK higher education's world-leading reputation for quality' (QAA, 2018). This version of the Code, which is still extant, is much shorter and lighter in touch, providing principles rather than detailed instructions. Safeguarding academic standards is not explicitly highlighted as a key purpose any more.

The current UK approach is very much in line with frameworks in other European countries; the Standards and Guidelines for Quality Assurance in the European Higher Education Area (EHEA, 2015) is descriptive rather than prescriptive. This document sets out expectations for national agencies to assure quality: they must adhere to these Standards and Guidelines for Quality Assurance in order to be a member of the European Network for Quality Assurance in Higher Education. These national organisations create their own system of quality review according to the Standards and Guidelines document, and these processes are then reviewed by external assessors across the EHEA network. How this tends to work in practice is that the national agency forms independent review groups, which include teachers and administrators from different universities, who look at documents and may also visit the universities (see, for instance, the Swedish process as a typical example; UKA, 2020). In Australia, the Tertiary Education Quality and Standards Agency (TEQSA) has a similar framework (TEQSA, 2021) (see also Chapter 4).

The US has a non-governmental system for quality oversight (called accreditation), which is similar to the EHEA approach, with some oversight from individual states of the agencies that accredit universities. There is said to be some variability between states in relation to quality standards (Kelly et al., 2015). We note that none of the examples given from outside the UK include a specific requirement to review academic standards, perhaps because they are not working on the basis of trying to show consistency of standards between and across institutions, which is an aim of the UK system.

One similarity between these schemes in different countries is that it seems to be considerably easier to develop systems for the oversight of quality standards than for academic standards. They all include processes for reviewing documentation, counting progression rates, and comparing syllabuses, but there are few, if any, processes or metrics for evaluating and comparing the quality of student learning, which is dependent on many variables such as the design, teaching, and assessment of individual modules, student support, library and information technology access, as well as students' own situation and ability to engage with their learning. This chapter will now focus on the two main quality assurance processes that are commonly used in the UK to specifically assure academic standards; external and internal moderation.

External moderation: external examining

External examining is a form of external moderation and explicitly focuses on the consistency of academic standards across institutions. External examiners have been a feature of the UK university system since the early nineteenth century (Brennan et al., 1996). They have a direct role in reviewing academic standards because they look at student outputs, rather than only looking at inputs such as teaching, processes, and documentation. External examiners are considered critical to ensuring academic standards because they are the only people outside a university who review student assessment performances or work (other than in some professionally accredited programmes where professionals may also be involved in reviewing students' work). In this role, they are expected to advise and, where necessary, challenge institutions as to how students are achieving threshold academic standards, verify comparability of standards between institutions, and act as critical friends to their peers (see also Chapter 6).

These aims are laudable, but there is no overarching system to review consistency between examiners or institutions (Warren Piper, 1994). There is no guarantee that external examiners are aware of national guidelines (Hannan & Silver, 2004), or that they have a comparable understanding of academic standards and their maintenance (Bloxham & Price, 2015). The assessment literacy of examiners has also been found to be variable (Medland, 2015) (see also Chapter 7).

In the UK, external examiners are peers from different universities who are employed by institutions according to the respective institution's own criteria and employment arrangements. There is no obligation to advertise the posts widely, as might be expected for more substantive posts, and external examiners may be appointed from a small pool of applicants within a subject area, often from similar institutions. In 1997, the Dearing Report recommended the creation of a national pool of external examiners, a proposal which was repeated by a parliamentary Select Committee (IUSS, 2009), a universities-led review of external examining (UUK, GuildHE & QAA, 2010) and a funding body review (HEFCE, 2015), but the system of individual appointments continues to the time of writing (2024). In our own work we have found that academics are often keen to become external examiners as it provides them with insight into the approaches taken by programmes similar to their own and, for better or worse, opportunities to influence another university's assessment practices. However, safeguarding academic standards is not necessarily high on their agenda.

External examiners exist in countries other than the UK, but many have different roles. Where they are used in mainland Europe, they have tended to look more at quality standards, such as reviewing examination papers or the relationship between programme outcomes and assessment in documentation (Kristensen, 1997; Myrhaug et al., 2004; Kohoutek, 2014). This oversight of quality standards may be organised and/or regulated by national bodies, for instance in Denmark and the Netherlands (Kohoutek, 2014), rather than individual universities.

This brings us back to the principal challenge of oversight of standards, which is that there is no real evidence to judge the effectiveness of external examiners or reviewers. In fact, many of the assumptions underpinning the rationale for external examination have been effectively questioned (Bloxham & Price, 2015; see also Chapters 6 and 7). There is an implication that external examiners will be able to judge academic standards by reviewing adherence to the quality frameworks. However, while these quality processes contain necessary factors for achieving and reviewing quality, they are not sufficient to assure academic standards. The academic standards for individual modules on individual degree programmes in individual universities can only be judged by someone who understands academic standards in that subject area through having sampled a reasonable number of student outputs (Bloxham & Boyd, 2011). This aspect of quality assurance needs to be explicitly included in quality frameworks, and external examiners need to be supported so that they really do understand academic standards (Medland, 2015, 2019) (see also Chapter 7).

Internal moderation

The other activity widely used to assure academic standards is internal moderation. Moderation has been described as a consensus-seeking activity 'intended to ensure that the mark a particular student is awarded is independent of which marker does the marking' (Sadler (2013, p. 5), and as 'a practice of engagement in which teaching team members develop a shared understanding of assessment requirements, standards and the evidence that demonstrates differing qualities of performance' (Adie et al., 2013, p. 968). Moderation thus involves both consensus and community. However, in reviewing a sample of UK university regulations, Poole (2022, p. 2) found variation in the definition and interpretation of the moderator's role, and potential confusion between marking and moderation practices. This would certainly mitigate against the development of shared standards and make quality assurance less reliable. Based on the descriptions of moderation cited above, it could be argued that a key function of the process is to assist in the social construction of standards as much as to provide quality assurance (Bloxham et al., 2015a). Effectively, it is a kind of peer observation of the marking process and, as has been shown for peer review of teaching (Hammersley-Fletcher & Orsmond, 2004; Gosling & O'Connor, 2006; Purvis et al., 2009; Thomson et al., 2015), is itself developmental. The repeated process of moderation improves our ability to interpret criteria and make judgements (Sadler 2013) and therefore is key to the development of assessment literacy in the context of academics' own disciplinary areas.

It can certainly be argued that conversations and interactions between individuals and groups of markers within the same disciplinary domain help to create a community in which there is a broad, shared understanding of academic standards (Crimmins et al., 2016). This is also argued in Chapters 8, 14 and 15. However, as Poole (2022) reported, and in our own experience, the degree to which these interactions and conversations occur and the ways in which these are undertaken will vary. In some contexts, there is no meaningful interaction of this type; the external moderator reviews samples of student work and provides a report which may lead to the adjustment of student grades (Gillis, 2020). The moderator is simply reporting back on their individual perception of the academic standards on the course.

Approaches to implementing moderation in UK higher education

To review the impact that quality assurance has on consistency in academic standards, we can consider the varying approaches to moderation used in the UK and their implications for standards. Moderators are expected to report back to the programme team and to other stakeholders about standards, showing that the requirements of national or university frameworks are being met in the programme and university. They may be internal to the programme team, from another department, or from another university, and they are asked to review individual or multiple assessment tasks.

Most of the exercises undertaken to ensure that marking is fair take place *after* students have completed the assessment task. While post-marking moderation does reassure students of the fairness of assessment, it is often time-pressured because marks need to be agreed and confirmed in advance of a looming decision-making board. Depending on the type of assignment and its credit value, the moderator may be asked to review all student work submitted or just a sample. They may be asked to review adherence to quality standards such as the type and quantity of feedback, and/or comment on the academic standards (i.e. whether or not they agree with the original marker's judgement on the quality of the student work). The processes for carrying out such a review can vary significantly between universities (Poole, 2022).

There are some apparently common approaches to moderation that are assumed to be effective at assuring standards, but are actually undertaken in very different ways. Second marking is a good example. Following grading by a first marker (something which is already subject to a great deal of variety), a second person is asked to give an opinion. They may or may not repeat the process undertaken by the first marker; they may or may not have access to the grade and feedback of the first marker; they may review some or all of the student scripts which were submitted to the first marker. If there were multiple first markers, the second marker may look at a sample from all of them. The outcomes of the second marking may lead to further conversations between markers or be undertaken independently; they may or may not be recorded and shared with the programme team, the head of department, or students. The process might also involve reference to mark distributions; across the current cohort, previous years, and/or different modules/units. Clearly, these are processes that are intended to assure quality, which should help to reassure students of the 'fairness' of marking. They will also have helped prevent many students from receiving 'rogue' marks that do not fully reflect the academic standards they have achieved. We are not suggesting that they should not be used. However, their value in the assurance of academic standards is less certain (Bloxham, 2009).

Repeated studies of independent marking under more idealised conditions have shown that consistency of judgement is difficult to predict or to achieve, however experienced the first and second markers are (Hartog & Rhodes, 1935; Ecclestone, 2001; Baird et al., 2004; Hanlon et al., 2005; Bloxham et al., 2015b;). Different markers use criteria in very different ways (Orr, 2010; Bloxham et al., 2015b).

Currently there is no research evidence that post-marking moderation exercises alone lead to a greater shared understanding of academic standards or about whether these processes are operated consistently, both within and across marking teams, discipline areas, and/or institutions. Questions can be asked as to how much attention, or otherwise, is paid to marking criteria or whether second markers end up deferring to more experienced colleagues, or simply end up agreeing to split the difference, i.e. averaging the marks arrived at by first and second markers (Partington, 1994). Hartley et al. (2006) showed that typographic variables such as font size could have an impact on grades. While such differences may be tempered in academic departments in which markers regularly, if often informally, discuss standards, there is no 'requirement' for such conversations to take place, or guarantee that they have. Put simply, it is not unreasonable for questions to be asked as to whether the development and operation of second marking moderation alone has added much extra value to our understanding (and the comparability) of academic standards in specific disciplines.

Staff perceptions of moderation

If we want to make moderation practices more effective at leading to consistent judgements about student work, it is crucial to understand academics' beliefs about moderation, since beliefs will impact on the way in which the role as internal moderator or external examiner is carried out. External examiners are usually asked to comment on moderation processes because one of their key duties is to ensure that 'assessment and classification processes…are reliable, fair and transparent (QAA, 2023, p. 3). This is why the AdvanceHE Professional Development Course (PDC) for External Examiners, part of the AdvanceHE Degree Standards Project (see Chapter 9 and Chapter 10), considered moderation practices in some detail. The course included an exercise in which participants were asked to rate the perceived effectiveness of strategies commonly used to assure academic standards across the UK sector. While the exercise was in part designed to highlight the critical role of external examiners as guardians of academic standards across the sector and to cover the range of strategies they might encounter, it also revealed some very different perceptions on the effectiveness of those strategies. Working in small groups, course participants were provided with a list of some of the strategies commonly used to assure academic standards (see Figure 5.1). By placing them on a matrix (see Figure 5.2), participants were asked to evaluate each strategy's effectiveness and the extent to which it focussed on local standards or allowed for comparability across institutions.

Strategies used to help assure academic standards

(A) Peer scrutiny of module assessment, instructions, criteria etc. (before start of module).
(B) Pre-teaching briefing to module team on expectations for the assessment.
(C) Pre-teaching module team exercise to mark and discuss exemplar assignments (e.g. from the previous year).

(D) Whole course team development and enactment of programme assessment strategy.
(E) Second marking of all work, resolving differences by discussion.
(F) Blind double marking (BDM) of all work, resolving differences by discussion or by averaging.
(G) Moderation discussion after first marking, involving all markers on a module.
(H) Sample second marking by module leader.
(I) Use of a detailed marking scheme.
(J) Provision of model answer.
(K) All markers mark and discuss a common sample of work before full marking process.
(L) Team marking session with markers able to discuss decisions particularly about 'unusual' work – marking bee.
(M) Moderation by comparing averages and distribution of marks given by each marker in the team.
(N) Exam board consideration of means and standard deviations of module marks.
(O) Institutions require module mark profiles to conform to a reasonable 'curve', requiring justification for variation.
(P) External examining.
(Q) Markers having experience as external examiners or as assessors at other institutions.
(R) Markers being members of a learned society or professional body.
(S) Markers being familiar with national reference points.

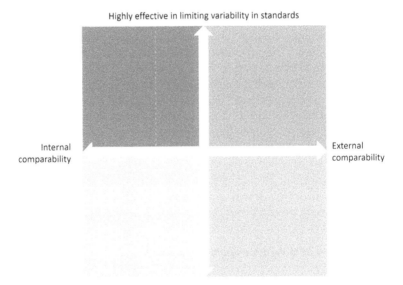

Figure 5.1 Matrix used to evaluate the effectiveness of the different moderation strategies (A-E), as used on the Professional Development Course.

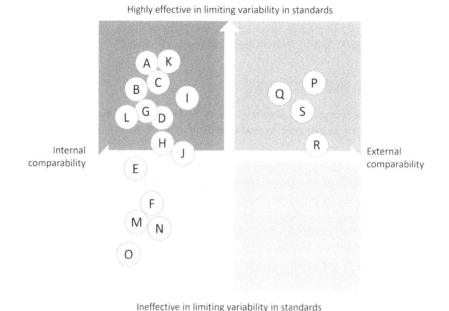

Figure 5.2 Mean position in which each moderation strategy was placed (based on 200 completed grids).

To understand academics' beliefs about these strategies, data collected from 200 grids completed by groups of course participants have been analysed. Figure 5.2 shows the mean position where the groups placed each strategy. The value of this exercise came in discussing why a strategy should be placed in a particular quadrant, and what made it effective. On the whole, external methods (P, Q, R and S) were highly rated in terms of effectiveness, particularly the role of external examiners as a guardian of academic standards across the sector. Methods undertaken in advance of marking (such as A, B, C, D and K), which typically involve discussion between markers, were also rated as effective. Norm-referencing of grades (such as M, N and O) was rarely seen as effective, which is unsurprising during a course where the importance of outcomes-based assessment is emphasised, as expected in the UK Quality Code. However, averaging the data conceals that each of the 21 strategies were, at some point, rated both the *most* and *least* effective. Many course participants suggested that the processes they themselves used must be the most effective, as they seemed to work fine in their contexts.

It was highly relevant to this discussion that quality assurance often involves a combination of strategies. While the distribution of results suggested that many markers recognise the value of pre-marking moderation strategies that include discussion across a marking team, participants frequently identified the need for a third axis on the matrix; time. The lack of this precious commodity was regarded as a barrier to effective moderation and explains why methods such as second and double marking (E and F) were not seen as more effective.

CRITICAL PERSPECTIVE

Box 5.1 Summary of the interplay between quality standards and academic standards and the role of moderation

The quality movement has highlighted the need for a focus on assessment standards. This includes quality standards, which are extensively documented in regulatory material, but it is also important that academic standards receive the attention needed to ensure that assessment is valid and reliable. In the UK, there is renewed emphasis on the comparability of awards within the QAA External Examining Principles (QAA, 2022). An effective way to assure this would be to place further emphasis on calibration, but this will need to be reinforced by guidance for both staff and students, and effective training for moderators and external examiners.

There is evidence for the value of social construction of shared standards, but regulatory documents rarely mention the practice. University policies need to be completely clear about the ways in which socially constructed standards are created, reviewed, and tested. Without a direct expectation that they engage in the activity, it is difficult for programme teams to make time for it, focusing instead on time-consuming but less effective processes, such as independent second marking. External examiners have an important part to play in this. They could review evidence of activities to support social moderation but are unlikely to do so if this is not explicitly included in quality processes. A good moderation policy should work from the basis that the purpose of moderation is to ensure that marking criteria have been fairly, accurately, and consistently applied during first marking. Setting out the requirements clearly will save programme teams considerable time and anxiety.

Conclusion

Reviewing the ways in which quality assurance processes have become a central feature of many higher education systems, it appears inevitable that pressure will remain on academic staff to ensure that student grades are fair and reliable. However, these are necessarily complex judgements, and this may not have been helped by the ways in which marking and moderation processes operate; often as single exercises that mix quality assurance of institutional processes (i.e. input measures) with the assurance of academic standards that can only be evident in student work (i.e. outputs). Disentangling these will require a greater focus to be placed on the assessment literacy of all staff, including those involved in quality assurance, and the development of ongoing conversations that will allow 'calibrated' academics (Sadler, 2013) to emerge (see Chapters 8, 14 and 15). However, this is not without its challenges. Not only may it require institutional policies and approaches to be reviewed, it will require time to be made available for academic staff to engage in pre-marking discussions (but this may in turn reduce the time spent on post-marking moderation), it will require further research into the efficacy of relatively new techniques such as consensus moderation (Mason & Roberts, 2024), and it will require a culture to be adopted in which these discussions can be held in a robust and respectful way, so that the views of all colleagues can be collectively taken on board. There is further work to be done.

References

Adie, L., Lloyd, M. & Beutel, D. (2013). Identifying discourses of moderation in higher education. *Assessment & Evaluation in Higher Education*, 38(8), 968–977. https://doi.org/10.1080/02602938.2013.769200.

AdvanceHE. (2018). *Professional Development Course for External Examiners. Facilitators' Guide*. York: AdvanceHE.

Baird, J. A., Greatorex, J. & Bell, J.F. (2004). What makes marking reliable? Experiments with UK examinations. *Assessment in Education: Principles, Policy & Practice*, 11(3), 331–348. https://doi.org/10.1080/0969594042000304627.

Bloxham, S. (2009). Marking and moderation in the UK: false assumptions and wasted resources. *Assessment & Evaluation in Higher Education*, 34(2), 209–220. https://doi.org/10.1080/02602930801955978.

Bloxham, S. & Boyd, P. (2011). Accountability in grading student work: securing academic standards in a twenty-first century quality assurance context. *British Educational Research Journal*, 38(4), 615–634. https://doi.org/10.1080/01411926.2011.569007.

Bloxham, S., Hughes, C. & Adie, L. (2015a). What's the point of moderation? A discussion of the purposes achieved through contemporary moderation practices. *Assessment & Evaluation in Higher Education*, 1–16. https://doi.org/10.1080/02602938.2015.1039932.

Bloxham, S., den Outer, B., Hudson, J. & Price, M. (2015b). Let's stop the pretence of consistent marking: exploring the multiple limitations of assessment criteria. *Assessment & Evaluation in Higher Education*, 1–16. https://doi.org/10.1080/02602938.2015.1024607.

Bloxham, S. & Price, M. (2015). External examining: fit for purpose? *Studies in Higher Education*, 40(2), 195–211. https://doi.org/10.1080/03075079.2013.823931.

Brennan, J., Frazer, M., Middlehurst, R., Silver, H. & Williams, R. (1996). *Changing Conceptions of Academic Standards*. Quality Support Centre Higher Education Report No. 4. London: Open University. https://files.eric.ed.gov/fulltext/ED393360.pdf.

Crimmins, G., Nash, G., Oprescu, F., Alla, K., Brock, G., Hickson-Jamieson, B. & Noakes, C. (2016). Can a systematic assessment moderation process assure the quality and integrity of assessment practice while supporting the professional development of casual academics? *Assessment & Evaluation in Higher Education*, 41(3), 427–441. https://doi.org/10.1080/02602938.2015.1017754.

Drennan, L. & Beck, M. (2001). *Teaching quality assessment scores: measuring quality or confirming hierarchy?* The Sixth QHE Seminar: The End of Quality? Birmingham, 25–26 May. www.qualityresearchinternational.com/papers/drennanpmv6.pdf.

Ecclestone, K. (2001). 'I know a 2:1 when I see it': understanding criteria for degree classifications in franchise university programmes. *Journal of Further and Higher Education*, 25(3), 301–312. https://doi.org/10.1080/03098770126527.

EHEA. (2015). *Standards and Guidelines for Quality Assurance in the European Higher Education Area (ESG)*. EHEA.

Gillis, S. (2020). Ensuring comparability of qualifications through moderation: implications for Australia's VET sector. *Journal of Vocational Education & Training*, 1–23. https://doi.org/10.1080/13636820.2020.1860116.

Gosling, D. & O'Connor, K.M. (2006). From peer observation of teaching to review of professional practice (RPP): a model for continuing professional development (CPD). *Educational Developments*, 7(3), 1–4. www.seda.ac.uk/resources/files/publications_18_eddev7_3.pdf.

Greatbatch, D. & Holland, J. (2016). Teaching quality in higher education: literature review and qualitative research. https://assets.publishing.service.gov.uk/government/uploads/system/uploads/attachment_data/file/524495/he-teaching-quality-literature-review-qualitative-research.pdf.

Hammersley-Fletcher, L. & Orsmond, P. (2004). Evaluating our peers: is peer observation a meaningful process? *Studies in Higher Education*, 29(4), 489–503. https://doi.org/10.1080/0307507042000236380.

Hanlon, J., Jefferson, M., Molan, M. & Mitchell, B. (2005). An examination of the incidence of 'error variation' in the grading of law assessments. www.education.uwa.edu.au/__data/assets/pdf_file/0006/1888611/Hanlon.pdf.

Hannan, A. & Silver, H. (2004). Enquiry into the nature of external examining. www.heacademy.ac.uk/ourwork/universitiesandcolleges/alldisplay?type=resources&newid=resource_database/id375_enquiry_into_the_nature_of_external_examining&site=york.

Hartley, J., Trueman, M., Betts, L. & Brodie, L. (2006). What price presentation? The effects of typographic variables on essay grades. *Assessment & Evaluation in Higher Education*, 31(5), 523–534. https://doi.org/10.1080/02602930600679530.

Hartog, P. & Rhodes, E. (1935). *An Examination of Examinations: Being a Summary of Investigations on Comparison of Marks Allotted to Examination Scripts by Independent Examiners and Boards of Examiners, Together with a Section of Viva Voce Examinations*. London: Macmillan.

Harvey, L. (2005). *A History and Critique of Quality Evaluation in the UK*. Quality Assurance in Education.

HEFCE. (2015). *A Review of External Examining Arrangements across the UK*. Report to the UK higher education funding bodies by the Higher Education Academy, June. HEFCE. https://dera.ioe.ac.uk/id/eprint/23541/1/2015_externalexam.pdf.

IUSS. (2009). Students and universities. www.publications.parliament.uk/pa/cm/cmdius.htm.

Kelly, A.P., James, K.J. & Columbus, R. (2015). *Inputs, Outcomes, Quality Assurance: A Closer Look at State Oversight of Higher Education*. American Enterprise Institute.

Kohoutek, J. (2014). European standards for quality assurance and institutional practices of student assessment in the UK, the Netherlands and the Czech Republic. *Assessment &*

Evaluation in Higher Education, 39(3), 310–325. https://doi.org/10.1080/02602938.2013.830694.

Kristensen, B. (1997). The impact of quality monitoring on institutions: a Danish experience at the Copenhagen Business School. *Quality in Higher Education*, 3(1), 87–94. https://doi.org/10.1080/1353832960030110.

Mason, J. & Roberts, L.D. (2024). Consensus moderation: the voices of expert academics, *Assessment & Evaluation in Higher Education*, 48(7), 926–937. https://doi.org/10.1080/02602938.2022.2161999.

Medland, E. (2015). Examining the assessment literacy of external examiners. *London Review of Education*, 13(3), 21–33. https://eds.s.ebscohost.com/eds/pdfviewer/pdfviewer?vid=1&sid=979db2d8-ae9f-4df7-9f15-dd85c0326e7c%40redis.

Medland, E. (2019). 'I'm an assessment illiterate': towards a shared discourse of assessment literacy for external examiners. *Assessment & Evaluation in Higher Education*, 44(4), 565–580. https://doi.org/10.1080/02602938.2018.1523363.

Myrhaug, D., Lian, W. & Gynnild, V. (2004). External examiners in new roles: a case study at the Norwegian University of Science and Technology. *Quality in Higher Education*, 10(3), 243–252. https://doi.org/10.1080/1353832042000299522.

Orr, S. (2010). We kind of try to merge our own experience with the objectivity of the criteria: The role of connoisseurship and tacit practice in undergraduate fine art assessment. *Art, Design & Communication in Higher Education*, 9(1), 5–19. http://dx.doi.org/10.1386/adch.9.1.5_1.

Partington, J. (1994). Double-marking students' work. *Assessment & Evaluation in Higher Education*, 19(1), 57–60. https://doi.org/10.1080/0260293940190106.

Poole, B. (2022). Moderation: concept and operationalisation in UK universities. *Quality Assurance in Education*. https://doi.org/10.1108/QAE-12-2021-0203.

Purvis, A., Crutchley, D. & Flint, A. (2009). Beyond peer observation of teaching. In D. Gosling & K.M. O'Connor (eds), *Beyond the Peer Observation of Teaching*, pp. 23–28. Staff and Educational Development Association. http://shura.shu.ac.uk/1497/.

QAA. (2015). UK Quality Code for Higher Education: general introduction. https://dera.ioe.ac.uk/19293/1/QC-general-introduction.pdf.

QAA. (2018). The revised UK quality code for higher education. www.qaa.ac.uk/quality-code.

QAA. (2022). QAA external examining principles. www.qaa.ac.uk/quality-code/external-examining-principles.

QAA. (2023). The UK Quality Code for Higher Education. www.qaa.ac.uk/docs/qaa/quality-code/revised-uk-quality-code-for-higher-education.pdf?sfvrsn=4c19f781_24.

Sadler, D.R. (2013). Assuring academic achievement standards: from moderation to calibration. *Assessment in Education: Principles, Policy & Practice*, 20(1), 5–19. https://doi.org/10.1080/0969594X.2012.714742.

TEQSA. (2021). Higher Education Standards Framework (Threshold Standards) 2021. www.teqsa.gov.au/higher-education-standards-framework-2021.

Thomson, K., Bell, A. & Hendry, G. (2015). Peer observation of teaching: the case for learning just by watching. *Higher Education Research & Development*, 34(5), 1060–1062. https://doi.org/10.1080/07294360.2015.1034349.

UKA. (2020). Vägledning för granskning av lärosätenas kvalitetssäkringsarbete / Guidance for review of higher education institutions' quality assurance work. www.uka.se/kvalitetssakring–examenstillstand/granskningar-av-larosatenas-kvalitetssakringsarbete/hur-gar-larosatesgranskningen-till.html.

Universities UK/GuildHE Joint Review Group. (2010). *Review of External Examining Arrangements in the UK: A Discussion Paper*. UniversitiesUK, GuildHE and the Quality Assurance Agency for Higher Education.

UUK, GuildHE & QAA. (2010). Review of external examining arrangements in the UK. https://dera.ioe.ac.uk/id/eprint/1180/1/ExternalExaminersDiscussionPaper.pdf.

Warren Piper, D. (1994). *Are Professors Professional? The Organisation of University Examinations* (Vol. 25). Jessica Kingsley Publishers.

Chapter 6

External examining
A peer-led system for guarding academic standards

Margaret Price

Introduction: external examining

The introduction of external examining in the UK in the early nineteenth century was probably the earliest response to potential variation in academic standards, but recent growth and diversification of the sector means that there is now an urgent need to critically evaluate and strengthen the system for current circumstances. This chapter describes, and then critically evaluates, an external examiner system designed to safeguard academic standards. It then explores ways to enhance the peer-led system in order to increase confidence in academic standards in the sector.

External examining is a peer review process designed to safeguard fairness in assessment and academic standards in higher education. Its most important characteristic is its focus on student performance as seen in student work (see definition of academic standards in Chapter 3), rather than on learning inputs such as course design or teaching. Peer-led systems of external examining have been adopted at various times in several other countries: Ireland, New Zealand, Denmark, India, Malaysia, Brunei, Malawi, Hong Kong and South Africa in order to provide confidence in academic standards in the sector. The external examining system in the UK, being the earliest and most established, will be the focus of this chapter but with broader lessons for assurance of academic standards. It will question the assumptions on which the external examiner system is built, in particular assumptions about the inherent existence of common understandings of standards and how they are shared. Bringing greater consistency to the inherently human judgements made by external examiners in the field matters because these judgements make up the rigour of the system. Unless the need for greater support for external examiners and the need for calibration is fully acknowledged and acted on, the system cannot reach its full potential to support national academic standards.

UK external examiner system

Unlike some other countries, the UK aspires to consistent national academic standards in higher education regardless of type or mission of the provider. This aspiration is reinforced through a national qualification framework and other supporting quality assurance procedures and processes including external examining (see Chapter 2). The external examining system is the one process that monitors the academic standards achieved by students. The current system is largely concerned with taught undergraduate and postgraduate programmes. While in many countries doctoral assessment also uses a variant of external examining, it has a focus on direct examination of the student's work. External examining operates through numerous academics acting as external reviewers within higher education institutions, which creates a complex network of oversight across the UK. For each higher education programme an academic from another institution, but with expertise in the relevant subject area, is appointed as external examiner for a limited period (usually 3–4 years) to oversee assessment for that programme of study or suite of courses, for example an undergraduate degree programme. Their role is to comment on and discuss the design and expectations of assessment tasks and examinations, scrutinise samples of marked student work at regular intervals (usually once or twice a year) and to approve marks awarded for all student cohorts. They periodically submit reports to the institution commenting on the academic standards used to judge student work and assessment procedures. In the case of vocational courses, some examiners may be practising members of the relevant profession rather than academics.

UK higher education institutions with degree-awarding powers are academically autonomous and thereby responsible for the academic standards they use. The external examining system is the means by which those autonomous academic standards are compared and mediated across the sector with a view to achieving national parity in awards from different institutions. One of the fundamental principles articulated in the UK Quality Code for Higher Education (QAA, 2018, p. 1) is 'ensuring external referencing is used to ensure the integrity of awards and the quality of provision'. External examining is the means by which this principle is met in practice and is the only element of quality assurance that 'specifically addresses the quality of student performance' (Bloxham & Price, 2013, p. 2).

The UK Quality Assurance Agency (QAA, 2022, p. 1) asserts that: 'The external examining system has been a key mechanism for upholding academic standards in UK higher education for almost 200 years, ensuring comparability across different institutions.' But to what extent does it live up to this claim and is there room for improvement?

The strengths of the system

The higher education sector has confidence in the system. As part of a review of external examining arrangements, responses to a Universities UK and GuildHE discussion paper indicated that '[t]he overwhelming body of opinion from the responses is that the external examining system works well on the whole, and does not require a major overhaul' (Universities UK & GuildHE, 2011, p. 6). In fact none of the numerous successive reviews, reports and research projects has rejected the external examiner model, although several have made recommendations focused on strengthening it.

The key factor in assuring the system's status as respected and trusted derives from its peer-led structure (see Box 6.1). This has a dual advantage in that the formal structure of the system is owned by the sector and that the practice of examining is carried out by academic peers from within subject communities. Ownership of the system by the sector means that the closely guarded autonomy of higher education institutions is respected. Institutions appoint external examiners for each programme of study and they retain the right to devise, manage and control their own processes to select and appoint the external examiners who will work with the institution. Formal and rigorous selection procedures are set up by institutions aimed at ensuring independent and highly regarded examiners are appointed. These seek to largely mitigate any accusations of appointing 'friendly' examiners (see Chapter 5).

The conceptual framework of peer review is dependent on the idea that academics from the same subject community will, by and large, hold similar understandings of academic standards. Therefore senior academics, each acting as external examiners to several institutions across the sector over time, will create a dynamic and interacting network covering the whole sector to oversee academic standards in use. Such a dynamic system exposes external examiners to the academic standards used by other academics in their community, acting not only as a means to 'test' the standards of an institution, but also to provide a 'check' on individual external examiners' academic standards.

CRITICAL PERSPECTIVE

Box 6.1 The importance of peer review in external examining

The peer-led structure of the external examiner system allows the sector to retain ownership of the academic standards used and endows trusted status on this quality assurance process.

Another advantage of a peer-led system is at the level of the practice. Those whose academic standards and assessment practices are being 'examined' know that the external examiner is an academic from within their own subject community. Consequently trust in external examiners' legitimacy to make judgements is likely to be enhanced by the tendency for academics to feel greater affinity with their subject community rather than their institution (Trowler, 2008). An external examiner from within the subject community is likely to engender far greater acceptability than an examiner imposed from outside the core discipline or even outside the sector.

Although holding a different 'status' from academics on programme teams, an external examiner usually tries to work with the team to assure academic standards rather than oversee them. The examiners are, generally, current practitioners and therefore having to make similar choices, decisions and judgements around assessment in their own day-to-day practice and, of course, will also be subject to external examining in their own institution.

Apparent problems with the system

Although the sector considers the system to work well, many reviews and reports have made recommendations for improvement. These recommendations largely concern the need to clarify and make more transparent aspects of the system such as: the process of appointments of examiners (e.g. BIS, 2009); guidance relating to examiner reports (e.g. Universities UK & GuildHE, 2011); institutions' support for the system and examiners (e.g. QAA, 2005); and examiner role definition (e.g. HEQC, 1996). Many of these are long standing issues and could, in theory, be largely addressed through greater written guidance or development of processes within the system. However, there are some problems that are more fundamental and not so easily fixed.

One possible weakness is that the system is under too much pressure in the current complex mass higher education to be effective (Universities UK & GuildHE, 2011). In its early stages, before higher education was vastly expanded in the late twentieth century, the system needed only to cover a relatively few universities and courses compared with the number and diversity of courses offered in the sector today. It has been suggested that in a smaller sector the limited number of academics could more easily represent standards of smaller, more close-knit subject communities (Silver & Williams, 1996). Unfortunately there is little evidence to determine whether the system was more effective in a smaller sector or whether examiners acted autonomously without much regard for any consensus that existed in their discipline communities. In terms of the diversity that now exists within the sector, can examiners from different types of universities (e.g. traditional research intensive versus employment focused) make judgements about academic standards used across such a divide? In practice, there is evidence that research intensive universities appoint 80% of their external examiners from similar institutions (HEA, 2015), belying the idea that the examiner network envisaged across the whole sector exists. This not only suggests that there may be fragmentation within the sector's standards but also that institutions' appointment systems may not guard against selection of 'sympathetic' externals as claimed (see also Chapter 5).

Regardless of size or complexity of the sector the peer-led structure, in theory, should provide a robust and effective system to safeguard academic standards. Common understanding of subject academic standards among external examiners (and indeed the wider community of academics) should provide a sound foundation for using those standards in a range of settings across a diverse sector by many examiners. However, the external examiner system rests on a number of untested assumptions that may not hold true, and this has led to its effectiveness being questioned.

First, the system depends on a common understanding of the role of the examiner (Universities UK & GuildHE, 2011) with the safeguarding of academic standards being of primary importance (QAA, 2022). The extent of such common understanding, however, is in some doubt (Bloxham & Price 2013). In 1996 the Higher Education Quality Council identified four conceptions of the role: examiner; moderator; calibrator; and consultant. However, the balance between these conceptions seems to be unclear, with a particular tension between consultant (or critical friend concerned with academic input or process) and examiner (concerned with the standard of output). The system currently allows institutions and examiners considerable autonomy in how they play the role. A study (HEA, 2015, p. 6) revealed '43% of examiners … perceive the role as largely a 'process checker', i.e. having a focus on quality standards rather than academic standards'. Without consistency in the role of external examiner it is likely that there will always be doubts about the system's efficacy.

Another assumption relates to the nature of academic standards and how common understanding can be established. As discussed in Chapter 3, the nature of academic standards makes defining and establishing a consensus extremely challenging and 'the simplistic and fixed notions of standards as portrayed in public debate deny the necessarily elusive and dynamic nature of academic standards which are continuously co-constructed by academics' (Bloxham & Price, 2013, p. 200). This may go a long way in to explain why external examiners tend not to rely on explicit national frameworks and documented statements of academic standards, preferring to rely on personal experience of academic standards (Colley & Silver, 2005).

The external examining system is built on the assumptions that subject community consensus on academic standards exists, examiners are fully aware of and are able to represent those community standards, and that they understand the complexity of professional judgement and higher education assessment processes. If these assumptions are unreliable, claims made about the effectiveness of the system are in serious doubt. There is further discussion about this issue in Chapter 8.

CRITICAL PERSPECTIVE

Box 6.2 The need for professionalisation of the external examining system

The historic 'cottage industry' approach to external examining has deprived it of professional approaches such as external examiner development and recognition of the importance of subject communities in informing the academic standards used by external examiners. Professionalisation is essential for a modern external examining system.

Despite the importance of these assumptions, Bloxham & Price (2013) point out that relatively few studies or reviews have addressed the issue of whether academic standards are well understood and consistently applied by external examiners, with examiners instead affording greater focus to the processes and procedures of the system. This may be because these processes and procedures are more straightforward to address and that the prominence given to explicit approaches to defining academic standards remains dominant in the sector. Unfortunately, evidence increasingly challenges reliance on the assumptions with external examiners using academic standards that are no more aligned than other academics across the sector (e.g. see Newstead & Dennis, 1994; Warren Piper, 1994; QAA & HEA, 2013).

In addition, the co-construction of academic standards that is assumed to take place within subject communities may also be in doubt: 'An assessment standards discourse is needed to support the functioning of assessment communities of practice but the development of such a discourse…seems to be limited by a lack of assessment scholarship' (Price, 2005, p. 226). Subject communities are largely autonomous and there are considerable differences between their approaches and level of activity. For example, some focus almost exclusively on research with little emphasis on learning, teaching and assessment, some have multiple formal groupings seeking to support the subject and some have strong links with professional bodies linked to their subject (see Chapters 14 and 15). The role of the subject community provides another focus for a professional approach as well as consideration of resources available to each community.

As a peer-led system, the effectiveness of external examining ultimately relies on the external examiners themselves. External examiners find themselves in the difficult position of having to negotiate tacit and contextual standards within a regime built on the promotion of transparency and accountability (Hudson et al., 2016). With the external examining system analogous to a 'cottage industry', relying on individual, isolated and largely untrained workers to collectively provide high quality, robust outcomes, this seems to be a careless approach for such an important aspect of assuring academic standards across a sector (see Box 6.2). Without dedicated training for their role and opportunities to engage with their subject communities to discuss and develop confidence about their understanding of academic standards there is no reason to expect that examiners will be able to provide consistent judgements about academic standards.

Recent developments in external examining

It is notable that many of the findings and recommendations of successive external examining reviews bear considerable similarity and it is disappointing that many of the recommendations are still unfulfilled. A recent report (HEA, 2015) and subsequent Degree Standards Project focused on the development needs and professionalisation of the examiners themselves rather than the policies and procedures of the system. See Chapters 9–12 for information on the Degree Standards Project, its implementation in practice, and its outcomes.

The most recent development was the publication of 'Principles of External Examining' (QAA, 2022), which were developed through consultation in the sector.

These emphasise the need for external examiners to 'advise and, where necessary, challenge the institutions' on their academic standards and, although there is an emphasis on explicit formal definitions of national standards, it is also suggested that '[w]herever possible, they [external examiners] take part in calibration activities within their discipline' (QAA, 2022, p. 2). This acknowledges the socially constructed nature of academic standards and that for examiners to represent their subject community standards they must engage in calibration activities within their communities (see Chapters 8, 14 and 15 for examples). The system cannot be effective if 'isolated' and unsupported academics act as external examiners.

In addition, to support their ability to judge standards, the QAA publication (QAA, 2022, p. 2) says, examiners should be 'assessment-literate and familiar with the current literature and research in assessment practice' (see Chapter 7 for further detail). It is also recommended that external examiners receive training to support their professionalisation. For their part, institutions need to clearly define the role examiners will play, appoint examiners to reflect the diversity of the sector as well as recognising and supporting their staff who take up external examining.

While not mandatory, it is hoped that these principles will be effective in developing and professionalising the external examining system. They encompass important ideas that can be applied in other systems of assuring academic standards and, particularly, highlight what is needed for the effective implementation of any peer-led system aiming to maintain academic standards. In a sector where there is a tension between institutional autonomy and the belief in a 'gold' standard of nationally agreed academic standards there will need to be a commitment to change as an important step in building a robust and fully effective external examiner system (see Box 6.3).

CRITICAL PERSPECTIVE

Box 6.3 Stakeholder commitment to the external examiner system

To claim that external examining upholds and safeguards academic standards it is critical that all key players in the system – regulators, institutions, examiners and subject communities – demonstrate their commitment to its robust operation. This requires willingness to support and resource a professional approach, particularly for examiners and subject communities.

Conclusion

The external examiner system in the UK has strong foundations and such a peer-led system, focused on comparing academic standards evident in student work, provides a conceptually robust model for any country to use. As seen in Chapter 3, academic standards are manifested in performance so the monitoring of outputs through the external examining system is a critical part of assuring those standards nationally. However, peer-led systems are only as strong as the individual examiners and the coverage of the national network. Until recently, the UK system has remained largely unchanged since its inception, relying on some dubious assumptions and a 'cottage industry' approach to its operation. Recent developments aiming to support the system to meet the needs of a mass and diversified sector are to be welcomed. The moves to professionalise the external examiner role and to recognise the importance of external examiners calibrating their own standards within their subject communities, should enable greater consistency in practice and judgements. These moves, however, still depend on the willingness of autonomous institutions to acknowledge and support a more professional system and for there to be much more support for the haphazard structures and resources that exist to support subject communities to successfully discuss and share academic standards. Any external examiner system needs to pay close attention to the key elements of the system to ensure it is not built on spurious assumptions and that it is structured and resourced in a way to enable it to operate professionally and independently.

References

BIS. (2009). *Higher Ambitions: The Future of Universities in a Knowledge Economy*. London: Department for Business Innovation and Skills. www.bl.uk/collection-items/higher-ambitions-the-future-of-universities-in-a-knowledge-economy-1

Bloxham, S. & Price, M. (2013). External examining: fit for purpose? *Studies in Higher Education*, 40 (2), 195–211. https://doi.org/10.1080/03075079.2013.823931.

Colley, H. & Silver, H. (2005). *External Examiners and the Benchmarking of Standards*. York: Higher Education Academy.

HEA. (2015). A review of external examining arrangements across the UK. https://radar.brookes.ac.uk/radar/file/642f577e-4a43-44b3-8bc5-a774ea2e25f/1/2015_externalexam.pdf.

HEQC. (1996). *Strengthening External Examining*. London: Higher Education Quality Council.

Hudson, J., Bloxham, S., den Outer, B. & Price, M. (2016). Conceptual acrobatics: talking about assessment standards in the transparency era. *Studies in Higher Education*, 42(7), 1309–1323. https://doi.org/10.1080/03075079.2015.1092130.

Newstead, S. E. & Dennis, I. (1994). Examiners examined: the reliability of exam marking in psychology. *The Psychologist: Bulletin of the British Psychological Society*, 7, 216–219. https://doi.org/10.2304/plat.2002.2.2.

Price, M. (2005). Assessment standards: the role of communities of practice and the scholarship of assessment. *Assessment and Evaluation in Higher Education*, 30(3), 215–230. https://doi.org/10.1080/02602930500063793.

QAA. (2005). *Outcomes from Institutional Audits: External Examiners and Their Reports*. Gloucester: Quality Assurance Agency. https://dera.ioe.ac.uk/9626/1/Outcomes1.pdf.

QAA. (2018). UK quality code for higher education. www.qaa.ac.uk/the-quality-code.

QAA. (2022). Principles of external examining. www.qaa.ac.uk/docs/qaa/quality-code/external-examining-principles.pdf?sfvrsn=fe91a281_12.

QAA & HEA. (2013). *External examiners' understanding and use of academic standards.* https://s3.eu-west-2.amazonaws.com/assets.creode.advancehe-document-manager/documents/hea/external-examiners-report_1581086309.pdf.

Silver, H. & Williams, S. (1996). Academic standards and the external examiner system. In J. Brennan, M. Frazer, R. Middlehurst, H. Silver & R. Williams. (Eds.), *Changing Conceptions of Academic Standards* (pp 27–48). London: Quality Support Centre, Open University.

Trowler, P. (2008). *Cultures and change in higher education: Theories and practice.* Basingstoke: Palgrave Macmillan.

Universities UK & GuildHE. (2011). *Review of External Examining Arrangements in Universities and Colleges in the UK: Final Report and Recommendations.* London: Universities UK. www.tcd.ie/teaching-learning/quality/assets/pdf/ReviewOfExternalExaminingArrangements%20UK.pdf.

Warren Piper, D. (1994). *Are Professors Professional.* London: Jessica Kingsley.

Chapter 7

Demystifying the role of the external examiner through the lens of assessment literacy

Emma Medland

Introduction

The external examining system has been a 'gold standard' of the quality assurance process in UK Higher Education (HE), as well as in countries where HE systems are based upon practices in the UK such as India, Denmark and New Zealand. Yet growing scrutiny of the external examiner system has resulted in a downgrading of the role of the external examiner through the language used to describe it by UK quality bodies such as the Quality Assurance Agency, or QAA, (Bloxham & Price, 2015). This is perhaps why countries such as Canada and the USA have opted for an accreditation system in preference to external examiners (see Chapter 4).

Subject and assessment expertise (or assessment literacy) form the key pillars upon which the role of the external examiner is built (Cuthbert, 2003; Medland, 2019), with the latter being described as an obligation of the role (Bloxham & Boyd, 2012). Yet national criteria for appointment of external examiners contains little emphasis on assessment literacy (Finch Review, 2011; Medland, 2019), and little evidence exists to support the assumption that external examiners are assessment literate (Medland, 2015, 2019). As noted in Box 7.1, assessment literacy represents one of several untested assumptions underpinning the external examiner role (Bloxham & Price, 2015) and, as one of the only quality assurance instruments that focuses directly on the quality of student work (Gaunt, 1999; also see Chapters 5 and 6), requires further interrogation.

CRITICAL PERSPECTIVE

Box 7.1 Two pillars of external examining

External examining is built upon the two pillars of subject expertise and assessment expertise, or assessment literacy. Yet scant attention or evidence supports the assumption of assessment literacy in external examiners.

This chapter will interrogate the role of the external examiner by focusing on the untested assumption that external examiners are assessment literate. The chapter will

DOI: 10.4324/9781003379768-9

draw upon research findings focusing on the assessment literacy demonstrated in UK external examiner written reports and reported practice (see Medland, 2015, 2019). In addressing this assumption, the chapter will illuminate how assessment literacy could be conceptualised as a means of demystifying the external examiner role. This conceptualisation could also lead to the development of a shared language, or discourse, which could support examiners and teachers alike, to surface and critique the often tacit understandings and beliefs that shape personal assessment practices.

External examining: the quality of the underlying practice?

Chapter 6 provides an insight into the strengths and apparent problems of the external examining system that rest upon a set of untested assumptions. A tentative downgrading of the system (Bloxham & Price, 2015) has been strengthened by the UK Quality Assurance Agency's (QAA's) use of the term 'external expertise' (QAA, 2018, p. 1) in preference to external examiner. The QAA is an impartial regulatory body working in partnership with HE institutions and colleges, in the UK and internationally, to support their quality assurance and enhancement processes (see www.qaa.ac.uk). While such organisations tasked with safeguarding and enhancing quality and standards produce guidelines for external examiners, their focus lies primarily with establishing reliability and comparability of procedures (e.g. appointment, induction, reporting), rather than interrogating the more fundamental question concerning the quality of the underlying practices (Bloxham, 2009).

Research focusing on the quality of underlying practices of the external examining system does not inspire confidence, with a wide range of challenges being identified. For example: issues with the effectiveness of the system (Silver et al., 1995), its impact (Murphy, 2006), reliability (Price, 2005), consistency (Brooks, 2012); the comparability and quality of standards (Bloxham, 2009; Bloxham & Price, 2015) and difficulty of codifying and assuring academic standards (Bloxham, 2009; Bloxham et al., 2016); and the limited impact on the development of assessment practices (Biggs, 2003). In essence, the focus of external examiner evaluations tends to overlook the substance of what is being evaluated in favour of the constituent processes or, using the terms introduced in Chapter 5, quality standards instead of academic standards. As one of the only quality assurance instruments that focuses directly on assessing the quality of student work, greater emphasis needs to be placed on the substance of what is being evaluated and on tackling the untested assumptions underpinning the external examiner role. In response to this need, Bloxham and Price (2015) have identified six untested assumptions underpinning the role of external examiners.

While attempts have been made to increase the transparency, accessibility and enhancement of the external examiner system's procedures, these have largely failed to address the six assumptions upon which external examining is built. These assumptions focus primarily on the challenges associated with a shared knowledge, understanding and application of academic and community standards (i.e. assumptions 1–

5), and on the assessment literacy of external examiners (i.e. assumption 6). While the first five assumptions focusing on academic and community standards are expertly interrogated throughout this book, the assumption that external examiners are assessment literate requires further interrogation. This chapter will focus on investigating the assumption that external examiners are assessment literate by tackling the three highly pertinent questions raised by Bloxham and Price (2015, p. 206):

1   What confidence can we have that the average external examiner has the 'assessment literacy' to be aware of the complex influences on their standards and judgement processes?
2   How likely are they to understand the provenance of their own standards and the influence of their background and experience?
3   How strong is the temptation to draw largely on their personal experience as an indicator of what standards should be rather than recognising the potential bias in that approach, or the influence of a particular context or student body or professional experience?

Prior to attempting to address these questions, some context needs to be provided in relation to what assessment literacy is, why it is considered important, and what the challenges associated with its use might be.

Assessment literacy: conceptualisations and challenges

There has been a sustained and increasing interest in assessment literacy across the overall education sector. Assessment literacy has been described as fundamental to educators (Popham, 2009) and an obligation for external examiners (Bloxham & Boyd, 2012). Indeed, Bloxham and Price (2015) identify assessment literacy as one of the two pillars upon which external examining is built, while also highlighting the inadequate focus on it, in preference to the subject expertise of external examiners.

CRITICAL PERSPECTIVE

Box 7.2 Assessment literacy is under-conceptualised

The concept of assessment literacy frequently appears within education-related discourse, but is poorly understood and conceptualised, leading to the unhelpful and over-simplistic literate - illiterate dichotomy.

Assessment literacy has been identified as one means of supporting universities to reverse the deterioration of confidence in academic standards (HEA, 2012, 2016). Nevertheless, it is often overlooked when recruiting new examiners, and is not adequately reflected in national criteria for the appointment of examiners (Cuthbert, 2003). As noted in Box 7.2, assessment literacy has also been described as a concept that is 'often used but rarely defined' (Willis et al., 2013, p. 242). This points to an assumption that a commonly held understanding of the concept has been achieved, or that it is transparent in its meaning. But the literature shows little consensus regarding how assessment literacy is defined or conceptualised, and highlights the promiscuity of use of the term literacy and its attachment to 'too many disparate practices' (Vincent, 2003, p. 341). Increasingly, it would seem, the addition of the term 'literacy' has been used to add gravitas to a concept, while concurrently concealing inadequate conceptualisation. Assessment literacy is no exception. For example, much of the pre-existing literature centres on establishing a simplistic dichotomy concerning whether it is present in practice (i.e. assessment literate), or not, and is often found to be lacking (i.e. assessment illiterate). This has resulted in a largely unhelpful distraction from the conceptualisation of assessment literacy, thus fuelling the widespread accusation of 'assessment illiteracy' across the compulsory education sector (Stiggins, 1991).

Within the HE sector assessment literacy is a relatively new concept enjoying increasing attention and appearing more frequently within sector wide discourses. Definitions of assessment literacy within the HE context tend to centre around staff and students, and focus on aspects such as rules, language, standards, knowledge, skills and attributes (HEA, 2012; QAA, 2013; Deeley & Bovill, 2017; Denton & McIlroy, 2018) and more recently on attitudes, actions and abilities (Chan & Luo, 2022). With the exception of Smith et al. (2013), few means of measuring the concept have been developed. This is perhaps not surprising in view of Wiliam's (2015) assertion that assessment literacy should be defined according to different practitioners various roles. From this perspective, assessment literacy should be a negotiated and fluid concept (Willis et al., 2013; DeLuca et al., 2016) requiring broadening beyond a focus on staff and students to include other assessment-related practitioners, such as external examiners.

Just as Chapter 6 notes in relation to assessment standards, to broaden focus requires the development of a shared language that will enable assessment-related practitioners to both critique their assessment practices as well as articulate and examine the values and beliefs that underpin them (Willis et al., 2013). The development of a shared language that focuses on a set of constituent elements could serve to circumvent the over-simplistic assessment (il)literacy dichotomy while providing a more nuanced and agile means of investigating the concept. It would also provide a means of addressing the first of Bloxham and Price's (2015, p. 206) questions concerning the assessment literacy of external examiners.

What confidence can we have that the average external examiner has the 'assessment literacy' to be aware of the complex influences on their standards and judgement processes?

To begin exploring the extent of assessment literacy in external examiners, a conceptualisation that underpins the possibility of a shared language of assessment literacy was developed. This was piloted in Medland (2015) and extended in Medland (2019). Both articles are grounded in a theoretical frame provided by a book on assessment literacy (Price et al., 2012), which serves to provide a more nuanced understanding of assessment literacy, involving a complex set of integrated elements. In Medland (2015), external examiner reports from a range of disciplines were thematically analysed against this theoretical framework, resulting in the identification of six constituent elements of assessment literacy of external examiners. These elements consisted of:

i community;
ii dialogue;
iii knowledge and understanding;
iv programme-wide approach;
v standards; and
vi self-regulation.

Framework analysis was then used to establish the extent of evidence for each element within these reports as the basis for the development of a shared language of assessment literacy. In Medland (2019) external examiners from across the UK with a range of experience and disciplinary backgrounds were interviewed to interrogate perceptions of their own assessment literacy based upon the six constituent elements, which was then used to initiate a discussion surrounding the development of a shared discourse of assessment literacy (see Medland, 2015, 2019 for further details).

The findings reported by Medland (2015, 2019) indicated that assessment literacy is a concept in its infancy and one that external examiners are largely unfamiliar with. For example, when asking external examiners what they understood by assessment literacy, responses included, 'I think I'm about to fail my external examiner 101', and 'I'm an assessment illiterate' (Medland, 2019, p. 10). So an initial reaction to the question that shapes the focus of this section would be that we can have little confidence that the average external examiner has assessment literacy. However, upon further investigation the six constituent elements of assessment literacy cited above were apparent in the self-reported perceptions of the role (see Box 7.3).

CRITICAL PERSPECTIVE

Box 7.3 External examiner perceptions of assessment literacy

While external examiner understanding of the concept of assessment literacy was poor, aspects of each of the six constituent elements of assessment literacy was apparent in the external examiners' perceptions of the role. Immersion in the community of practice provided insight into the standards of that community. While a poor programme-wide overview interfered with immersion, dialogue with its members supported immersion and an insight into the co-constructed standards shaping that practice. Implicit knowledge and understanding of relevant assessment theory was apparent but required explicit articulation to avoid compounding the gap between theory and practice, which could be supported through self-regulation grounded in a commitment continuing professional development.

Standards are typically considered to live within local cultures (Orr, 2007; Medland, 2010) and immersion within another programme's community is a central benefit of the role. However, integration within the target community is challenging, principally due to resource and time restrictions that an external examiner can commit to the role, fuelled by the typically insufficient recognition and reward of the role across the sector. In addition, a programme-wide overview, while vital to the development of assessment literacy, is generally not achieved in the role, and actively discouraged by some institutions. However, the informal dialogue that external examiners engage in with a programme team, and sometimes the students too, supported their integration into the community. It also provided insight into the co-constructed nature of standards, although the outcomes of this informal dialogue were generally not shared at the institution-level. It became evident that the assessment knowledge and understanding of external examiners needs to be brought out more explicitly if the external examiner system is to avoid compounding the gap between what theory calls for and how this is enacted in practice, that is currently present in HE. A further tension related to the extent of integration achieved by each external examiner. If full integration were to be achieved, how might this impact on the examiners ability to compare local standards with national standards and challenge them? Finally, self-regulation via continuing professional development is an aspect of the role that has received increasing interest and support, as reported within Part IIIA of this book.

As such, of the six constituent elements of the concept of assessment literacy identified in Medland (2015), standards and dialogue were most frequently discussed. However, these two elements were discussed primarily in relation to the challenges experienced such as the difficulties associated with developing a shared understanding of standards. The remaining elements of community, knowledge and understanding, programme-wide approach, and self-regulation require attention for the assessment literacy of the external examiners involved in this research to develop in a more explicit manner. This might be achieved through greater consistency relating to how the role is perceived and enacted, and greater support from both home and host institutions. Therefore, one means of developing the assessment literacy of external examiners requires recognition of the provenance of their own internal standards and the influence of their background and experience (Bloxham & Price, 2015). The inclusion of a reference to the importance of assessment literacy in the recently published 'Principles of External Examining' (QAA, 2022, p. 2) is a step in the right direction, but appears to focus largely on only one of the constituent elements (i.e. knowledge and understanding) of assessment literacy requiring development. Further support is therefore required for this principle to be acted upon in a consistent way.

How likely are external examiners to understand the provenance of their own standards and the influence of their background and experience?

In Medland (2019) a key distinction emerged between the internalised standards of the external examiners interviewed and external standards, which Bloxham et al. (2015, p. 1080) describe as the difference between a 'personal standards framework and national standards'. In contrast to the assumptions of academic standard community consensus and external examiners' ability to both represent and acknowledge the complex influences upon these standards as outlined in Chapter 6, the examiners interviewed by Medland (2019) explained how national standards were 'translated' into the local practices of programme teams to which they were not fully familiarised. As a result, differences and idiosyncrasies emerged between teams of markers, which Bloxham and Boyd (2012, p. 200) have referred to as the 'invisibility and variability of tacit standards', and which HEFCE (2015, p. 5) concluded led to 'limited use of formal reference points in making … judgements'. In other words, the very experience of acting as an external examiner resulted in greater cognisance of the variance of tacit standards, and with such recognition comes a greater possibility of understanding the provenance of one's own standards.

After exposure to the idiosyncrasies of other academics' tacit standards, the external examiners interviewed in Medland (2019) highlighted how this experience supported them to reflect upon their own tacit and idiosyncratic internalised personal standards. It also exposed each external examiner to diverse practices that could be used to inform their personal development, with Hudson et al. (2017, p. 1321) acknowledging that such recognition of difference 'underpins external examiners' ability to contribute to comparable standards across institutions'. What this revelation demonstrates is how engagement in the role of external examining serves to make internal standards more explicit to the individual so that they are more likely to understand the provenance of their own standards and the influence of their background and experience. For example, one external examiner noted how acting as external examiner had 'opened my eyes to what I consider normal'. Interestingly, several external examiners also explained how they avoided applying their own internal standards by adapting them to the context of the programme for which they were employed to oversee, referring to the 'different rules of the game'. As a result and outlined in Box 7.4, for the external examiners who have the foresight to reflect upon the differences in assessment practices to which they are exposed, the role can support the articulation of their internal personal standards and recognition of their provenance. However, this was by no means an aspect of the role that all external examiners discussed and so the answer to this question indicates inconsistency across individuals.

CRITICAL PERSPECTIVE

Box 7.4 Inconsistent recognition of internal standards

Exposure to differences in assessment practices can instigate internal comparisons and the articulation of internal standards and recognition of their provenance, but this is not consistent across external examiners.

How strong is the temptation for external examiners to draw largely on their personal experience as an indicator of what standards should be rather than recognising the potential bias in that approach, or the influence of a particular context or student body or professional experience?

This question focuses on the interconnections between national frameworks, local practices and tacit standards, and which has the greatest influence over assessment practices. In Medland (2019), the most pertinent findings relating to these interconnections concerned what role the external examiners felt they fulfilled. Perceptions of role were far more diverse than the *Handbook for External Examining* (HEA, 2012, p. 5) would have us believe, in which it is stated that:

> The critical friend approach is now more or less universal with the expectation that the external examiner will identify strengths, weaknesses and good practice of the provision and play a role in quality enhancement.

In Medland (2019), tensions arose when comparing external examiners perceptions of their role with those of the employing institution, thus highlighting tensions between tacit standards and local practices. What became quickly apparent in the interviews was that there is a lot of mystery and diversity of practices and understanding surrounding the role. Some respondents felt that their main concern lay in supporting quality enhancement, such as informing the development of particular aspects of the programme in question, whereas others felt that their primary concern lay in supporting quality assurance, such as acting as a champion for a programme. There was also inconsistency relating to what was considered to be the primary purpose of external examiners, responses ranging from a 'governance role' to a 'mouthpiece for the programme team'. Some examiners viewed a primary responsibility residing in the provision of 'advice', while others noted that 'my role is to point out where there are deficiencies. It is not my role to specify how to put them right'. Responses also highlighted a diversity of institutional perspectives of the role, ranging from critical friend to a rubber stamp or tick box exercise. This diversity is identified in Chapter 6 as a result of the considerable autonomy that examiners and institutions are afforded.

Internal examiners were often observed as not being clear of the remit of external examiners, highlighting the potential for clashes between the internal standards of the programme team compared to the external examiner. But there was also an indication of how internal standards could be adapted to suit the particular local context in which the external examiners were employed. For example, one external examiner noted that 'despite the platform you're put on, you are not God and must accept they are running the programme *and that you can be wrong*'. So how the role is perceived and enacted is far from consistent and where inconsistencies are apparent, this strengthens the temptation to use personal experience as an indicator of what standards should be. As outlined in Box 7.5, it is also perhaps worthwhile to acknowledge the role of experience in response to this question.

CRITICAL PERSPECTIVE

Box 7.5 External examiner experience, internal standards, and confidence in the system

As the level of experience that individual external examiners have increases, so too does the influence of their internal standards, leading to greater inconsistency concerning the primary purpose and role of the external examiner. This in turn, leads to greater inconsistency, which further undermines confidence in the external examining system.

For example, Eraut (1995) noted how increasing levels of assessment expertise is typically characterised by a reduction in reference to codified external standards, in preference to a more instinctive approach based largely on internalised standards. As a result, greater expertise can result in a reduction in ability to articulate one's personal internal standards. Therefore, as the external examiner gains more experience, the temptation to draw upon personal experience and internal standards can increase and have a greater influence upon understanding of what standards should be.

Conclusion

The external examining system is viewed as 'a cornerstone of how academic staff confirm standards and quality across the sector', providing one of the only quality assurance instruments that focuses directly on the quality of student work. However, the system has faced mounting criticism resulting in its downgrading. Several flawed assumptions underpinning the external examining system have been identified by Bloxham and Price (2015), the majority of which focus on the challenges associated with a shared knowledge, understanding and application of academic and community standards, which this book interrogates throughout. The final assumption requiring interrogation relates to the assessment literacy of external examiners. As summarised in Box 7.6, research by Medland (2015, 2019) served to identify six constituent elements of assessment literacy as a means of developing a shared language that could support examiners and teachers alike to surface and critique the often tacit understandings and beliefs that shape personal assessment practices. The findings highlighted the mystery, and diversity of practices and understanding, that surround the role of the external examiner, its primary purpose and key responsibilities. In other words, there were inconsistent levels of assessment literacy exhibited by a group of external examiners.

PRACTICAL STRATEGY

Box 7.6 The importance of developing a shared language of assessment literacy

The development of a shared language of assessment literacy could enable the effective sharing of standards and development of a more common approach to the external examiner role. This could reduce the inconsistencies resulting in greater reliance upon personal standards, thereby reversing the deterioration of confidence in academic standards.

A key distinction drawn by Medland (2019) related to one of the six constituent elements of assessment literacy, namely standards. Findings distinguished between the internal standards of each external examiner, and the external standards developed to underpin the quality assurance regime shaping the HE sector (Jarvis, 2014). Engagement in the role of external examiner was evidenced to increase awareness of the diversity of assessment practices typical in HE that, in turn, could support the articulation of internal standards and recognition of their provenance. However, this was not consistent across all external examiners and was dependent upon each individual engaging in a self-reflective process. Perceptions of how the role is conceived and enacted were also found to be far from consistent (Medland, 2019), with tensions sometimes emerging between institutional, programmatic and individual views of the role. Where perceptions differed and perceived expertise increased, there was a greater temptation to draw upon external examiners' personal standards, with less reference to codified external standards, which could result in greater inconsistency thus fuelling calls for downgrading the role of external examiners.

It would seem that organisations tasked with safeguarding standards and improving the quality of HE, such as the QAA in the UK, have put into motion the calls for a downgrading of the external examiner system. This has been achieved by replacing use of the word external examiner with 'external expertise'. In other words, external examiners are no longer a requirement for the assurance of standards in HE and, therefore, not something that institutions must have. However, to replace the external examining system with a broader diversity of external expertise for the purpose of assuring standards and quality assurance processes, would seem to concurrently compound issues surrounding quality assurance, while avoiding tackling the challenges identified in relation to the external examining system. These are challenges that are likely to be reflected and perhaps exaggerated through the use of a broader diversity of external experts such as external advisers, employers and alumni.

A much more efficient approach surely lies in tackling the challenges identified in relation to the external examiner system via a sector-owned and led response, such as that outlined in the UK Degree Standards Project. Here, the focus rests on developing the quality of the underlying practices of external examiners through the professionalisation of the role (see Chapters 9–12). One aspect of this response should focus on enhancing the assessment literacy of all practitioners involved in the assessment process, from internal and external examiners, through to quality assurance personnel involved in drafting relevant codes of practice and overseeing programme validations. This could be achieved via the development of a 'shared language' of assessment literacy that will empower those involved to question their role in the assessment process, articulate and interrogate the internal standards that shape their practices, and reduce the level of inconsistency that underpins the external examining system.

References

Biggs, J. (2003). *Teaching for Quality Learning at University* (2nd ed.). Open University Press.

Bloxham, S. (2009). Marking and moderation in the UK: false assumptions and wasted resources. *Assessment & Evaluation in Higher Education*, 39(2), 209–220. http://dx.doi.org/10.1080/02602930801955978.

Bloxham, S. & Boyd, P. (2012). Accountability in grading student work: securing academic standards in a twenty-first century quality assurance context. *British Educational Research Journal*, 38(4), 615–634. http://dx.doi.org/10.1080/01411926.2011.569007.

Bloxham, S., Hudson, J., den Outer, B. & Price, M. (2015). External peer review of assessment: an effective approach to verifying standards? *Higher Education Research & Development*, 34(6), 1069–1082. http://dx.doi.org/10.1080/07294360.2015.1024629.

Bloxham, S., Hughes, C. & Adie, L. (2016). What's the point of moderation? A discussion of the purposes achieved through contemporary moderation practices. *Assessment and Evaluation in Higher Education*, 41(4), 638–653. http://dx.doi.org/10.1080/02602938.2015.1039932.

Bloxham, S. & Price, M. (2015). External examining: fit for purpose? *Studies in Higher Education*, 40(2), 195–211. http://dx.doi.org/10.1080/03075079.2013.823931.

Brooks, V. (2012). Marking as judgement. *Research Papers in Education*, 27(1), 63–80. https://doi.org/10.1080/02671520903331008.

Chan, C.K.Y. & Luo, J. (2022). Investigating student preparedness for holistic competency assessment: insights from the Hong Kong context. *Assessment & Evaluation in Higher Education*, 47(4), 636–651. http://dx.doi.org/10.1080/02602938.2021.1939857.

Cuthbert, M. (2003). The external examiner: How did we get here?http://78.158.56.101/archive/law/resources/assessment-and-feedback/cuthbert/index.html.

Deeley, S.J. & C. Bovill (2017). Staff student partnership in assessment: enhancing assessment literacy through democratic practices. *Assessment & Evaluation in Higher Education* 42(3), 463–477. https://doi.org/10.1080/02602938.2015.1126551.

DeLuca, C., LaPointe-McEwan, D. & Luhanga, U. (2016). Teacher assessment literacy: a review of international standards and measures. *Educational Assessment, Evaluation and Accountability*, 28(3), 251–272. https://link.springer.com/article/10.1007/s11092-015-9233-6.

Denton, P. & McIlroy, D. (2018). Response of students to statement bank feedback: the impact of assessment literacy on performances in summative tasks. *Assessment & Evaluation in Higher Education*, 43(2), 197–206. http://dx.doi.org/10.1080/02602938.2017.1324017.

Eraut, M. (1995). *Developing Professional Knowledge and Competence*. Falmer Press.

Finch Review. (2011). *Review of External Examining Arrangements in Universities and Colleges in the UK: Final report and recommendations*. UniversitiesUK and GuildHE.

Gaunt, D. (1999). The practitioner as external examiner. *Quality in Higher Education*, 5(1), 81–90.

HEA. (2012). *A Handbook for External Examining*. Higher Education Academy.

HEA. (2016). *Framework for Transforming Assessment in Higher Education*. Higher Education Academy. www.heacademy.ac.uk/sites/default/files/downloads/transforming-assessment-in-he.pdf.

HEFCE. (2015). *A Review of External Examining Arrangements across the UK: Report to the UK Higher Education Funding Bodies by the Higher Education Academy*. Higher Education Funding Council for England.

Hudson, J., Bloxham, S., den Outer, B. & Price, M. (2017). Conceptual acrobatics: talking about assessment standards in the transparency era. *Studies in Higher Education*, 42(7), 1309–1323. https://doi.org/10.1080/03075079.2015.1092130.

Jarvis, D.S.L. (2014). Regulating higher education: quality assurance and neo-liberal managerialism in higher education – a critical introduction. *Policy and Society*, 33(3), 155–166. http://dx.doi.org/10.1016/j.polsoc.2014.09.005.

Medland, E. (2010). Subjectivity as a tool for clarifying mismatches between markers. *The International Journal of Learning*, 17(7), 399–412.

Medland, E. (2015). Examining the assessment literacy of external examiners. *London Review of Education*, 13(3), 21–33. http://dx.doi.org/10.18546/LRE.13.3.04.

Medland, E. (2019). 'I'm an assessment illiterate': towards a shared discourse of assessment literacy for external examiners. *Assessment & Evaluation in Higher Education*, 44(4), 565–580. https://doi.org/10.1080/02602938.2018.1523363.

Murphy, R. (2006). Evaluating new priorities for assessment in higher education. In C. Bryan & K. Clegg (eds), *Innovative Assessment in Higher Education*, pp. 37–47. Routledge.

Orr, S. (2007). Assessment moderation: constructing the marks and constructing the students. *Assessment & Evaluation in Higher Education*, 32(6), 645–656. http://dx.doi.org/10.1080/02602930601117068.

Popham, W.J. (2009). Assessment literacy for teachers: faddish or fundamental? *Theory Into Practice*, 48(1), 4–11. https://doi.org/10.1080/00405840802577536.

Price, M. (2005). Assessment standards: the role of communities of practice and the scholarship of assessment. *Assessment & Evaluation in Higher Education*, 30(3), 215–230. https://doi.org/10.1080/02602930500063793.

Price, M., Rust, C., O'Donovan, B. & Handley, K. (2012). *Assessment Literacy: The Foundation for Improving Student Learning*. The Oxford Centre for Staff and Learning Development.

QAA. (2013). *The UK Quality Code for Higher Education, Chapter B6: Assessment of Students and Recognition of Prior Learning*. Quality Assurance Agency.

QAA. (2018). *UK Quality Code for Higher Education. Advice and Guidance: External Expertise*. Quality Assurance Agency. www.qaa.ac.uk/docs/qaa/quality-code/advice-and-guidance-external-expertise.pdf.

QAA. (2022). *Principles of External Examining*. Quality Assurance Agency. www.qaa.ac.uk/docs/qaa/quality-code/external-examining-principles.pdf?sfvrsn=fe91a281_12.

Silver, H., Stennett, A. & Aldrich, R. (1995). *The External Examiner System: Possible Futures (Report Commissioned by the Higher Education Quality Council)*. London: Open University Quality Support Centre.

Smith, C.D., Worsfold, K., Davies, L., Fisher, R. & McPhail, R. (2013). Assessment literacy and student learning: the case for explicitly developing students 'assessment literacy. *Assessment & Evaluation in Higher Education*, 38(1), 44–60. https://doi.org/10.1080/02602938.2011.598636.

Stiggins, R.J. (1991). Assessment literacy. *Phi Delta Kappan*, 72, 534–539.

Vincent, D. (2003). Literacy literacy. *Interchange*, 34, 341–357. https://doi.org/10.1023/B:INCH.0000015908.37414.aa.

Wiliam, D. (2015). Foreword: assessment literacy. *London Review of Education*, 13(3), 3–4. http://dx.doi.org/10.18546/LRE.13.3.02.

Willis, J., Adie, L.E. & Klenowski, V. (2013). Conceptualising teachers' assessment literacies in an era of curriculum and assessment reform. *Australian Educational Researcher*, 40(2), 241–256. http://dx.doi.org/10.1007/s13384-013-0089-9.

Chapter 8

Using social processes to maintain academic standards

Social moderation and calibration

Nicola Reimann and Ian Sadler

Introduction

Standards are co-constructed and internalised through active participation in communities of practice (Bloxham & Boyd, 2007). This socio-constructivist model of standards underpins the ideas and practices presented in this book (see Chapters 2 and 3) and is also the foundation for those discussed in this chapter. If standards are created and learnt socially, social processes also need to be employed to address the problem of inconsistency between markers. This is exactly what social moderation aims to do. As the name suggests, it is essentially a social and collaborative approach to discussing and agreeing standards, with the aim of influencing and aligning individually held academic standards and future marking practices so that they become standards owned by the academic community. The focus is on dialogue, negotiation and joint decision making. Since standards are learnt in and through practice when assessment judgements are being made (Shay, 2005), concrete exemplars of student work are central to the discussions which social moderation generates. According to Sadler, repeated participation will produce 'calibrated academics … able to make grading judgements consistent with those which similarly calibrated colleagues would make' (Sadler, 2013, p. 5).

This chapter will discuss the nature of social moderation and calibration, their potential benefits, how they have been, and can be, implemented, and their associated challenges. It will provide an overview of the different ways in which social moderation has been carried out, with practitioners in mind who may want to implement this approach in their own contexts, departments and disciplines. Existing examples and the current evidence base will be reviewed to offer advice and different models that can be used as a basis for incorporating social moderation and calibration into contemporary higher education policy and practice.

What are social moderation and calibration?

Moderation more broadly has been described as an approach to agreeing, assuring and checking standards (Bloxham et al., 2015). Moderation is essentially a quality assurance process (Beutel et al., 2017), already widely used in contemporary higher education (HE), aimed at ensuring the validity and reliability of assessment decisions and grades (Sadler, 2013; Beutel et al., 2017). While moderation practices commonly involve scrutinising and finalising assessment decisions that have already been made, more recent conceptualisations of moderation and associated practices include a wider range of approaches (Bloxham et al., 2015; see also Chapter 5). In contrast to conventional post-assessment moderation, social moderation tends to be detached from marking as the focus is on standards rather than the actual award of grades. Interestingly, elements that could be described as 'social' have been shown to be inherent in conventional moderation practices too. Orr's (2007) research, for instance, has surfaced the negotiation and 'bargaining' processes which are part of real-world moderation dialogue in the arts. This research suggests that even conventional post-assessment moderation may not necessarily be the objective mechanism it purports to be and may therefore not be diametrically opposed to social moderation, but rather a variation of what has been going on already, albeit less manifest.

Social or consensus moderation is a dialogic process of peer review carried out by members of a disciplinary and/or professional community who discuss, review and compare exemplars of student work in order to reach a shared understanding of the academic standard that such work needs to meet. An early analysis of social moderation carried out by Lim (1993) stresses that it is based entirely on professional judgment, rather than relying on statistical procedures which are commonly used when making the results of different assessments comparable, such as, for example, papers testing the same learning outcomes set by different exam boards in the school sector. Social moderation, by contrast, entails a consensus on standards and on performances that meet those standards. Discrepancies between markers are reviewed in order to achieve a shared understanding of the criteria as well as an agreement on what Lim calls a benchmark or 'anchor product' that exemplifies the criteria. Social moderation thus always involves interaction between two key elements: (implicit or explicit) standards and concrete exemplars of student work. Sadler (2013) likens consensus moderation to the academic peer review process and describes it as a process during which private standards are made public and agreed intersubjectively. A key aim is to achieve more convergence between assessors in their assessment judgments and in the reasons underpinning them. Sadler suggests that this process can be applied both internally by reviewing judgements about student responses to one single assessment task within one course, as well as across course boundaries.

Sadler (2013) uses the term 'calibration' – normally associated with statistical methods for achieving consistency (Lim, 1993) – to refer to consensus moderation that focuses on developing, agreeing and internalising collective knowledge about the standards relevant to cognate courses in different institutions. This type of calibration has been described as a type of inter-institutional external referencing process which complements institutions' own internal processes for marking and moderation (Sefcik et al., 2017). Sadler (2013) argues that repeated participation in social moderation and calibration will ultimately lead to assessors' confidence in their own judgements and those of their colleagues and, as a consequence, to closer alignment of standards and improved consistency. A key purpose of calibration is therefore to assure degree standards at national level and avoid 'standard slippage' (Sefcik et al., 2017), thus reassuring higher education stakeholders such as students, employers and the wider community that national standards are consistent with expectations and across institutions. In addition, calibration offers important collaborative learning and professional development opportunities to academics (Watty et al., 2014).

The term social moderation has been used in slightly different ways by different authors. In the context of this chapter, it is regarded as a generic concept that subsumes a range of activities situated on a continuum. Consensus seeking dialogue is core to all variants, while the exact purpose of this dialogue can vary somewhat. If responses to more than one task type are considered and the dialogue is totally detached from the award of grades, the attention shifts from marking towards developing a shared understanding of the standards that underpin judgements about the quality of student work. This kind of social moderation, situated at one end of the continuum, is not about preparing, justifying or negotiating grading decisions, it is about clarifying standards and reaching an agreement on what performances that meet these standards might look like, beyond the concrete piece of work and the task under consideration. Such shared understanding of standards is the key characteristic of the 'calibrated academic' described by Sadler (2013), who is able to make future grading decisions aligned with the community standard. All social moderation activities focus on standards to a certain extent, but some more so than others. At the other end of the continuum are dialogues during which judgements about student work are negotiated and agreed on, while the ultimate purpose is to agree a grade, albeit in a social, consensus-focused manner. In another variant academics are brought together prior to marking student work, to discuss a small sample of actual submissions or exemplars from prior cohorts. Here, the attention is on standards, but with a view to supporting actual grading decisions which are coming up, rather than standards more broadly. For instance, the example by Crimmins et al. (2016) which is described below, is of this kind.

Social moderation is different to what is known as 'standard setting', a process common in medicine and other health disciplines (e.g. Pell et al., 2011). Standard setting is informed by the principles and practices of educational measurement, where psychometric data and statistical procedures are used to ensure consistency of marking. While on the surface calibration looks similar to standard setting, calibration does not focus on reliability and validity of a specific assessment instrument and its components, nor does it employ numerical data or seek to identify reasons for error variance between individual items, groups or assessors. Instead, it aims to facilitate dialogue between individuals who actively agree on and buy into a collective community standard, using discursive methods which enable consensus formation.

What are the benefits of social moderation and calibration?

The benefits of social moderation and calibration have been repeatedly highlighted in the literature and there is empirical evidence to support this. One important argument that has been made – perhaps the most important argument – is that social moderation and calibration enhance consistency between markers and reduce variation. However, there are surprisingly few studies that have investigated this empirically. Why might this be the case? Since social moderation and calibration have not been embedded systematically into HE policy and are therefore not widely practised, few naturally occurring data that could be used to evidence their impact on consistency are available. In addition, studies which convincingly demonstrate impact, in particular on judgements made over longer periods of time, require complex longitudinal designs that are neither easy to develop nor easy to implement on the ground. Interesting advances were made by the Australian 'Achievement Matters' project in Accounting. O'Connell et al. (2016) used an experimental design to investigate whether academics' judgments were influenced by participating in calibration activities. Two groups of research participants individually graded the same three exemplars twice, with the experimental group undertaking calibration activities between the two rounds of grading. The researchers found significantly reduced variation between assessors following calibration, demonstrated by a reduction in the standard deviation of the scores awarded and in the gap between minimum and maximum ratings in the experimental group. There were limitations, such as the small sample size, which affected the reliability of the significance tests, and the fact that the same exemplars were graded again in the second round rather than testing whether the shared understanding gained through calibration affected future judgments. Despite these limitations, this study is noteworthy since it provides empirical evidence of enhanced consistency between assessors. Additional self-reported data arising from the same project showed that participating academics also believed that engaging in calibration facilitated consistency (Watty et al., 2014).

Similar findings to O'Connell et al. (2016) are reported by Crimmins et al. (2016), and in earlier investigations such as the small-scale study in medical education conducted by Pitts et al. (2002) and unpublished practitioner research on UK-based calibration in Law by Hanlon et al. (2004). Chapters 14 and 15 offer further examples of calibration in practice across two different subject communities, presenting new findings, and critiquing the processes and outcomes. More research is needed, however, to investigate if social moderation and calibration enhance consistency between assessors, in particular once assessors grade their own students' work, and over longer periods of time.

Another important benefit is the increase in assessors' confidence that results from participation in social moderation and calibration activities. Participants have reported repeatedly that they feel more confident in making assessment judgements and that these judgments are more in line with those of other assessors. This has been identified by several studies and project reports (Hanlon et al., 2004; Watty et al., 2014; Crimmins et al., 2016; O'Connell et al., 2016) and is closely linked to the finding that academics appreciate the professional development opportunities that social moderation and calibration offer (Crimmins et al., 2016; Sefcik et al., 2017; see also Chapters 14 and 15). This is perhaps unsurprising since assessment judgments are discipline specific and learnt informally 'on the job', and as a consequence there are few formal opportunities to undertake professional development in this area. Educational development workshops and courses tend to focus on broader assessment concepts (Kandlbinder & Tai, 2009) and are usually not discipline specific. University assessment policies tend to be based on the assumption that codifications such as learning outcomes, assessment criteria and rubrics provide sufficient guidance for assessors so that professional development about standards and grading is not needed. However, making judgements about student work is a high stakes aspect of academic work, and academics, in particular early career academics, often feel left alone when learning how to make such judgements (Handley et al., 2013; Reimann, 2018). Participation in social moderation and calibration has been described as resulting in collegial relationships (Crimmins et al., 2016) and ultimately a community of practice which opens up future opportunities for exchange and collaboration between peers and institutions (Sefcik et al., 2017). Participants in the study by Watty et al. (2014) also stressed that social moderation stimulated them to reflect on their own assessment practices.

How have social moderation and calibration been implemented?

As has already been pointed out, two broad types of social moderation activities exist. One is organised internally within an institution and focuses on specific course units/modules, often those with large numbers of students and multiple markers, and on the specific assessment tasks used within them. The other type takes place across institutions and is frequently referred to as calibration. Calibration activities tend to be organised by professional, statutory and regulatory bodies (PSRBs) or subject associations as professional development for academics in a specific discipline, often aimed at senior academics with responsibility for standards and course design such as programme directors. Unfortunately, little information is available on how many activities of this kind take place, where they are held, who organises them, how frequent they are and who participates. Some of this information can be accessed in reports which summarise and review projects that have experimented with social moderation and calibration. There are a handful of academic publications which capture relevant research and practice, with a larger proportion focusing on calibration rather than social moderation within modules/course units (see also Chapters 14 and 15).

The examples that follow, based on published literature, have been included to assist readers who wish to organise social moderation events in their own contexts and may be interested in the details of practical implementation. The principles of social moderation have been implemented in a variety of ways and in different disciplinary and national contexts, and examples have been selected in order to showcase contrasting types of implementation. Early experiments were conducted in the UK under the auspices of the then Subject Centres: first the Subject Centre for Hospitality, Leisure and Tourism (Buckley, 2011), later-on the Subject Centre for Law (Hanlon et al., 2004). In Australia, where an external examining system does not exist, policy has focused increasingly on developing a system of external referencing / peer review of assessment. As a consequence, calibration has gained momentum in Australia (see Chapter 4), and several of the examples provided below originate from there.

PRACTICAL STRATEGY

Box 8.1 Within-module social moderation as a developmental opportunity for staff on casual part-time contracts, Australia

This social moderation activity was organised in the context of a large module comprising over 800 students. Twenty-one tutors taught and marked student work and most of them (i.e. 18) were on 'casual' short-term, part-time contracts. In a staged process, pre-marking social moderation was combined with post-marking 'expert' feedback on grades and their justification, based on a model by Klenowski and Adie (2009). Since the module comprised three pieces of assessed work, a total of three social moderation workshops were held, each several weeks before the respective assignment was due to be marked. During these workshops all casual tutors marked the same exemplar individually first, using a rubric. Comments and grades were discussed in pairs, then in small groups and finally in plenary. The exemplar and the rubric were discussed in detail, with the aim of reaching a consensus on the classification to be awarded and the reasons for this classification. In the second stage of the process, once initial marking had been completed individually, the casual tutors submitted samples of their marked work to the module coordinators (i.e. the 'experts'), who provided them with feedback on their marking. Once a tutor's marking was deemed to be in line with the standards of the coordinators and one other tutor, marks and comments were uploaded onto the learning management system. The third and final stage consisted of the coordinating team randomly selecting assignments and checking comments and grade against what had been agreed in the social moderation workshop, potentially suggesting changes in grades or comments and discussing the rationale with the tutor concerned.

Source: Crimmins et al. (2016)

PRACTICAL STRATEGY

Box 8.2 Calibration workshops in accounting, Australia

Several universities were invited to commit to a series of calibration workshops. Each university contributed assessed work by final year accounting students, from which a random sample was selected and de-identified. Each workshop that was part of this calibration pilot focused on one of several national threshold standards (e.g. 'written communication skills'), with subsequent workshops being devoted to another standard. Prior to each workshop individual participants graded three pieces of work on a continuous scale from 0 to 100, from 'meeting' to 'not meeting' this standard, as well as providing written reasons for the grade awarded, suggestions for ways in which the work could be improved and ratings for the validity of the assessed task as set by the academics that provided the exemplar. This was done anonymously and facilitated by an electronic repository which revealed and analysed all participants' responses prior to a face-to-face workshop. During the 3–6-hour workshop the collated responses were used as a basis for discussion of the task and of the sample of student work, both in small groups and in plenary, with the ultimate purpose of achieving a shared understanding of the threshold standard coupled with a consensus on the quality of each piece of work. Within two weeks of the workshop, all participants reassessed the initial sample of three, in order to evaluate whether their judgements converged more than prior to the calibration activities. The same process was repeated in subsequent workshops. The calibration activities were complemented by 'live review of student work' in which module/unit and assessment documentation as well as marked work by final year students were scrutinised by reviewers from other universities, but only once they had been calibrated through participation in at least three calibration workshops (Hancock et al. 2015).

Sources: Watty et al. (2014); Hancock et al. (2015); O'Connell et al. (2016)

PRACTICAL STRATEGY

Box 8.3 External peer review of standards in pairs and threes, multiple disciplines, Australia

Based on calibration projects conducted earlier, this approach to external referencing of standards was deliberately small scale in order to be efficient and cost-effective. It took place in small cross-institutional groups. Leaders of comparable final year modules were matched and held an initial web conference in twos or threes during which they talked each other through their modules and accompanying module and assessment documentation. A random sample of previously marked and de-identified work was then selected and shared, including sound passes, low passes and fails. The module leaders reviewed each other's samples to evaluate whether the assessment was suitable to allow students to achieve and evidence the learning outcomes of the module. They then exchanged draft reports with each other in which they made judgements about the appropriateness of the outcomes, the assessment practices and the grades awarded. A second web conference was held to discuss these reports which were finalised afterwards to include priorities for implementation in the respective home institution. While participants were initially concerned that the process might be time consuming, they found it quicker than they had initially expected (on average just under 15 hours in twos, and 18.5 hours in threes), while there was variation depending on discipline.

Source: Sefcik et al. (2017)

PRACTICAL STRATEGY

Box 8.4. Characteristics of student work in hospitality, sport, leisure and tourism at different grade levels, UK

In this calibration pilot three workshops were held, each of them focusing on the characteristics of student work at different levels of the grading scale, namely:

1   First class work, i.e. work at the highest level.
2   A marginal pass and what distinguished it from a fail.
3   The remaining two categories (in the UK known as a 2:1 versus 2:2) and what distinguished them from each other.

Prior to the workshop, participants were asked to assess work that had been marked by other institutions and to write a commentary on whether or not they agreed with the grades awarded and their reasons for this judgement. Grading criteria and comments provided by the original markers were not provided. During the calibration workshop, areas of agreement and disagreement were identified, with the aim to achieve a consensus on the quality characteristics of work at the specified level. To conclude the third workshop, which focused on final year dissertations, students participated in a question-and-answer session during which they shared their understanding of a good dissertation and distinction between the different grade bands.

Sources: Buswell (2010); Buckley (2011)

As will have become evident, the concrete implementation of social moderation can differ considerably. The approaches summarised above exemplify some key aspects and principles that influence the ways in which social moderation and calibration are carried out in practice.

Expert versus community understanding of standards

Social moderation is based on the premise that standards are open to negotiation and that all participants have equal opportunities to influence the collective consensus-seeking process. In practice, however, some approaches incorporate elements of 'expert' input, as illustrated by the example of Crimmins et al. (2016). Here, social moderation is used to support marginalised markers through a social moderation process, but their subsequent marking decisions are checked and, if deemed necessary, adjusted by course coordinators as guardians of standards, albeit in a collegial and dialogic manner. This example takes account of the large differences in experience and familiarity with the specific context of the module/course unit, but implicitly assumes that there is a 'correct' way of interpreting and assessing the standard, namely that of the more experienced course coordinators. Some authors would refute that such a 'correct' way exists and would argue that disagreements among the more experienced coordinators are also likely.

Including or excluding a discussion of task validity

In the example by O'Connell et al. (2016), scrutiny of the assessment task is included in the calibration process, while other calibration examples only consider examples of student responses to tasks, not the task itself. The Australian Achievement Matters project highlights the importance of task design and its validity as a key outcome since students can only successfully demonstrate their achievement of the standards if a valid task allows them to do so. However, according to Hancock et al. (2015), achieving consensus on what exactly constitutes a valid task is a particularly challenging component of calibration and requires expert facilitation.

Pre-determined criteria as input versus reaching collective agreement on attributes of quality

Most of the social moderation activities outlined above provide participating academics with explicit criteria. This makes sense in the context of contemporary HE assessment which is overwhelmingly based on the principle of criterion referencing. However, as previous chapters in this book have shown (see particularly Chapter 13), codifications have limitations as they cannot make the tacit knowledge that underpins assessment judgments explicit. In the example by Buckley (2011), criteria were not included. Not doing so foregrounded participants' own implicit quality criteria, and it could be argued that this draws attention to aspects of student work which have not been, or are not normally, included in formal codifications. According to our own experience, in instances where there are no criteria participants formulate their own collective criteria during the social moderation process, whereas social moderation with explicit criteria focuses participants' attention on comparing each other's differing personal interpretations of the given criteria.

What are the challenges of implementing social moderation and calibration?

Implementing social moderation and calibration also involves paying attention to a range of practical problems and challenges. These tend to arise from the selection, preparation and distribution of exemplars as well as the relationships and group processes which influence the discussions that will take place. A brief overview of the challenges is provided below for readers wishing to set up such activities.

Selecting, preparing and distributing exemplars

Identifying appropriate exemplars can be difficult (Hancock et al., 2015), but project reports and publications do not offer much advice on how to select them. If the social moderation process involves consideration against pre-determined standards or criteria, exemplars clearly need to relate to these. Conciseness is also crucial in order for reviewing not to be onerous, but not much work of this kind appears to exist, in particular at final year level. On the other hand, Sefcik et al. (2017) caution that exemplars should not only be selected because they can be easily read and shared. Once selected, de-identifying exemplars, i.e. removing student and institutional information, is described as time consuming, but important for the calibration discussion to be as detached as possible from the influence of reputation and potential loss of face. Even if exemplars have been de-identified, participating academics occasionally reveal during the discussion where an exemplar comes from, and this may influence the social moderation process unduly (Hancock et al., 2015). The importance of a suitable online system for sharing, reviewing and making outcomes of the reviews available has also been stressed. Since such systems outdate quickly, no specific recommendations are made here. It has also been noted that sharing documentation, tasks and student work raises intellectual property rights (Sefcik et al., 2017), more so when academics are inspired to adopt practices they gleaned in calibration activities.

Group process, power dynamics and relationships

The notion of consensus underpins social moderation and calibration, but how easy is it to achieve consensus in practice? Hancock et al. (2015) comment on the wide diversity of views and understandings of the standards and the difficulties of reaching a consensus. Interestingly, standards that focused on the knowledge students need to demonstrate appeared to be easier to agree on than standards that focused on skills such as written communication. Hancock et al. (2015, p. 54/55) make several recommendations for designing and leading calibration events. These include:

> pre-workshop peer review of both input assessment data (e.g., task requirements) as well as output assessment data (e.g., sample student work; distributing de-identified judgements and reasoning for review and interrogation prior to face-to-face workshops; using small group consensus prior to seeking consensus of the entire group at workshops; confirming understandings with new samples of student work that allow individual judgement, small group consensus and large group consensus). To avoid possible bias all markings and identifiers should be removed from inputs, outputs and reviewers.

For social moderation to be successful, relationships must also be actively managed. Care must be taken when allocating participants to groups or partners since hierarchies, fear of being judged and different levels of experience may interfere with the consensus-seeking process (Mason & Roberts, 2024). As reported by Sefcik et al. (2017), participants can feel nervous and evaluated, although research has shown that repeated participation in social moderation makes participants feel increasingly comfortable with revealing their own uncertainties. In Crimmins et al. (2016, p. 434), for instance, one participant emphasised how repeated participation made them change from only revealing grading decisions they were certain about to opening up and discussing uncertain ones. In the example by Sefcik et al. (2017), participants were allocated to groups of two or three. Matching proved to be difficult and the size of both groups were found to have advantages and disadvantages. Groups of three resulted in 'more candid and in depth' discussions as they offered broader perspectives and greater opportunity for quality enhancement of assessment. However, groups of three were also more labour intensive to set up and administer.

Conclusion

This chapter has offered a discussion of social moderation and calibration as approaches with the potential to reduce variability in the judgement of academic standards. To date, several pilots and projects have been conducted, some of which have informed this chapter. The academic literature and the examples that have been included have shown that social moderation and calibration can be, and have been, successfully implemented in higher education. By drawing on existing publications and reports we hope that this chapter has inspired interested practitioners to get involved, academic leaders to organise relevant activities and events, and policy makers to incorporate social moderation and calibration requirements into policies which in the past have focused on prescribing ever more codification.

This chapter has offered advice on why and how to make social moderation happen. Much more needs to happen, and we would like to encourage the readers of this chapter to have a go.

The current evidence on social moderation and calibration in higher education is promising, but still in its infancy, limited to a few projects in selected disciplines with relatively low numbers of participants. Clearly, more research is needed. There still exists relatively little research into the different ways in which social moderation and calibration can be implemented, the nature of the dialogue it generates, the ways in which individuals' constructions of standards are affected by it, the impact of repeated participation and its longer-term influence on practice. We also do not know how many module teams, subject associations and professional bodies actually practise social moderation, in what ways such opportunities have been made available, and what the respective communities make of them. More work is also needed to embed these practices into institutional and national policies, and again there is scant evidence whether and where this is taking place.

This chapter has focused on social moderation and calibration carried out with academics. Similar initiatives have taken place with students. By using exemplars or peer review processes, students are also confronted with concrete pieces of work and tasked with appraising their quality (e.g. Nicol et al., 2014; To & Yiqi, 2018; Knight et al., 2019; see also Chapter 13). Ultimately, the same goals and processes apply: as with staff, students also need to develop a concept of quality, and in order to be successful in their studies, this needs to converge with that of the academic community in their respective disciplines. However, the fact that academics themselves do not necessarily agree on what constitutes quality tends to be hidden from students – but sub-consciously they may already be aware. A vision for future developments is thus to bring staff and students together in negotiating and developing a consensus on standards.

References

Beutel, D., Adie, L. & Lloyd, M. (2017). Assessment moderation in an Australian context: processes, practices, and challenges. *Teaching in Higher Education*, 22(1), 1–14. http://dx.doi.org/10.1080/13562517.2016.1213232.

Bloxham, S. & Boyd, P. (2007). *Developing Effective Assessment in Higher Education: A Practical Guide*. McGraw-Hill Education.

Bloxham, S., Hudson, J., den Outer, B. & Price, M. (2015). External peer review of assessment: an effective approach to verifying standards? *Higher Education Research and Development*, 34(6), 1069–1082. http://dx.doi.org/10.1080/07294360.2015.1024629.

Buckley, J. (2011). 'Upper or Lower?' Unpublished report of a workshop to identify standards which could apply to dissertations at 2:1 and 2:2 grades in HLST programmes, 5 April, The Higher Education Academy Hospitality, Leisure, Sport and Tourism Network, Oxford Brookes University, Oxford.

Buswell, J. (2010). Assessment Standards in Hospitality, Leisure, Sport and Tourism. Unpublished report of a workshop to identify and agree standards which could apply to marginal pass work at level 6 in HLST programmes, 1 July, Higher Education Academy Hospitality, Leisure, Sport and Tourism Network, Oxford.

Crimmins, G., Nash, G., Oprescu, F., Alla, K., Brock, G., Hickson-Jamieson, B. & Noakes, C. (2016). Can a systematic assessment moderation process assure the quality and integrity of assessment practice while supporting the professional development of casual academics? *Assessment & Evaluation in Higher Education*, 41(3), 427–441. https://doi.org/10.1080/02602938.2015.1017754.

Hancock, P., Freeman, M., Abraham, A., De Lange, P., Howieson, B., O'Connell, B. & Watty, K. (2015). *Achievement Matters: External Peer Review of Accounting Learning Standards*. Australian Government, Office for Learning and Teaching, Department of Education and Training.

Handley, K., den Outer, B. & Price, M. (2013). Learning to mark: exemplars, dialogue and participation in assessment communities. *Higher Education Research & Development*, 32(6), 888–900. http://dx.doi.org/10.1080/07294360.2013.806438.

Hanlon, J., Jefferson, M., Molan, M. & Mitchell, B. (2004). *An Examination of the Incident of 'Error Variation' in the Grading of Law Assessments*. United Kingdom Centre for Legal Education (UKCLE).

Kandlbinder, P. & Tai, P. (2009). Key concepts in postgraduate certificates in higher education teaching and learning in Australasia and the United Kingdom. *International Journal for Academic Development*, 14(1), 19–31. https://doi.org/10.1080/13601440802659247.

Klenowski, V. & Adie, L. (2009). Moderation as judgement practice: reconciling system level accountability and local level practice. *Curriculum Perspectives*, 29(1), 10–28.

Knight, S., Leigh, A., Davila, Y.C., Martin, L.J. & Krix, D.W. (2019). Calibrating assessment literacy through benchmarking tasks. *Assessment & Evaluation in Higher Education*, 44(8), 1121–1132. http://dx.doi.org/10.1080/02602938.2019.1570483.

Lim, R.L. (1993). Linking results of distinct assessments. *Applied Measurement in Education*, 6(1), 83–102. https://doi.org/10.1207/s15324818ame0601_5.

Mason, J. & Roberts, L.D. (2024). Consensus moderation: the voices of expert academics. *Assessment & Evaluation in Higher Education*, 48(7), 926–937. https://doi.org/10.1080/02602938.2022.2161999.

Nicol, D., Thomson, A. & Breslin, C. (2014). Rethinking feedback practices in higher education: a peer review perspective. *Assessment & Evaluation in Higher Education*, 39(1), 102–122. https://doi.org/10.1080/02602938.2013.795518.

O'Connell, B., De Lange, P., Freeman, M., Hancock, P., Abraham, A., Howieson, B. & Watty, K. (2016). Does calibration reduce variability in the assessment of accounting learning outcomes? *Assessment & Evaluation in Higher Education*, 41(3), 331–349. https://doi.org/10.1080/02602938.2015.1008398.

Orr, S. (2007). Assessment moderation: constructing the marks and constructing the students. *Assessment and Evaluation in Higher Education*, 32(6), 1–12. http://dx.doi.org/10.1080/02602930601117068.

Pell, G., Fuller, R., Homer, M. & Roberts, T. (2011). How to measure the quality of the OSCE: a review of metrics. *Medical Teacher*, 32(10), 802–811. https://doi.org/10.3109/0142159X.2010.507716.

Pitts, J., Coles, C., Thomas, P. & Smith, F. (2002). Enhancing reliability in portfolio assessment: discussions between assessors. *Medical Teacher*, 24(2), 197–201. http://dx.doi.org/10.1080/01421590220125321.

Reimann, N. (2018). Learning about assessment: the impact of two courses for higher education staff. *International Journal for Academic Development*, 23(2), 86–97. http://dx.doi.org/10.1080/1360144X.2017.1375413.

Sadler, R. (2013). Assuring academic achievement standards: from moderation to calibration. *Assessment in Education: Principles, Policy & Practice*, 20(1), 5–19. http://dx.doi.org/10.1080/0969594X.2012.714742.

Sefcik, L., Bedford, S., Czech, P., Smith, J. & Yorke, J. (2017). Embedding external referencing of standards into higher education: collaborative relationships are the key. *Assessment & Evaluation in Higher Education*, 43(1), 45–57. http://dx.doi.org/10.1080/02602938.2017.1278584.

Shay, S. (2005). The assessment of complex tasks: a double reading. *Studies in Higher Education*, 30(6), 663–679 https://doi.org/10.1080/03075070500339988.

To, J. & Yiqi, L. (2018). Using peer and teacher–student exemplar dialogues to unpack assessment standards: challenges and possibilities. *Assessment & Evaluation in Higher Education*, 43(3), 449–460. http://dx.doi.org/10.1080/02602938.2017.1356907.

Watty, K., Freeman, M., Howieson, B., Hancock, P., O'Connell, B., de Lange, P. & Abraham, A. (2014). Social moderation, assessment and assuring standards for accounting graduates. *Assessment & Evaluation in Higher Education*, 39(4), 461–478. http://dx.doi.org/10.1080/02602938.2013.848336.

Part IIIA

Professional development to reduce variation in academic standards

Chapter 9

Strengthening professional development provision for external examiners

The UK Degree Standards Project

Geoff Stoakes and Erica J. Morris

Introduction

The Degree Standards Project, which ran from 2016 to 2021, was designed to enhance the professional development of external examiners across the UK. The Project had to face challenges both of a contextual and of a political nature. This chapter explores how these were addressed and the lessons learnt.

The Project formed part of the Revised Operating Model for Quality Assessment introduced by the Higher Education Funding Council for England (HEFCE) in 2016. The invitation to tender for the Project summarised the rationale behind it:

> We ... wish to investigate a range of approaches designed to improve arrangements for the maintenance of degree standards and their reasonable comparability. In particular, we believe that it would be beneficial to the sector and its stakeholders to consider further strengthening the external examining system ... However, we wish to develop this area in a way that is credible to the academic community and respects the autonomy of providers.
> (HEFCE, 2016, pp. 7–8)

The primary purpose of the Project was to address doubts about the efficacy of external examining as part of the quality assurance system across the UK (see Chapters 6 and 7 for further discussion regarding external examiners). In 2009, a House of Commons Select Committee had expressed concern about the evidence, which the sector provided, regarding (a) the maintenance of academic standards over time, and (b) the comparability of standards between providers and subject areas. The subsequent Finch Report concluded that the external examining system was still working well, but also made a series of recommendations aimed at improving the consistency of practice (in particular, the recruitment, selection and induction of external examiners) and increasing the transparency of the system with regard to students (Universities UK, 2011). These recommendations were largely incorporated into the UK Quality Code for Higher Education in 2011,

DOI: 10.4324/9781003379768-12

especially chapter B7, which described external examining as 'one of the principal means of maintaining UK threshold academic standards' (QAA, 2011, p. 2). However, in 2015, amid continuing concerns about grade inflation and the 'impact of increased competition and the role of leagues tables on the robustness and independence of the work of external examiners' (HEFCE, 2016, p. 11), the Higher Education Academy (HEA) was commissioned to conduct a nationwide review of external examining arrangements. The brief was to consider how far the Finch recommendations had been implemented, how effective the system was in safeguarding standards and whether further reforms were necessary.

The ensuing review concluded that the recommendations of the Finch Report had been implemented in large measure. In particular, there was the establishment of clear and consistent appointment criteria for external examiners and more transparent processes for reporting and responding to external examiner reports produced for institutions (HEFCE, 2015). However, while the review found the sector confident that external examiners played an effective role in helping to assure fair and robust procedures (*quality standards*), there was much less confidence in their ability to reliably assure *academic standards*. The assurance of academic standards referred to the consistent judgement of actual student work against explicit agreed standards and the reasonable comparability of such judgements across higher education providers. The report therefore recommended (inter alia) the acceleration of the professionalisation of external examiners, firstly, by their engagement in regular calibration of their standards through disciplinary communities, and secondly, by 'more systematic training to develop further knowledge and more consistent perspectives on the role, standards, assessment literacy and professional judgement' (HEFCE, 2015, p. 12). These recommendations directly informed the specification of the Degree Standards Project proposed by HEFCE.

The rationale for the Degree Standards Project also acknowledged the need to ensure that the process of change towards more systematic training sustained credibility among the academic community. The external examining system was (and is) dependent on the willingness of academics to undertake this additional form of work, usually at their busiest time of year. Finally, the rationale strove to communicate that, in launching the Degree Standards Project, HEFCE was acting in accord with the established policy of collaboration between funder and university, respecting the latter's institutional autonomy.

The purpose of the Degree Standards Project was therefore to:

- Design and pilot different approaches to the training of external examiners;
- propose evidence-based and cost-effective longer-term approaches to ensuring that external examiners operating across the UK higher education system are appropriately trained;
- deliver ongoing training for external examiners;
- explore approaches to the calibration of standards, and present recommendations for any future work in this area (HEFCE, 2016, p. 21).

This chapter explores the strategies adopted in realising the goal of enhancing the professional development of academic staff engaged in external examining, alongside navigating significant changes in UK higher education policy. There are lessons learnt which can be beneficial for other contexts where, for example, political power is devolved or where governmental intervention is perceived as conflicting with institutional autonomy.

Professional development provision for external examiners

The Degree Standards Project was set up to explore evidence-informed and sector-owned processes for the professional development of external examiners in UK higher education. A key purpose of this initiative was to establish a professional development provision that was sustainable and use approaches that were credible, valid and reliable across different modes of delivery. It became clear early on that working in partnership with higher education institutions was pivotal in ensuring that the design of a course was engaging and relevant to academics from a range of professional, subject and disciplinary areas. It was also apparent that the course needed to be relevant to those with different levels of experience from aspiring or new external examiners to those who had worked as external examiners for several years across different institutions. Based on this, the strategies adopted for the initiative involved:

- Designing and piloting a generic Professional Development Course with a group of eight higher education institutions (project partners).
- The iterative design of the course, including piloting and formative evaluation with participants.
- An exploration of different course models (e.g. face-to-face, online and remote) and ways of delivering them (e.g. regionally, institutionally).
- Establishing a 'Develop the Developer' process, so that staff in institutions could be trained as course facilitators to run the course within their institutional contexts.

In the first year of the Project (2016–2017), a generic Professional Development Course was developed, trialled and evaluated. This was done by a team of higher education assessment experts as HEA (later AdvanceHE) associates, through working with eight partner institutions and supported and managed by AdvanceHE. This first phase involved the implementation of a face-to-face course in terms of design (i.e. a one-day in-person workshop with online preparation), which was offered regionally on an open recruitment basis and delivered by facilitators within the project team (see Chapter 10 for details of the course). To allow delivery within adopting institutions, facilitators were trained through a Develop the Developer programme (see below). This was an important part of the approach to ensure quality assurance of the delivery of the course as it was rolled out across the higher education sector.

In addition, an online version of the course was developed. The delivery of this course took the form of synchronous and asynchronous activity, which participants could engage with over a period of up to forty days. This online alternative to the face-to-face course was considered essential with regard to supporting differing learning preferences, helping to ensure inclusivity, and enabling flexibility for academics in terms of the time they could commit to their professional development. Online courses were held for open cohorts (i.e. participants from a range of institutions) and cohorts of staff within the same institution. With the onset of the pandemic and the introduction of social distancing restrictions in 2020, the online course became an ideal mode of delivery and was adapted for larger cohorts. However, to further respond to these changing demands, the face-to-face course was adapted for remote delivery. This took the form of two half-day synchronous sessions (meetings), supported by video communication technology, typically scheduled on consecutive days or one-week apart (see Table 9.1).

An important point of reference for the design of the Professional Development Course for external examiners was the AdvanceHE Professional Standards Framework, initially the 2011 version (AdvanceHE, 2011), then the updated version in 2023: for those seeking recognition of their professionalism at any level of fellowship of AdvanceHE, the course provides evidence of the enhancement of practice though continuing professional development. External examining itself helps to evidence 'influencing the practice of those who teach and/or support high quality learning' and 'practice that extends significantly beyond direct teaching and/or direct support for learning', which is required for those seeking recognition as a Senior Fellow (AdvanceHE, 2023, p. 9). The course is also directly informed by the Advice and Guidance on External Expertise of the UK Quality Code for Higher Education.

Table 9.1 Modes of delivery for the Professional Development Course.

Face-to-face	Online	Remote
Face-to-face over one day, with a small amount of prior online preparation.	Synchronous and asynchronous activity with up to 40 days to complete.	Two half-day synchronous meetings (typically over consecutive days), supported by video technology, including a small amount of prior online preparation.
Delivered initially by AdvanceHE associates, later by institutional facilitators trained via the Develop the Developer programme.	Delivered by AdvanceHE associates.	Delivered initially by AdvanceHE associates, later by institutional facilitators trained via the Develop the Developer programme.
Either open recruitment or internal recruitment (institutional courses).	Open recruitment.	Either open recruitment or internal recruitment (institutional courses).

The Degree Standards Project was successful in establishing a Professional Development Course. A total of 3,893 participants from 250 institutions providing higher education completed the course during the Project in one of the three design models (face-to-face, online or remote), which were delivered either by the HEA (later AdvanceHE) associates or by institutional facilitators. Course completion was monitored through attendance and engagement with the pre-course activities and the formative summary logs that participants were asked to complete throughout the sessions. Participants who completed the course were issued with a course completion certificate and were included on the register of course completers maintained by AdvanceHE.

An independent evaluation undertaken by DEWR Ltd assessed the credibility, validity and reliability of the professional development provision for external examiners. This drew on a variety of evidence sources, including course participant feedback, institutional case studies and interviews with key stakeholders. It was found that the course was regarded as high quality, with feedback on the course having been 'consistently positive' throughout the duration of the Project, as well as across different models and modes of delivery (DEWR, 2021, p. 7). Furthermore, in relation to the course learning outcomes, it was found that knowledge and understanding of the purpose of external examining were developed reliably across the different delivery modes. The outcomes tended to depend on level of external examining experience. For example, 'Seven out of ten respondents to the post-course survey ... indicated their ability to explain the nature of standards in the higher education context had improved (71% of those with no or little examining and 65% of experienced examiners)' (DEWR, 2021, p. 18).

The evaluation also considered the impact of the course on changes in external examiner practice. Almost nine out of ten (89%) respondents to the post-course survey indicated that they felt more confident than before in the role of an external examiner. In the 2021 follow-up survey, 85% of respondents who had gone on to externally examine indicated that participation in the course had made them more effective in the role. They referred to improvement in their ability to deal with challenges, increased reference to national standards and frameworks, the ability to engage in dialogue and to develop a shared understanding collegiately with a programme team (DEWR, 2021) (see Chapter 12 for further discussion of the course evaluation).

Develop the developer programme

The Develop the Developer programme was devised to train individuals to be able to effectively facilitate the delivery of the course. This was to enable institutions to offer the course in-house to their staff, including it as part of their relevant continuing professional development provision. A total of 50 higher education providers became institutional adopters of the course, with 90 facilitators having completed the Develop the Developer programme since its inception in 2016–

2017. With the completion of the Professional Development Course a prerequisite for entry, the developers programme involved the following:

- Stage A – online activities and reading to prepare for the role of facilitator.
- Stage B – a workshop with prospective facilitators from other institutions.
- Stage C – an assisted course, in which new facilitators deliver the face-to-face course with staff at their institution, working with an AdvanceHE mentor.
- Stage D – an observed course, in which new facilitators deliver the face-to-face course at their institution, with support from an AdvanceHE mentor.

In response to the pandemic, the programme was adapted for synchronous remote delivery, with stage B entailing two half-day online workshops, and remote-delivery courses deployed, if needed, for stages C and D. An accelerated route through the programme was also made available using the online course, with new facilitators being able to meet the requirements of the assisted and observed courses by being online tutors (see Table 9.2).

Quality assurance was a vital consideration when devolving responsibility for the delivery of the Professional Development Course to institutional facilitators. The Develop the Developer programme was designed to ensure that new facilitators were supported in their development to effectively run the course, and that they were suitably knowledgeable and competent. Key elements of the quality assurance process included:

- Successful completion of the Professional Development Course. Completion of a self-assessment log to reflect on what they brought to the role (part of Stage A).

Table 9.2 Stages of the recognition process for new facilitators: face-to-face and remote delivery.

Stage	Method	Details
Stage A	Online self-study.	Reading and activity to prepare for the role of facilitator.
Stage B	One-day workshop (face-to-face delivery of programme) or two half-day synchronous online workshops (remote delivery).	Workshop with prospective facilitators from other institutions to reflect on course activities and questions to self-assess learning.
Stage C	Assisted course: assisted facilitation of the course either face-to-face or via the online course (accelerated route).	Delivery of the course by two or three new facilitators, usually working in their own higher education institution, and one mentor who is an experienced facilitator of the course.
Stage D	Observed course: observed facilitation of the course either face-to-face or via the online course (accelerated route).	Observation of the new facilitators running the course. This observer is an experienced course facilitator, but not the mentor involved in Stage C.

- Attendance at a workshop with other facilitators to reflect on the course activities and consider questions that helped them to self-assess their learning (Stage B).
- Joint delivery of the course with a mentor who was an experienced facilitator and a follow-up feedback discussion to assess progress against the learning outcomes of the Develop the Developers Programme (Stage C).
- Observation of prospective facilitators delivering the course by an experienced facilitator who was not the mentor in Stage C, and a feedback discussion as part of the assessment process, resulting in a recognition decision (Stage D).

On successful completion of the programme, facilitators were issued with a certificate and their names added to an AdvanceHE list of recognised facilitators.

Overall, the feedback on the programme was 'very positive' and the facilitators reported that they felt relatively well prepared to deliver the course (DEWR, 2020, p. 30). The online preparatory work and the workshop (Stages A and B) were considered particularly valuable in developing more fully their understanding of the course and building confidence. The assisted course (Stage C) with the 'safety net' of support from an AdvanceHE associate was considered to be a good idea, although being observed delivering the course (Stage D) was inevitably felt to be challenging for some. A further issue seemed to be the length of time between the facilitators completing the workshop, delivery of the assisted and then the observed courses (the scheduling of the latter being at the convenience of the institution). This led some to worry that they had forgotten what they had learnt between each stage of the development process (DEWR, 2020, pp. 11–15). Despite this and an initial concern of the project team that the shift to institutional provision might affect the quality of delivery, the evaluation data indicated that there was no indication of a difference in the skills and expertise of facilitators (DEWR, 2021, p. 8; see also this volume, Chapters 10 and 11, for discussion of implementation from institutional perspectives, and Chapter 12 for further evaluation of the developer programme).

The Degree Standards Project delivered an approach to the professional development of external examiners that was well received. The training of facilitators through the Develop the Developer process created the capacity for institutions to provide professional development of their staff (see Chapter 11 for further analysis). The purpose of this was to ensure that the provision was sustainable beyond the end of the funded project. Other mechanisms were also put in place to support this, which included: establishing a regional consortium of institutions to facilitate collaborative arrangements in running the course (a particular boon to small and specialist institutions unable to regularly recruit a viable cohort); creating a community of practice for course facilitators, supported by an online forum; and ongoing development opportunities, such as webinars on course updates. However, continued commitment was dependent on the priority accorded by institutions to this form of continuing professional development. It became clear that it would be beneficial for a centralised sector body to coordinate the oversight, continuing quality assurance and delivery of the provision. Fortunately, in 2021 the Office for Students granted AdvanceHE a three-year non-exclusive licence to do this.

Calibration of academic standards

The purpose of calibration activity is to help ensure that academic and assessment standards in subjects or disciplines are reasonably comparable across institutions within a region or nation by creating or using existing community processes to establish, share and develop an agreed understanding of standards (see Chapter 8 for a fuller discussion).

It is important to note that the project's brief was to *explore* approaches to the calibration of standards, and present recommendations for any future work in this area. The main priority for the funders was the development and delivery of professional development for external examiners and the funding reflected this priority. However, recognising that research, as well as feedback from course participants, clearly indicated that subject-based calibration was essential in ensuring consistent standards for judging student work, additional funding was provided after the first year to support some piloting of calibration activities.

During the Project, it became clear that consensus seeking dialogue was likely to be the most effective approach to calibrating academic standards across institutions. This required the facilitation of a process of peer review carried out by members of a subject, discipline or professional community, to discuss and compare student work in order to reach a shared understanding of the academic standards. In partnership with a number of professional bodies and subject associations, the viability and effectiveness of different models of subject-based calibration was explored. The aim, in these collaborative explorations, was to work with bodies, such as the British Association of Sport and Exercise Sciences (see Chapter 14), the Royal Geographical Society (see Chapter 15) and Conservatoires UK, to develop exemplars for the way in which academic standards can be calibrated.

Three models of delivering calibration activity were trialled in a range of different subject areas:

1 Stand-alone calibration events, in which workshops were designed and held with the Royal College of Veterinary Surgeons, the Royal Society of Chemistry, the Royal Geographical Society (with the Institute of British Geographers) and Conservatoires UK.
2 An integrated model, in which the Professional Development Course for external examiners and calibration activities were linked (i.e. a subject-focussed Professional Development Course followed by a calibration event). This model was employed for sport and exercise science, geography, and law.
3 A revised model, where the generic Professional Development Course for external examiners was a prerequisite for participants to attend a calibration

activity that was delivered remotely. Working with the British Psychological Society, and the Chartered Association of Business Schools, this approach was trialled and developed in 2020–2021.

As part of the work to develop these different models of calibration, case studies and toolkits were produced to exemplify calibration activity conducted in the subject areas, which could be emulated by other subject communities. A synthesis report on calibration was published, designed to help professional bodies and subject associations undertake their own calibration activities (Bloxham, Reimann & Rust, 2018).

The scope and nature of the calibration activity deployed is influenced by the subject in question. In particular, it is important to consider the disciplinary specific standards, priorities of the collaborating professional bodies and the subject-relevant form of student assessment to be scrutinised. Each delivery model has advantages from a pragmatic perspective. For example, the stand-alone model, involving preparatory activity and a one-day workshop, is relatively easy to arrange and serves to highlight disparity in marking, but allows less time for the building of consensus around academic standards. The integrated model has the benefit of utilising a subject-focussed Professional Development Course, which provides the underpinning rationale for the subsequent calibration activity and as a two-day event offers more time for reflection and debate. The main benefit of the revised model is that it removes the need for designing a subject-focussed Professional Development Course, while still ensuring that participants involved in calibration activity have experienced the learning from the generic Professional Development Course.

The experience of designing, running and evaluating calibration activity has been invaluable in refining the model for delivery, as well as suggesting that additional events could provide further benefits. For example, achieving consensus about the academic standards in one form of assessment (e.g. a musical recital) does not necessarily mean that these would apply to a different one (e.g. in musical composition). It is envisaged that subject communities can use the model of calibration multiple times with a range of assessment types as part of ongoing professional development. In general, participants were keen to take forward calibration by, for example, arranging activity in their own institution or engaging with their professional body about calibration. However, there was a recognition that there is a need for involvement of key subject experts to facilitate the engagement of professional bodies that are critical in ensuring sustained and cross-institutional delivery. Calibration is best understood as a long-term process, which is reflected in the revised model of calibration. Further in-depth overviews of the ways in which calibration was implemented in sport and exercise science (see Chapter 14) and geography (see Chapter 15) draw out some of the considerations and practical challenges of planning and running such events.

The independent evaluation work (DEWR, 2021) indicated a high level of interest in cross-institutional calibration and that bespoke calibration workshops were effective for creating interest in calibration activity among the subject communities involved. Participants recognised the value of calibration workshops:

> There is potential for relatively small-scale workshop events to have a big impact in highlighting the issues amongst subject communities and generating enthusiasm for calibration activities to continue and be driven within the existing networks.
>
> (DEWR, 2021, p. 69)

Although there was much interest in conducting calibration exercises in subject groups, there was recognition of the challenge of engaging academics with significant workloads in such exercises, and the engagement of professional bodies depended on their size and ability to prioritise these. Calibration activity aims to ensure comparability of academic standards across institutions and stability of standards over time. However, more sustained engagement and long-term evaluation is needed to assess the impact of calibration activity on generating consistent standards and their application. There is clearly a need for subject specialist involvement in the design of calibration activity, and ideally professional body or subject association support and endorsement.

Changes in higher education policy impacting on the Degree Standards Project

The Degree Standards Project also faced challenges arising from the political and educational context in which it was operating. The process of political devolution of the United Kingdom and the tension between institutional autonomy and a growing desire for regulation on the part of the UK government, all had an impact on the delivery of the professional development provision and, in particular, on its reach and potential sustainability.

Since the creation of legislatures in Scotland, Wales and Northern Ireland in the 1990s, responsibility for higher education policy has been determined by the funding agencies established in each nation. As a result, different approaches to funding, delivery and quality assurance have been adopted across the UK. Of particular relevance to the Project was the pattern of divergence over quality assurance. In England, the system of institutional review by peers was replaced by a data-driven approach to monitoring quality with institutions required to publish a range of information on quality and standards, including external examiner reports. Scotland and Wales, on the other hand, retained cyclical institutional review in slightly differing formats, but both with an emphasis on quality enhancement. There was no requirement to publish external examiner reports in either Wales or Scotland (Brown & Carasso, 2013). The divergent approaches were crystallised in the Revised Operating Model for Quality Assessment outlined by HEFCE, which applied only to England, Wales and Northern Ireland, although there was a commitment to continuing 'to work with the Scottish

Funding Council in areas of particular UK-wide importance' (HEFCE, 2016, p. 4). A UK Standing Committee for Quality Assessment (UKSCQA), with representatives (inter alia) from all four funding councils, was set up to provide 'sector-led oversight of higher education quality assessment arrangements that continue to be shared across the UK' (UKSCQA, 2023).

One of these shared arrangements was ensuring the reliability of degree standards and this included the professional development of external examiners. This meant that all four nations provided the financial resources for the Degree Standards Project, managed by HEFCE in 2016. As a result, each year a project report was Provided to HEFCE and a strategic report to the UKSCQA. During the first year, the Professional Development Course was, therefore, piloted in all four nations. However, the following year, the Scottish Funding Council (SFC) decided not to continue funding the Project. The decision by the SFC may have been affected by the on-going tension between its continued commitment to enhancement-led quality *assurance* and HEFCE's quality *assessment*. The decision had important implications for the Project, as it was unable to allow applicants from Scottish institutions to undertake the course, or the Develop the Developer programme. This limited the geographical reach of the Project in the remaining four years.

The Degree Standards Project was also caught up in the issue of universities being autonomous in the setting and maintenance of the standards of their awards, and a UK government increasingly inclined towards greater regulation. The funding councils had historically functioned as a mediator between government and universities in a system of co-regulation. However, the basis of HEFCE's regulatory powers in England largely ended with the increase in full-time undergraduate fees to £9,000 and the removal of subsidies for teaching to universities in 2012. But the UK government was already of 'the view that "quality" is an inescapable part of an overall approach to regulation' (HEFCE, 2016, p. 5). Consequently, following the Higher Education and Research Act (2017), HEFCE was replaced by the Office for Students, a regulatory body for England with statutory responsibility for quality and standards, and the management of the Project was transferred to this body.

As the Office for Students has a statutory duty to prioritise student interests, it has responded to governmental concerns about controversial issues like grade inflation. In 2017, grade inflation data were added as a 'supplementary metric' to the Teaching Excellence and Student Outcomes Framework (TEF) with institutions being required to declare the number of first, upper second class and other undergraduate degrees awarded in the review period compared with previous years. In 2018, the Office for Students made controlling grade inflation a condition of continued registration in its Regulatory Framework (Office for Students, 2018). Faced with this governmental concern about the erosion of standards and a perceived threat to institutional autonomy, sector bodies representing the whole of the UK, decided to support a programme of work related to strengthening the comparability and reliability of degree standards. In 2019, the UK Standing Committee for Quality Assessment published a 'statement of intent' signed by sector representatives across the UK to protect the value of qualifications; it included an explicit commitment (one of four) to 'support and strengthen the external examiners system' (UKSCQA, 2019).

In the same year, the QAA published a set of common degree classification descriptors developed with the sector, as an annexe to the new UK Quality Code for Higher Education (QAA, 2019). Universities UK published six fundamental 'principles for effective degree algorithm design' to promote more uniformity in processes for determining degree classification (Universities UK, 2020). However, the take-up of the professional development provision seemed to fluctuate in relation to priority accorded to external examining. Initially, it appeared that the significance of the role of external examiners had been diminished when external examining was subsumed within advice and guidance on 'external expertise' in the new UK Quality Code (2018). However, it may have been simply that, rather than a perceived diminution of the importance of external examining, institutional priorities changed where, for example, the writing of TEF submissions took precedence (AdvanceHE, 2019, p. 7).

While the 'statement of intent' had included specific commitments designed to protect the value of UK degrees, the way in which these commitments were to be met differed. The Office for Students required that English institutions produce 'degree outcomes statements', setting out how student outcomes data had been scrutinised, and associated regulations and processes reviewed. By contrast, in the case of Scotland, Wales and Northern Ireland, the statement of intent was to be secured by their particular quality assessment frameworks. In the event, however, all the Welsh higher education providers opted to produce degree outcomes statements. The English, Welsh and Northern Irish implementation plans referred to 'AdvanceHE's training programme for external examiners' as an option for institutions to consider (UKSCQA, 2019, p. 5), however the Scottish one did not.

The divergence between England's approach to external quality assurance and that of the other three nations of the United Kingdom limited the geographical reach of the Degree Standards Project. The incorporation of external quality assurance within the regulatory system in England, may have caused tension between the universities and the government, and made, for some, the adoption of the training of external examiners a political as well as educational decision. The Degree Standards Project illustrates in microcosm the challenge of implementing a uniform approach to tackling a problem common to all.

Conclusion

The Degree Standards Project managed successfully a number of key challenges in leading change in higher education. These included:

- Ensuring quality control and assurance when professional development is coordinated and maintained by a centralised body but is delivered through a devolved model involving institutions and regional consortia.
- Establishing viable solutions for course delivery across a diverse group of institutions, some of which are relatively small and specialist.

- Producing a course with content relevant to external examiners from a range of disciplines or tailoring the approach to offer subject-based courses integrating calibration activity.
- Building a sustainable provision, where the course might be embedded within institutional continuing professional development pathways or where course completion is a requirement in the appointment criteria for external examiners.

The Project had to navigate significant changes in UK higher education policy. Firstly, the increasing divergence of quality assurance policies across the four nations, which culminated in the Higher Education and Research Act (2017) and the setting up of a regulator (the Office for Students) for England only. Secondly, an increasing concern about the comparability of degree standards across the UK, and in particular, government concerns about undergraduate grade inflation.

The sector has persevered with attempting to reform itself from within; in 2022, the QAA published a set of 'External Examining Principles' as an addition to the 'statement of intent' (QAA, 2022). These reinstated and went beyond the guidance in the UK Quality Code (2018). While advisory, they demonstrate a continuing desire to improve the system of external examining. External examining does, after all, provide a measure of accountability (in terms of externality), while upholding institutional autonomy. Nonetheless, the professional development of external examiners requires sustained commitment by institutions, individuals and governments, as well as resourcing to contribute effectively to the maintenance of academic standards. The experience of delivering the Degree Standards Project has relevance in countries, such as Germany where power is devolved, and, for example, Australia, where there is on-going tension between governmental regulation and institutional responsibility for quality and standards.

PRACTICAL STRATEGY

Box 9.1 The development and delivery of large-scale professional development provision

- Engage stakeholders in the higher education sector by means of annual conferences and presentations to relevant sector bodies (built into the project plan), and regular articles or blogs, ideally from course participants or delegates.
- Involve the target constituency in project development, including co-designing the course with a number of partners and regular meetings of a representative steering group.
- Devolve responsibility for delivery of the course by trained institutional facilitators, but maintain quality control through a centralised body.
- Involve the funders in all key decisions including conference planning.

References

AdvanceHE. (2011). UK Professional Standards Framework. https://s3.eu-west-2.amazonaws.com/assets.creode.advancehe-document-manager/documents/hea/private/ukpsf_2011_0_1568037208.pdf.

AdvanceHE. (2019). Strategic Report on the Degree Standards Project, 2018–19. Unpublished project report prepared for the UK Standing Committee for Quality Assessment.

AdvanceHE. (2023). UK Professional Standards Framework. www.advance-he.ac.uk/knowledge-hub/uk-professional-standards-framework-ukpsf.

Bloxham, S., Reimann, N. & Rust, C. (2018). Calibration of standards: what, why and how?www.advance-he.ac.uk/sites/default/files/2022-01/Calibration%20synthesis%20report_0.pdf.

Brown, R. & Carasso, H. (2013). *Everything for Sale? The Marketization of UK Higher Education*. Routledge.

DEWR. (2020). Report on Develop the Developer Activities. Unpublished report, April.

DEWR. (2021). *Evaluation of the Degree Standards Project: Final Report to AdvanceHE*. (unpublished report).

HEFCE. (2015). *A Review of External Examining Arrangements across the UK. Report to the UK Higher Education Funding Bodies by the Higher Education Academy*. HEFCE.

HEFCE. (2016). *Revised Operating Model for Quality Assessment*. HEFCE.

Office for Students. (2018). *Teaching Excellence and Student Outcomes Framework Specification*. Office for Students.

QAA. (2011). UK Quality Code for Higher Education. www.qaa.ac.uk/quality-code.

QAA. (2019). Annex D: outcome classification descriptions for FHEQ Level 6 and FQHEIS Level 10 degrees. www.ukscqa.org.uk/wp-content/uploads/2019/10/Frameworks-Annex-with-Degree-classification-descriptions.pdf.

QAA. (2022). External examining principles. www.qaa.ac.uk/docs/qaa/quality-code/external-examining-principles.pdf?sfvrsn=fe91a281_12.

Universities UK. (2011). Review of external examining arrangements in universities and colleges in the UK. www.universitiesuk.ac.uk/highereducation/Documents/2011/ReviewOfExternalExaminingArrangements.pdf.

Universities UK. (2020). *Principles for Effective Algorithm Design*. Universities UK.

UKSCQA. (2019). *Degree Classification: Transparency, Reliability and Fairness – a Statement of Intent*. Universities UK.

UKSCQA. (2023). Who we are. https://ukscqa.org.uk/ (accessed 24 May 2023).

Chapter 10

Designing and developing the Professional Development Course for External Examiners

Andy Lloyd and Rachel Forsyth

Introduction

Based on the research findings and policy developments discussed elsewhere in the book, this chapter gives an overview of the design, content and delivery of the Professional Development Course for External Examiners (PDC). The PDC was designed based on the review of external examining carried out in 2015, which had shown a lack of consistency in external examiners' understanding and use of academic and quality standards in their work. Specifically, the course was designed to support one of the main recommendations in the 2015 report; to professionalise external examining 'so that those conducting the role are skilled and knowledgeable about assessment and the assurance of academic and quality standards' (HEFCE, 2015, pp. 92–93).

A secondary aim of the PDC was to contribute to the development of assessment literacy of academics to encourage more robust and informed discussion of both quality and academic standards. The course was therefore conceived as a way to provide consistent scholarly information about marking and standards nationally, while respecting disciplinary norms and approaches.

As outlined in Chapter 9, the contract to develop and facilitate the PDC was awarded to AdvanceHE, a UK organisation that supports the development and enhancement of the higher education sector. On behalf of AdvanceHE, a project team of experienced assessment researchers and course designers was recruited to design and deliver the course.

Designing the PDC

The initial design of the course was undertaken through a two-day workshop held in London during September 2016, attended by an initial core team of seven consultants and representatives from the three institutions who subsequently piloted the course. The planning drew on the background research into the social construction of standards (see Chapter 3), assessment criteria and rubrics (see Chapter 13) and the external examiner role and assessment literacy (see Chapters 6 and 7). In addition, the course design had several key requirements in that it needed to be:

- Situated firmly in the research literature – to allow the key messages to be supported by evidence and help participants understand and appreciate the course's scholarly background.
- Useful for participants from all disciplinary areas, with varied professional experiences of standards, teaching and examining in different types of institution; recognising the value of the course to both existing and prospective external examiners and the need for it to be relevant to academic staff from all disciplinary backgrounds.
- Accessible to teaching staff who would be giving up time to complete the course, being aware of the busy environment in which we all work and understanding the workload implications of engaging in continuous professional development (CPD) activities that often arise.
- Accessible to as many as possible, delivered consistently, and sustainability is built in beyond the original period of funding.

These requirements influenced the course design in several ways. Initially a one-day face-to-face course was developed. This delivery mode also required participants to complete online pre-course activities. This enabled the course to be delivered over a single day and allowed participants some flexibility with their time for undertaking the preparatory activities. Throughout the face-to-face day, the course fostered active learning where the participants engaged with activities that replicated some of the core tasks undertaken by an external examiner. The discursive and shared nature of these activities encouraged colleagues who had already worked as external examiners to share and reflect upon their experiences with participants aspiring to undertake this role. The design of the activities also expected participants to work both with colleagues in the same subject area and with others, to show potential differences and similarities across disciplines. In addition, the activities provided a varied pace to the day to keep participants engaged. The course was largely self-assessed by giving participants regular opportunities to record key learning points and reflect on what they had learnt within a reflective log. Finally, a key aspect of the design was to develop high quality facilitator and participant materials. The attention upon the development of the materials for the facilitator (e.g. facilitator handbook, key messages, course reader, and extensive notes for each slide) were to ensure that delivery was sustainable through the training of new facilitators (see Chapter 9 for further explanation of the Develop the Developer programme).

As an initial step, the development team identified a set of intended learning outcomes for the PDC. These were that having successfully completed the course, the participants would be able to:

1 Explain and discuss the nature and purpose of the external examiner role, its function for quality assessment in higher education, including the

importance within it of their contribution to safeguarding academic standards.
2 Explain the nature of standards in the higher education context.
3 Draw on practical and scholarly knowledge of assessment as appropriate to the role, including:

- professional judgement;
- assessment reliability;
- assessment validity;
- purposes of assessment;
- principles of assessment;
- programme coherence in assessment.

4 Recognise the varied provenance and uniqueness of individuals' standards and the challenge this brings to examiners representing the standards of their subject, discipline and/or professional community.
5 Explain the importance and use of key reference points for academic standards in the relevant subject, discipline and/or professional area.
6 Explain the purpose and value of ongoing calibration activities in supporting the use of common 'discipline community' standards.
7 Recognise the importance of their continuing professional development in assessment and external examining.

Structure of the PDC

An important aspect of the course structure were the activities and materials that participants were required to engage with and complete in advance of the face-to-face delivery. As well as a short briefing paper that participants were asked to read, which covers and captures a number of the key research findings in relation to external examining and academic standards, they were also requested to complete two short exercises. The first was to review or moderate three pieces of assessed work and the second was to consider and make decisions on several scenarios related to being an external examiner. The outcomes of these activities were then used at various points within the face-to-face part of the course and will be described in more detail within the relevant sessions below.

The face-to-face course was divided into eight sessions. Generally, each session was structured in a way that contained a short introductory presentation to outline the key ideas, concepts and research. Most sessions then had a related task that the participants were put into small groups to complete. The activities varied, to keep the day lively and motivating, but they all aimed to facilitate discussion about making judgements about academic and quality standards and dealing with potentially difficult situations in external examining practice. Sessions ended with and short plenary discussions, which allowed course participants to report back from their group, queries to be raised and facilitators to gauge understanding and reinforce key messages. The following provides and overview of the contents and related tasks for each of the eight sessions.

Session 1: Background and introduction

The initial session of the course is concerned with both the research and policy background for the course itself. In particular, the 'core' duties of a UK external examiner, as set out in chapter B7 of the 2018 UK Quality Code, are foregrounded. This context immediately highlights to participants some of the tensions embedded in the role and the need to balance the four key duties of an external examiner, which are:

- maintainer of academic standards;
- guardian of national standards;
- process checker; and
- critical friend.

As well as highlighting the findings from research (HEFCE, 2015), which suggest that many external examiners are more comfortable in the 'critical friend' role, participants are given the opportunity to discuss how they would respond to typical examiner scenarios. This draws upon one of the pre-course activities where participants have been asked to make decisions on what they might do in a range of external examining scenarios. The exercise helps participants to reflect upon the challenges inherent in the different roles and responsibilities that an external examiner has. Specifically, it helps participants to recognise the need for UK external examiners to focus on the overarching importance of academic standards, the part of the role that the 2015 research suggested has become less important for some practitioners.

Finally, the first session seeks to distinguish between 'academic standards' and 'quality standards'. This distinction is important to (a) foreground academic standards as core to the role of an external examiner, and (b) emphasise the need for external examiners to have confidence that their own sense of academic standards is comparable with others. Drawing both on the literature and the structure of the 2018 Quality Code, academic standards are defined in the course as an output measure; one that focuses on student achievement and that is only visible in students' work. In contrast, quality standards are defined as the input and process measures that focus on all other aspects of the assessment cycle such as the resources and procedures used. The session concludes by highlighting that good quality standards, while important in themselves, do not automatically lead to, or guarantee, good academic standards.

CRITICAL PERSPECTIVE

Box 10.1 Key messages in session 1 of the PDC

Although the external examiner has four main roles, safeguarding standards must be the primary concern. This role involves tensions and dilemmas, which the course is designed to help external examiners to manage.

As an external examiner, there needs to be a critical awareness of the key distinction between academic and quality standards.

Session 2: Variability in academic standards

The second session of the course introduces the concept of variability as a consequence of different people or markers holding different standards and the implications of this for external examining. In groups, the participants are asked to discuss the three pieces of work they have reviewed (moderated) prior to the course. This replicates one of the key activities that external examiners commonly undertake, which is to confirm the judgements or standards made on student work for the programme that they are the external examiner for. The three pieces of work participants were asked to review were essays about assessment practice, which are a typical assessment on the postgraduate courses in academic practice in higher education. These are qualifications in the UK that have been developed for newly appointed academic staff in higher education and focus on issues related to learning, teaching and assessment practice. While course participants are rarely specialists in academic development, this type of Postgraduate Certificate course is something many are likely to be familiar with from their own experience of undertaking such a course. This allows participants to consider marks in an area that they should all be familiar with and further helps to develop their assessment literacy. Supported by a facilitated discussion about the existence of variability and the challenges this presents for making consistent judgements about students' work, the activity clearly demonstrates the influence that initial marks and feedback comments can have on our judgements, and how 'groupthink' can similarly impact on our decisions. Fundamentally, the activity reveals the wide and disparate judgements that different markers can make about the same sample of scripts. As discussed in Chapter 5, this variability is clearly supported in the literature but can come as an unwelcome surprise to course participants.

The session concludes with participants working in small groups to consider potential sources of variation within a particular scenario. The scenario outlines a situation whereby markers in two partner institutions appear to have treated the same assignment quite differently in the ways in which judgements about academic standards were reached. Participants are asked to draw up a list of factors that contributed to the situation; again, a task that UK external examiners might be expected to undertake. Facilitators collate their responses, which are then divided into the three potential sources of variability that research has identified: people, tools, and tasks. It is a further exposition of these sources of variability that forms the focus of the next three sessions in the course.

CRITICAL PERSPECTIVE

Box 10.2 Key messages in session 2 of the PDC

Variability in academic standards is common and is not necessarily a result of poor practices. It is more likely a consequence of the complexity of assessment in higher education and the nature of academic standards themselves. There are significant

implications for variation in standards including fairness to students and the value of awards.
There are three main sources of variation: people, tools, and tasks.

Session 3: People as a source of variation

Drawing on the social constructivism model originally formulated by Vygotsky, this session begins with a short presentation that focuses on the nature of academic standards and the ways in which academic communities develop these (see Chapter 3 for further discussion). The presentation highlights both the tacit nature of academic standards, their fundamentally imprecise nature, and the ways in which we progressively develop our own understanding of academic standards over time. Specifically, the session highlights the frequent use of terms open to different interpretation, both those that seek to define relative performance (e.g., 'fair', 'good'), and those that seek to define the skills and attributes that students are asked to demonstrate (e.g. 'critically evaluate'). Such terminology is commonplace in the documents used to articulate academic standards. While recognising that 'academic socialisation' within individual academic programmes can lead to some common and shared understanding of academic standards, the session further highlights the research that demonstrates how differences in standards can often widen as we become less conscious of the frameworks developed to guide us as markers.

Following the introduction of the ideas and concepts above, the participants are asked to briefly reflect on the different influences that have contributed to their individual sense of standards. Drawing on an HEA/QAA study (Bloxham & Price, 2014), in which practising UK external examiners identified a wide range of influences on the development of their own understanding of academic standards, the exercise prompts course participants to review the list of influences this research identified and consider it against their own experiences. These influences are broadly grouped into influential people/groups, experience and personal values/beliefs. It is not uncommon for participants to identify factors that they had not considered previously; often ones that have had a profound impact on individual tacit knowledge and academic standards. These have included participant experiences of working internationally with different grading systems and cultures, as well as participants' personal beliefs, values, and backgrounds. It is the myriad of different influences that participants identify, which helps to convince them of the significant differences in the social construction and tacit understanding of academic standards.

The session concludes by summarising the implications of the nature of academic standards on the role of the external examiner. In particular, it warns against not relying on our informal learning for ensuring that we share similar standards to our wider academic community. It is at this point that calibration as a potential solution is first introduced in preparation for a greater focus in session 7.

CRITICAL PERSPECTIVE

Box 10.3 Key messages in session 3 of the PDC

Even when we use similar tools (such as marking criteria) and tasks, people are a key source of variation in standards. This is because standards are socially constructed and involve tacit knowledge. External examiners need to take a critical perspective and ensure that their standards are calibrated with others in their subject community.

Session 4: Tools and tasks, part A (formal guidance)

Sessions 4 and 5 are designed to help external examiners to consider and review the different documents and processes (the 'tools') used in the UK for the management of assessment, marking and academic standards. Session 4 begins by highlighting the range of documents and frameworks that are used across the UK higher education sector; focusing on both those that operate sector wide and the local guides and documents that exist at institutional and programme level. The potential limitations of these reference points are then discussed. The research indicates that external examiners often do not use key documentary points of reference and that many markers and external examiners choose to focus on their own tacit understanding of standards; something already shown to lead to variation (Silver, 2006). In addition, these reference points, in themselves, contain ambiguities of language and context that offer some of the same challenges of interpretation that were considered in session 2.

The activity in this session requires small groups of participants (typically two or three in similar disciplines or subject areas) to review examples of module documents and assessment briefs that they were invited to source from their own departments and bring to the session. Again, this aims to mirror a typical external examining activity where they are required to scrutinise assessment tasks and documentation. However, in this instance a key focus is upon how easily the academic standards for an assessment can be observed at this stage. It is an exercise that participants rate highly, allowing them to share examples of practice and discuss assessment design and documentation from the perspective of academic standards.

The plenary in this session restates the importance of the sector wide reference points but highlights their limitations and the fact that these documents, together with university-specific regulations and documentation, are not sufficient to indicate academic standards; something that will only be visible in student work. As highlighted earlier, while the quality standards these documents represent are clearly important, they do not by themselves guarantee appropriate academic standards.

At this point in the course, participants are often feeling concerned by the considerable challenges to the role which have been presented so far. The second half of the course aims to build their confidence by presenting tools which will reduce variability, and to give them practice in managing some of the typical dilemmas that UK external examiners often face.

CRITICAL PERSPECTIVE

Box 10.4 Key messages in session 4 of the PDC

External examiners should be familiar with external reference points and ensure that local reference point reflect them.

It is important to critically evaluate these tools and be aware that standards are open to different interpretation. External examiners need to pay attention to the combination of assessment tasks, criteria and students' performance.

Session 5: Tools and tasks, part B

A matrix task where participants are asked to evaluate a range of tools for assuring academic standards forms the basis of this session. There are nineteen different tools which are each presented on a separate card. Examples of these tools include: second marking of all work, resolving differences by averaging; use of a detailed marking scheme; all markers mark and discuss a common sample of work prior to full marking process; exam board consideration of means and standard deviations of marks; markers being a member of a learned society or professional body. In groups the participants discuss the tools and place them accordingly on a matrix that has two axes (see Figure 5.1). The placement on the matrix is based on their judgement about the tool in terms of (a) whether it allows for internal or external comparability (x-axis) and (b) whether it is highly effective or ineffective in limiting variability in standards. An example completed matrix and further discussion on the types of judgements is provided in Chapter 5.

The main value of this activity which forms the basis of session 5 is the discussion and consensus building within the groups. It provides participants with an opportunity to talk about the tools in relation to their own experiences, but also alongside the concepts presented in sessions 1 to 4. Groups are then encouraged to compare their results with those from others, which leads to a short plenary discussion. To close the session, participants are given a short summary of the main findings from this exercise and directed to a detailed expert commentary on each of the tools and activities (see also Chapter 5).

CRITICAL PERSPECTIVE

Box 10.5 Key messages in session 5 of the PDC

There are many tools in use to limit variability in academic standards in higher education. As an external examiner it is important to have a critical awareness of the level of internal/external focus and the potential differences in levels of effectiveness of these tools.

Many of the tools tend to be focussed on internal rather than external comparability and those tools that have a level of social construction of standards by individuals are likely to be more effective.

Session 6: Professional practice in the external examiner role and decision making

In this session participants are given the opportunity to apply what they have learned from the previous sessions. A game is used to promote discussion about how external examiners might approach realistic scenarios in their work. Participants work in groups to consider a number of dilemmas that an external examiner might encounter. Each individual has a set of four voting cards (A–D) that they use to indicate the decision that they would take in this situation. The first dilemma is read out, followed by the four proposed actions that an external examiner could take. Each participant individually selects an option and does not share it with other members of the group. Once everyone has decided, all participants reveal their selection at the same time so as not to be influenced by the decisions of others. At this stage the group discusses the range of options selected in terms of level of agreement and individuals can then defend and provide a rationale for the option that they have selected. Once the group have discussed and considered each other's point of view, there is then a second round of voting in which participants can either stick with their original choice or change their mind based on what they have heard. This acts as an example of social calibration and the group are encouraged to consider if there is reduced variability in the choices following the group discussion.

In the session plenary, the facilitator points out that there are not any correct or incorrect options, but there are a number of things that an external examiner needs to be aware of that means they are more likely to take an appropriate course of action for a specific context. This includes: an awareness of the important role of the external examiner as the only check on student outputs and the comparability of standards; that it may not always be possible to please everyone in the role; being confident that one's academic standards are representative of the subject community; being well informed about the evidence for effective assessment; and understanding the complexity of academic standards.

CRITICAL PERSPECTIVE

Box 10.6 Key messages in session 6 of the PDC

External examiners are likely to encounter a range of complex and difficult situations. There is rarely a single best approach and it is important to use professional judgement based on their understanding of academic standards and their subject expertise.

It is important for external examiners to be aware that they are the only check on comparability of academic standards across institutions. Therefore it is important to be confident that their standards are representative of the subject community to which they belong and that they have a good grasp of the evidence for effective assessment.

Session 7: Social moderation and calibration of standards

In this session, participants see how colleagues can work together to make professional judgements and develop a better shared understanding of academic standards. They compare two different approaches to start to draw out the differences between social moderation and calibration. Social moderation is generally focussed upon the agreement of marks, which often immediately follows marking decisions on specific pieces of summative work of students that contributes to their award. Calibration is about developing shared knowledge of standards, often through social moderation of a variety of different types of student work, in a continuous and ongoing manner in order to create 'calibrated' academics. The first approach is provided within a written case study (Saunders & Davis, 1998), which describes a process that a programme team went through as a pre-assessment activity. The second approach is captured in a video provided by the Royal Northern College of Music in which a team of examiners discuss the assessment of a live trumpet performance to agree a mark.

Following this discussion, participants are shown a second video that demonstrates an example of calibration, undertaken within the accountancy community in Australia (Watty et al., 2014). The example is drawn from the 'Achievement Matters' project that was supported by the Australian Government Office for Learning and Teaching (Booth et al., 2015). The video shows how a subject community can undertake structured calibration in order to socially construct standards which are appropriate to the tools and tasks used in the discipline. Key points to emerge from this exercise is that effective calibration activity should: be a collegial process within subject communities; work with exemplars of student work; have robust but respectful conversation; be structured and facilitated around sharing, moderating and agreeing standards.

CRITICAL PERSPECTIVE

Box 10.7 Key messages in session 7 of the PDC

Social moderation and calibration are approaches, which support consensus-building in relation to the interpretation of quality standards and the judgement of academic standards. Both are important ways to develop shared understanding of assessments.

Calibration has a broad range of application and can be used both within programme teams and between different assessors in the same discipline area.

Session 8: Conclusion

In this brief concluding session, the facilitator reiterates the key messages of the course, and gives time for any final thoughts or questions. Participants are then asked to complete their final reflections and are encouraged to identify how they can take forward the key messages from the course. This exercise often reveals participants' enthusiasm and willingness to become involved with or establish calibration activity, although this is often focussed upon internal calibration within departments. After the course, participants are asked to complete a final reflection, which is sent to and then reviewed by the course facilitators. As well as providing an opportunity for the facilitators to provide some feedback comments and confirm understanding of the key messages, this process enables facilitators to confirm whether participants can be added to the register of course completers maintained by AdvanceHE. This register is now used by a number of UK institutions to guide their appointment of external examiners.

CRITICAL PERSPECTIVE

Box 10.8 Key messages in session 8 of the PDC

The role of an external examiner is multifaceted and there is a need to balance the critical friend/process checker role with a robust approach to maintaining and safeguarding academic standards.

Academic standards are complex and there are multiple sources of variation including: the *people* involved; the assessment *tasks* involved; and the *tools* that we use to support judgements.

There are a range of difficult examining decisions that we are likely to encounter and professional development regarding external examining, academic standards and subject expertise is important to support the judgements and decisions taken.

Social moderation and calibration offer a way forward for reducing variation by ensuring that assessors and external examiners share their academic standards.

Course delivery formats

The original one-day (face-to-face) format for the course was subsequently adapted into an online distance-learning version that was designed to be delivered entirely online over a five-week period. The same learning outcomes and content was covered, but the online version of the course was divided into five self-study sections of roughly equal length. The course was punctuated with optional online sessions facilitated by two course tutors that provide an opportunity to reiterate key messages and answer questions. The benefits of the online course were partly in the flexibility that it offered participants, but also the opportunity to offer the course to very large groups due to the self-study nature (i.e. up to 160 at a time). The role of the facilitator was to encourage participants to keep up with the pace of the course, check-in on discussions, address any misconceptions and ensure that the key course messages were surfaced in discussions.

As detailed in Chapter 9, as a consequence of the coronavirus pandemic, a further remote variation of the course was developed in 2020. The remote version of the course was virtually identical to the original face-to-face course other than the synchronous remote delivery through a video conferencing tool. Some of the activities were adapted for remote delivery and the course was re-designed slightly to be delivered over two half days. This was to avoid issues with extended periods of screen time and the slightly more intense nature of remote delivery platforms for both participants and facilitators. The pre-course activity that participants were required to do for the remote version were identical to those described above for the face-to-face format.

Conclusion

It was originally expected that the course might be controversial and provoke participants to be quite vocal, critical of the content and defensive. This thinking was due to a sense that many of the key messages and research that is presented may contradict the participants' beliefs regarding the accuracy of marking and the effectiveness of processes. However, this did not prove to be the case. Rather an overwhelming majority of course participants reported that the content was extremely helpful and relatable in terms of their personal experiences as assessors and external examiners. While the formal evaluation on the strength and impact of the course is discussed more fully in Chapter 11, there have been many positive and unsolicited comments made to facilitators. The following provides an example of how the course has been received:

> I think this has been a really useful course. It is well designed, well executed and makes the case for what you are trying to achieve in terms of learning outcomes and understanding very robustly. I am very much convinced and wish I had known some of the things you have demonstrated here several years ago.
> (PDC participant feedback via email, 2020)

> I have thoroughly enjoyed this course and have found it to be of huge benefit in both my roles as Programme Leader and External Examiner. I feel the course has also helped me develop the confidence to pursue the opportunity of the role of validation panel member also - I have just sent off my first expression of interest!
> (PDC participant feedback via email, 2020)

Thank you for such an interesting course. It will definitely change my practice and inspired me to get my team to do more calibration.

(PDC participant feedback via email, 2020)

In addition to participant feedback, the team of facilitators met regularly during the project period to discuss their own experiences of working with the course materials and participants. These discussions led to ongoing modifications to the course throughout its delivery across the UK. The Professional Development Course for external examiners shows that it is possible to design and facilitate a course that is rigorous, challenging and can be used across diverse disciplinary areas and institutions. It should provide a model for future initiatives to support assessment literacy and the maintenance of academic standards.

References

Bloxham, S. & Price, M. (2014). External examiners' understanding and use of academic standards. http://insight.cumbria.ac.uk/id/eprint/3954.

Booth, S., Beckett, B., Saunders, C., Freeman, M., Alexander, H., Oliver, R., Thompson, M., Fernandez, J. & Valore, R. (2015). *Peer Review of Assessment Networks: Sectorwide Options for Assuring and Calibrating Achievement Standards within and across Disciplines and Other Networks.* Office for Learning and Teaching, Australia Government.

Broad, B. (2003). *What We Really Value: Beyond Rubrics in Teaching and Assessing Writing.* University Press of Colorado.

Crisp, V. (2008). Exploring the nature of examiner thinking during the process of examination marking. *Cambridge Journal of Education*, 38(2), 247–264. https://doi.org/10.1080/03057640802063486.

HEFCE. (2015). *A Review of External Examining Arrangements across the UK Report to the UK Higher Education Funding Bodies by the Higher Education Academy.* Bristol: HEFCE.

Hunter, K. & Docherty, P. (2011). Reducing variation in the assessment of student writing. *Assessment & Evaluation in Higher Education*, 36(1), 109–124. https://doi.org/10.1080/02602930903215842.

Saunders, M.N. & Davis, S.M. (1998). The Use of Assessment Criteria to Ensure Consistency of Marking: Some Implications for Good Practice. *Quality Assurance in Higher Education*, 6(3), 162–171. https://doi.org/10.1108/09684889810220465.

Silver, H. (2006). External Examining: Aspects of induction and briefing 2004–6. www.advance-he.ac.uk/knowledge-hub/external-examining-aspects-induction-and-briefing-2004-6-silver-2006.

Watty, K., Freeman, M., Howieson, B., Hancock, P., O'Connell, B., De Lange, P. & Abraham, A. (2014). Social moderation, assessment and assuring standards for accounting graduates. *Assessment & Evaluation in Higher Education*, 39(4), 461–478. https://doi.org/10.1080/02602938.2013.848336.

Chapter 11

The institutional impact of the Professional Development Course for External Examiners

A case study

Amanda Pill

Introduction

Sector buy-in and long-term sustainability were key aims of the Degree Standards Project. An important feature of the Project was therefore to involve higher education providers directly by enabling their own staff to deliver the Professional Development Course for External Examiners in-house. In 2017, the University of Gloucestershire became an early adopter of the course, supporting some staff to train as facilitators and committing to rolling out the course to its own academic staff who were acting as external examiners for other institutions. Later on, the course was also delivered to external academics who act as the university's external examiners, and, finally, it was opened up to any other university staff, i.e. those from academic and professional services departments, who although not external examiners, had a professional interest in external examining. This chapter explores each of these models of delivery, outlining the experiences of the facilitators and the delegates. In addition, the chapter explores the positive impact that has resulted from the university's deep engagement with the Professional Development Course for External Examiners.

Institutional context

The University of Gloucestershire (UoG) is a small teaching intensive, but research-informed, post-1992 institution (i.e. an institution with a more vocational focus), located in the SouthWest of England. The university has around 11,500 students in total, approximately 7,600 of which are studying at undergraduate level (mainly first degrees with most undergraduates studying full-time). There are 517 staff on academic contracts (excluding part-time, hourly paid (PTHP)), with 168 of these colleagues on fractional contracts (excluding PTHP). There is therefore a certain expediency to delivering professional development to a small staff body but there are nevertheless challenges presented to maintain consistency in the delivery of standards across a high number of part-time colleagues.

As an institution, we have been keen to develop the assessment literacy of our staff, including staff understanding of academic standards. There are a number of

DOI: 10.4324/9781003379768-14

reasons for this. At UoG, and across UK higher education more generally, an increasingly high percentage of students declare a disability, particularly specific learning difficulties, such as dyslexia or dyspraxia. National Student Survey data over several years shows that students with specific learning difficulties express lower levels of satisfaction around assessment and feedback. To this end, the university is committed to providing a course assessment experience for all students that is rigorous but also transparent, fair, consistent and that provides helpful feedback/forward because we believe this creates conditions within which all students may flourish.

The provision of an excellent assessment experience also underpins the university's Education Strategy (2022–2027) as it is central to an outstanding education, has a positive impact on student wellbeing, and enables students to achieve their potential within and beyond their course. Additionally, achieving reasonable comparability of academic standards over time is important to assure the credibility, reliability and value of the qualifications awarded by the institution. The opportunity to become an early adopter of the Professional Development Course for External Examiners came as an institutional review of assessment was being planned. The review was intended to focus on securing significant developments to assessment practice and once the university became aware that the course offered a means of improving the assessment literacy and practice of external examiners and the university's own staff who support the university's assessment processes, becoming an early adopter of the course was the obvious next step.

Involvement in the Degree Standards Project: background and timeline

The initial decision to participate as an early adopter in the Professional Development Course for External Examiners (PDC) was taken by the university secretary and academic registrar, and was supported by senior colleagues in both academic development and quality assurance. Participation was driven by several factors, but primarily by a desire to address growing national concern regarding degree standards, and a recognition that professional development for staff and institutionally appointed external examiners is an important contributor to achieving comparability of standards over time and between institutions. The timing was also good because our involvement in the Project complemented perfectly a planned institutional review of assessment to address areas of weakness we perceived in academic standards (student performance outcomes) and quality standards (assessment input and process measures).

Developing the developers

Five members of staff attended the Develop the Developer training courses run by the Degree Standards Project team (see Chapter 10) that ran in January and March 2018. Two of these colleagues went on to successfully complete all the elements of training, including the assisted and observed runs of the course. In January 2020, a new Head of Learning and Teaching Innovation (HLTI), who was already trained, took up an appointment at the university. As two trained staff members are required to run the course, this increased our ability to offer the course in the short term.

The PDC remains one of the most outstanding professional development courses that the author has undertaken. She took the course herself (November 2017) and she was determined to complete the training required, to enable her to run the course at UoG. At that time, she was an experienced institutional lead for assessment, who was keen to learn more but did not expect the transformational experience that she received when she signed up for the Develop the Developer training. The quality of the materials, particularly the carefully selected background reading, much of it journal articles authored by members of the project team, the activities, the balance between discussions around course content on the one hand and the opportunity to practise how to teach each session on the other, and post-activity reflection was far better than anything she had experienced previously. The training was followed by a period of carefully observed practice, and the feedback received during the assisted and observed sessions was rigorous but always constructive. Throughout this period, participants of the training reflected upon their own developing practice and these reflections were used as a starting point for feedback discussions with our observer.

Looking back, it was really at this point, having completed the Develop the Developers training day, that the benefits of opening the course to a wider group of staff, beyond external examiners, was first considered. The author began to appreciate the value of the course as professional development for academic colleagues who held academic responsibility for a subject, a course, or a module, regardless of whether they were an external examiner. There were a multitude of benefits: unpicking the assumptions made about academic standards and the external examining scheme in UK higher education (Bloxham & Price 2015); the opportunity to unpack and specifically develop the different elements of assessment literacy (Medland 2015); the chance to revisit existing moderation activity and reconceptualise the nature and timing of the most valuable moderation practices (Bloxham, Hughes & Adie 2015); and by gathering a greater insight into the external examining role, gaining a clearer understanding of the role and responsibilities of those responsible for assessment internally.

A timeline of PDC development at University of Gloucestershire

Between November 2017 and June 2019 UoG initially hosted and then taught the PDC several times (see Table 11.1). Plans to run the course in spring 2020 were derailed due to the COVID-19 pandemic. The online version of the course was not designed to run institutionally and, therefore, it was only in the 2022–2023 academic year that the institution managed to get back on track, delivering the course once in each term.

Table 11.1 Timeline of PDC delivery at the University of Gloucestershire.

November 2017	First Advanced HE facilitated PDC delivered (22 completers)
January 2018	Three members of staff start the DtD process
March 2018	An additional two members of staff start the DtD process
April 2018	Assisted course takes place (15 completers)
June 2018	Observed course takes place (6 completers)
April 2019	First institutional course held (17 completers)
June 2019	Second institutional course held (17 completers)
Spring 2020	Planned institutional course cancelled due to COVID-19
2021/22	Intention to relaunch the PDC with delivery each term

Initially, the course was promoted to university staff holding a current external examiner appointment. However, demand from aspiring externals meant that course recruitment was widened, and across all the runs of the course to date, there has been a good balance of experienced and inexperienced external examiners in attendance.

The course is seen to benefit thinking around assessment and has supported work related to our three-year long review of assessment practices across the institution. In addition, senior staff recognised that professional development for staff and institutionally appointed external examiners is an important contributor to achieving comparability of standards between institutions.

Models of delivery of the PDC

UoG adopted three models of delivery, which it has termed the export, import and internal models. Each of these will now be explained in turn.

Export model

Information about every run of the course is circulated to UoG academic staff who are acting as external examiners for other institutions. Those who take up this opportunity are very positive about the experience and believe it will help them to fulfil their external examining duties more effectively. Early on, we noticed these colleagues were equally enthusiastic about the positive impact of the course on their assessment practice internally. This feedback was a key factor in our decision to explore the possibility of offering the course more widely internally, particularly with course leaders and others who have academic leadership roles relating to assessment.

Import model

External academics who act as the external examiners for UoG are invited to take the course in addition to the general external examiner induction meeting, which focuses on UoG operational issues. External examiner uptake of the PDC has been steady. These colleagues are surprised and often very pleased to have the opportunity to take the course at no charge. They are impressed by the quality of the content and its delivery. When asked what aspects of the PDC they have found most useful, responses have included:

- 'The opportunity to reflect critically on my own practice as an external examiner and an increased awareness of how bias can creep into the marking and moderation of student work.'
- 'A better understanding of standards at national and subject level.'

When asked what changes they were planning to implement into their practice because of the workshop, the following responses were received:

- 'Reflective practice [on assessment], increased social moderation, promotion of calibration practices.'
- 'I plan to have a more holistic approach to the way I manage my current external examining role, reflecting on all that I've learned I will try to utilise the calibration techniques both in my own teaching and in advice I give to others.'

When asked about further professional development needs, responses included:

- 'Though this was a fantastic course it felt very advanced for a relatively new external examiner or someone starting out. I would love to have an intermediate session where you can gain advice on how to manage an EE role from the initial stages. Otherwise, it was great thanks!'

Internal model

In this model, the course is delivered to any university staff with an interest, across both academic and professional departments. In line with all higher education institutions, UoG is proud to employ academic colleagues with a wide range of experience. Some have many years of experience as academics, while others have years of professional or industry experience but are more recent arrivals into academic life in higher education. All new academic colleagues on appointments of greater than 0.4 full time equivalence, who do not already hold an HE-specific teaching qualification or equivalent, are subject to probationary arrangements that include successful achievement of a higher education teaching qualification. This provides a solid introduction to assessment in higher education.

Upon arrival, many new colleagues find they are quickly dealing with complex marking and assessment issues, and some are soon involved in course development activity, in which assessment is always a central element. These experiences often lead colleagues to request further development and the PDC is a superb resource for providing a holistic view of assessment practice, with a focus on academic standards.

Professional services colleagues often have a deep understanding of a particular aspect of assessment e.g. providing student support for assessment, leading on key arrangements such as UoG's Course Assessment Scrutiny Process or the administration of exam boards. The opportunity to take the course enabled these colleagues to see how their work sits within the overall context and develop a more complete understanding of the entire assessment process. With support where necessary to gain wider experience of assessment, these colleagues can successfully complete the course. Feedback from these colleagues has been positive.

Feedback from internal participants who are not external examiners is overwhelmingly positive but suggests, for some colleagues at least, there may be a gap between the work on assessment completed as part of the higher education teaching qualification (completion of this award or the equivalent is required as part of probation) and the content of the PDC course. The former focuses upon the theoretical underpinnings of assessment, assessment design, support for assessment and marking, but offers less on academic standards and quality arrangements, e.g. moderation, calibration and the responsibilities of boards of examiners. This is something that the university should explore further and, if found to be a more widely held view, address. The feedback comments below illustrate personal views from participants and hint at the need for further work on assessment to take place in-house prior to commencing the PDC.

'The workshop gave me a much better understanding of the Academic Standards and Quality frameworks on a national level, which I have not experienced in previous training.'

'I thought the whole session was wonderful. I think at times some of the activities did feel a little rushed and it would have been nice to have more time for discussion and reflection.'

The impact of the PDC for the institution

Being an early adopter of the PDC means that UoG has had time to develop its institutional strategies, operational processes and development activities to align with the course and to progress a diversity of staff into and on from it. This section highlights six key development aspects.

Reshaping of the external examiner induction programme

Once we had completed the training to be able to run the PDC at UoG, we began, as noted above, to invite our current external examiners to take the course. When we started to do this, we had not realised what a good opportunity this presented to clarify expectations around the external examining role at UoG. The pre-sessional work, teaching, and practical activities that form the participant experience on the PDC facilitated many focused and fruitful conversations between UoG colleagues and external examiners. We anticipate that as more internal and external colleagues complete the PDC, the shared language and shared understanding of the external examining role will enable these rich conversations to continue as UoG external examiners work with internal staff. As external examiners have been appointed, they have been made aware of the opportunity to take the PDC and these colleagues often take the course at the start of their period of tenure. It has been a natural next step to adapt the general external examiner induction to reflect the language and key themes of the PDC. The general induction cannot cover the same ground as it is more operational in nature, but we have reviewed it to make sure nothing jars (i.e. key messages align) and the general induction provides a natural opportunity to promote the PDC.

Redesign of the university's external examiner report form

Another way in which the PDC led to tangible changes to practice within the university can be seen within the university's external examiner reporting template. For many years we had required a rather traditional report that was felt to cover our bases in relation to quality assurance. The PDC was a catalyst for our internal reflections on the role of the external examiner and among the many changes that resulted from these reflections was a realisation that our external examining reporting template mainly focused on two of the four external examiner roles (process checker and guardian of national standards). As a result, we reviewed our expectations of the role of the external examiner at UoG and used this to inform our requirements for their reports. Our revised external examiner reporting template explicitly reflects the four roles of the external examiner.

The opening section of the external examiner's report template clearly introduces the four elements of the external examiner's role (Box 11.1). The template contains four sections, each of which has a title and an introductory statement that is aligned with one of the four elements of the role.

PRACTICAL STRATEGY

Box 11.1 Opening section of University of Gloucestershire's external examiner report template

In their report, external examiners are requested to comment on the following aspects of the course, as appropriate. These aspects are informed by the UK Quality Code, particularly Advice and Guidance on External Expertise, and AdvanceHE Professional Development for External Examiners, particularly the role of external examiners as:

- Guardian of national standards: The academic standards and the achievements of students are comparable with those in other UK higher education institutions of which the external examiners have experience.

- Maintainer of academic standards: An institution is maintaining the threshold academic standards set for its awards in accordance with the frameworks for higher education qualifications and applicable subject benchmark statements.
- Process checker: The assessment process measures student achievement rigorously and fairly against the intended outcomes of the programme(s) and is conducted in line with the institution's policies and regulations.
- Critical friend: Good practice and innovation relating to learning, teaching and assessment observed by the external examiners; opportunities to enhance the quality of the learning opportunities provided to students.

We believe these changes have delivered significant improvements to the quality and general usefulness of the external examiner reports we receive because the new report template provides a timely reminder of the different roles and encourages external examiners to provide feedback across all four elements of the role. The new template makes it difficult to act purely in a single role, e.g. as a critical friend or as a process checker. The changes to the reporting template have facilitated balanced reporting that is more likely to identify strengths and drive improvements across the four elements of the role. It is also much easier for a Subject Leader, or a centrally based colleague with a responsibility around enhancement, to look across reports and identify priority areas for development in relation to the four focus areas. One example of this is the way the new approach has enabled us to be proactive in relation to any specific challenges around degree inflation.

External examiners feeling part of the university community

We have valued the opportunity to invite external examiners to work alongside our own UoG colleagues also taking the PDC. There is no doubt that this mixture of internal and external colleagues enriches the dialogue around assessment practices and provides a little extra time to develop professional relationships. The feedback we have received from external examiners taking the PDC at UoG is that they feel welcomed, and they leave at the end of the day feeling much more confident about their role. External examiners have also commented about their increased awareness of our institutional commitment to getting assessment right, in terms of doing everything we can to provide a positive assessment experience for students and staff; and how much we want to use the insights into our assessment practice that our external examiners provide as the basis for genuine continuous improvement.

We believe that a key outcome of running the PDC is a stronger, more meaningful relationship with our community of external examiners. Put simply, we believe the course makes a difference to the quality of their work as external examiners at UoG and that the institution, as well as the course teams individual external examiners work with, really benefits from this.

Academic colleagues convening social moderation events

A key outcome of running the PDC at UoG, and encouraging colleagues who may not be external examiners to participate, is the level of interest in social moderation the course has sparked internally. Our Head of Learning and Teaching Innovation, who became a member of the project team prior to joining UoG, has delivered a range of assessment and feedback workshops, following up on key concepts introduced within the PDC. This has included social moderation workshops in two subject communities involving large numbers of staff. The university's Sport and Exercise Science Subject Community has integrated social moderation into their marking process and disseminated this process to other staff at the university's annual Festival of Learning. The social moderation workshop for subject communities has proved so successful that it has become part of the central professional development offer, with more subject communities keen to take up this opportunity in the current and forthcoming academic years. Additionally, the need for more sharing of good practice has been identified and is being addressed as an outcome from the course.

Addressing specific course level assessment issues

We have a couple of examples where courses have achieved low National Students Survey (NSS) scores for assessment and feedback (alongside other related areas, e. g. organisation and management). In these circumstances, course teams asked to review their scores and identify improvement actions sometimes struggle to ascertain the core issues that have resulted in the low satisfaction scores. In these circumstances, we have run the PDC course for a specific course team to help colleagues to really get to grips with the issues, which enables them to identify and take ownership for the actions they need to take in order to improve. We have found using the assessment themes introduced within the PDC provides a strong conceptual framework that enables course teams to transform their knowledge of NSS scores and the student feedback comments into insight that can be used to identify the underlying issues and commit to actions that will address them.

Widening participation in the course

Over time, we have allowed a wider range of colleagues to join the course if they have a professional role that involves assessment, and they are ready and willing to engage fully and meet the requirements for joining the course. We can create opportunities for them to gain new assessment experiences that allow them to participate fully in the course. Colleagues from the student achievement team are a good example of a professional group that has benefitted from taking the course. Our former academic registrar also drew upon aspects of the course with specific groups (e.g. academic services managers), who may not be able to take the entire course, but who benefit from developing a greater understanding around key themes within the PDC (e.g. the multi-faceted role of the external examiner).

Conclusion

Looking back over our involvement in the PDC, we are delighted with the impact the course has had to date, but we are also aware there is more we could do. To finish, this chapter shares our thinking about next steps and offers some concluding thoughts.

We are considering two next steps:

1 At present, we strongly advise new course leaders to take the PDC and a number do. We are keen, however, to make the course a mandatory part of induction for all course leaders and believe this would bring considerable benefits in relation to improving professional practice and increasing consistency in the management of assessment.
2 We wish to provide further/earlier guidance for external examiners, to encourage them to consider the four elements of the external examining role (see Box 11.1) as they review assessment documentation and student work and meet with staff and students. In this way, they will be more able to use these lenses during their visits and discussions, including their verbal report to the exam board, rather than only adopting this perspective when they come to writing their report.

In terms of final thoughts, the PDC is a highly valuable course that has had significant impact on the student and staff experience of assessment at the university. External examiners who have taken the course have also been very impressed by the quality of the content and overall design. We remain delighted that we grasped the opportunity to commit key colleagues to undertaking the Develop the Developers training and to seeing their training through to completion so that we can continue to run the course at the university. As is to be expected, those originally trained are gradually moving on or retiring. Very shortly, we will be down to just one colleague, fully trained and able to lead the course. How future staff can be trained as funding ends for the national Degree Standards Project and how resources can be maintained in terms of currency and consistency across institutions remains a concern for us (as noted more widely in Chapter 12).

As two qualified staff members are required to run the course, we remain concerned about our staffing arrangements and our ability to sustain the delivery of the course. This issue is highlighted more broadly in the evaluation report discussed in Chapter 12. The availability of trained staff presents real challenges to the continuation of delivery, but in the short term, as noted in the introduction, we are focusing on the benefits to be gained from a reciprocal arrangement with other local universities in similar positions to ensure each run of the course continues to be taught by two trained colleagues. While there may be administrative and operational challenges involved, the opportunity to work closely with assessment experts from other institutions will bring many benefits for UoG colleagues. There are also benefits for our institutional PDC leaders who will gain experience of running the workshops with colleagues in other institutions. However, the success of our in-house delivery depends on the Develop the Developers training programme being available on a regular basis, to allow us and other higher education institutions to offer more staff the opportunity to be trained. At UoG, this would enable us to build capacity and create a resilient PDC leadership team, something we would dearly love to do.

To date, we still receive updated course materials online, we can also access the website, which contains valuable resources, and we continue to receive support from the central project team to organise each run of the course and to ensure successful completers are added to the AdvanceHE Register of External Examiners. This support is essential, but it comes at a cost. In principle, despite tight budgets, we would be willing to pay a reasonable fee to ensure this support continues. Removing it would present a significant risk to the continuation of the PDC at the university and we believe, over time, and without alternative initiatives being introduced, this would undermine the student and staff experience of assessment at the university.

Acknowledgement

We are indebted to Andrea Chalk, former Academic Registrar at UoG, without whom this chapter would not have been written. Andrea fully supported the university, becoming an early adopter of the Professional Course for External Examiners, and, prior to her departure, was one of the two colleagues who successfully completed the training to run the PDC.

References

Bloxham, S., Hughes, C. & Adie, L. (2015). What's the point of moderation? A discussion of the purposes achieved through contemporary moderation practices. *Assessment & Evaluation in Higher Education*, 41(4), 638–653. https://doi.org/10.1080/02602938.2015.1039932.

Bloxham, S. & Price, M. (2015). External examining: fit for purpose? *Studies in Higher Education*, 40(2), 195–211. https://doi.org/10.1080/03075079.2013.823931.

Medland, E. (2015). Examining the assessment literacy of external examiners, *London Review of Education*, 13(3), 21–33. https://doi.org/10.18546/LRE.13.3.04.

Chapter 12

Lessons learnt from the evaluation of the Degree Standards Project

Joanne Moore

Introduction

External examining is a distinctive feature of the model for quality assessment in UK Higher Education (HEFCE, 2016), and a central aspect of what Jarvis (2014, p. 160) categorised as the 'professional self-regulation' strand of quality assurance. The direct focus which external examining has on the quality of student work makes it a particularly useful tool. Strengthening of the external examiner system was referred to in the statement of intent for the revised operating model, as part of the UK quality assessment system (UK and Northern Ireland) (HEFCE, 2016). The Degree Standards Project (DSP) was a response to key criticisms of the UK external examining system regarding the multi-faceted nature of the examiner role, the importance of examiners having knowledge and understanding of assessment practice and the need for pre-assessment calibration due to the socially moderated nature of academic standards (see also Chapter 9). The Project put the focus of attention clearly on the underlying practices and assessment literacy skills of examiners (see Chapter 7), through the development, piloting and rolling-out of professional development for external examiners. Recognising that standards are socially constructed (Shay, 2008; Bloxham et al., 2011; Stowell et al., 2016), the DSP was also tasked to create or use existing mechanisms for calibration – defined as a 'process of peer review carried out by members of a disciplinary and/or professional community who discuss, review and compare student work in order to reach a shared understanding of the academic standard which such work seeks to meet' (AdvanceHE, 2018).

The long-term vision of the DSP was for a sector-wide sustainable and sector-led process of professional development for new and existing external examiners, which would enable staff to become more effective external examiners, and to test mechanisms for calibration in relation to academic standards, with a view to improvements in arrangements for the maintenance and comparability of degree standards across UK higher education. Key concepts underpinning the DSP, namely the importance of examiners' assessment literacy (Bloxham & Boyd, 2012) and the need for social moderation processes (Sadler, 2016), were relatively emergent topics in higher education, and as such subject to debate and ongoing refinement. The Project was designed to take account of the different quality assurance arrangements across the UK nations and sought to respect the responsibility of the degree awarding institutions for setting and maintaining standards. The approach needed to be feasible across a diverse sector. Moreover, the outputs needed to be credible to higher education stakeholders, and valid in terms of addressing the challenges around comparability of academic standards and the impact of external examiners on standards.

Chapters 9–11 discuss, in detail, the background, design and local impact of the DSP from 2016 to 2021. This chapter presents the findings of the DSP evaluation, focusing on conclusions about the feasibility, credibility and impact of the developments for external examiners provided through the Project. This chapter aims to investigate the outcomes for the understanding and practice of external examining, drawing upon perspectives from participants and institutional stakeholders. The chapter also discusses what has been learnt about how professional development for external examiners might best be approached in the UK context.

The importance of evaluation

Between 2016 and 2021 the Professional Development Course for External Examiners (PDC) was refined and adapted for different delivery modes which included regional blended courses (mainly face-to-face with some online activities), an online course, and an institutional roll-out model whereby staff members in adopter institutions were trained to deliver courses to their colleagues in-house (see Chapters 9 and 11 for further detail). From 2020, there was also remote delivery of courses due to the COVID-19 pandemic. Evaluation was important from the point of view of accountability to the funders to generate new knowledge on the effectiveness of professional development for external examiners and through identification of the models which would deliver professional education in an acceptable, effective, efficient and sustainable manner. Evaluation also served a formative function, drawing the attention of project leaders to the need for potential improvements. The evaluation sought to assess the evidence on the credibility, feasibility, reliability, validity, and impact of the PDC. Measures of success included the extent to which the PDC was taken up as part of continuing professional development (CPD) across sector providers, indicators of sector endorsement of the course, and evidence of impact in terms of learning and changes in understanding as a result and the contribution to greater comparability of degree standards.

Evaluation methodology

ARC Network and subsequently DEWR Ltd were commissioned to undertake external evaluation, starting in 2017. Aspects of process and impact evaluation were built into the DSP from the outset, and an evidence base was built-up over time. In agreement with the project team, the evaluators set out a model for the evaluation drawing on the Kirkpatrick approach (Kirkpatrick, 2006), which conceptualises professional development outcomes as a series of levels through which the professional development participants progress (satisfaction, learning, behaviour, and results/effects of behaviour) (Freeth et al., 2005). A key challenge when undertaking evaluation of the implications for practice of professional development is the difficulty in attributing professional development programmes outcomes to behavioural change – even for strongly built courses and in engaged learners. Additionally, there is the issue of showing a causal relationship between or among the levels in the Kirkpatrick approach (Tamkin et al., 2002; Haupt & Blignaut, 2007; Arthur et al., 2010; Tamkin et al., 2002). To address these issues, as far as possible, the evaluation used multiple measures and drew on multiple perspectives. The evaluation sought to capture both individual level and institutional/sector level benefits, and to take account of contextual factors, such as the levels of previous experience of external examiners and institutional types.

A mixed methods approach was adopted in order to be able to triangulate findings and explore the underlying processes involved in receiving and applying the learning. The key information sources, which informed the analysis, are discussed in turn within the following sub-sections.

Participant feedback questionnaires

Demographic and evaluative data were collected using pre-course questionnaires ($n = 2,579$) and post- course questionnaires ($n = 1,688$). The questionnaires were designed to track whether participants were sufficiently exposed to and engaged in the programme to learn and then apply the new knowledge. Likert scales were used to assess participants' satisfaction with some of the components, and to assess whether the professional development for external examiners achieved the desired short-term learning goals. The changes in the matched pre and post questionnaires were calculated for participants for whom there was both before and after data ($n = 852$).

In-depth semi-structured interviews

To further explore the implications of professional development for external examiners in practice, the research team conducted confidential one-on-one virtual interviews (by phone or online). Each interview lasted about 45–60 minutes. Respondents were a cross-section of professional development participants ($n = 158$), stakeholders and developers in institutions ($n = 27$), participants in calibration activities ($n = 27$), and other stakeholders ($n = 23$). The in-depth interviews with individual external examiners were used to shine a light on changes in examining behaviour. The research team summarised the qualitative data using a grounded theory approach (Bryant & Charmaz, 2007; Birks & Mills, 2015) and then categorised and analysed the recurring themes. Interview-based case studies were further developed with a sample of PDC participants. The qualitative interviews and case studies were used to evaluate the learning outcomes of professional development and subsequent changes in examining behaviour, in ways that extended beyond the results of the usual survey-based methods of evaluation. These supplementary methods allowed the evaluators to determine whether the professional development was affecting examiners in ways that were unanticipated and to provide novel insights into the processes underpinning changes in external examining practice. The evaluators also tried to collect experiential data, from participants who held external examiner posts, through the use of reflective logs between 2019 and 2020 (n = 20). Some informative examples were collected from these logs of examiners adapting their examining practice as a result of the professional development, although the resource limitations of the evaluation did not allow for large scale use of participant reflection data.

Institutional-level research

A series of institutional case studies (n = 11) were undertaken to investigate the inputs and emergent outcomes at institutional level and the implications of institutional context for the professional development programme. The cases were chosen to represent a range of provider profiles and different institutional types. Information was drawn from course monitoring and feedback data, and interviews with institutional PDC facilitators and other stakeholders involved in quality assurance (n = 23).

Yearly participant follow-up survey

Participants were followed up on an annual basis through an online survey administered with the help of the Degree Standards team. This was important to assess the number of professional development graduates who secured positions as external examiners and reported using the knowledge and learning in the role. The final follow-up survey in 2021 achieved 482 responses (13%) which is relatively high for surveys of this nature, and impressive considering that 40% of respondents had participated more than two years prior to the survey.

PRACTICAL STRATEGY

Box 12.1 Approach to the evaluation of the PDC

The evaluation of the PDC utilised a mixed-methods approach, which included:

- Collection of baseline data against learning outcomes and feedback as part of the PDC delivery
- Pre and post-course questionnaires

- One-to-one in-depth virtual interviews with course participants, institutional staff and participants of calibration events
- Detailed case studies of individual participants
- Reflective logs of course participants who were external examiners
- Institutional interview-based case studies
- Longitudinal follow-up to assess the learning and capture resulting changes in participants' behaviour
- Annual follow-up surveys

Strengths and limitations of the evaluation approach

The evaluation benefitted from a number of design features:

- The analysis was designed to respond to a cycle of quarterly and annual reporting to the funders. Data collection was embedded into the delivery, good relations were built up between the evaluators and the delivery team, and the data analysis was used formatively as well as summatively.
- The mixed methods approach was able to triangulate different types of data collected through quantitative and qualitative assessment tools developed by the evaluators and agreed with the Degree Standards team.
- Evaluation data was collected at different stages to allow for cumulative and longitudinal analysis. The evaluation included data from all the cohorts from 2016 up to and including the 2021 cohort in the analysis for the evaluation.
- Comparative analysis was undertaken to assess outcomes across different delivery modes.
- Consideration was given to both individual and institutional level outcomes.

There were some limitations to the evaluation. Respondents in the evaluation were self-selected, and therefore there was potential for response bias if participants in the evaluation group were more positively disposed. The outcomes of the professional development for external examiners were based on their own perceptions. The perceived benefits were measured at different points of time to show impacts across four levels (satisfaction, learning, behaviour, and results), but basing conclusions on the perceptions of the participants themselves was subjective, which affected the reliability of the results. The evaluation did not attempt to use objective instruments for measuring knowledge and understanding, such as improvements in assessment literacy (which in any case is a fluid and contested field). Neither did it collect objective data on how the learning was transferred into the external examining relationship. Observation of behaviours or drawing on perspectives of the programme teams that were being examined were not part of the brief. Another limitation was that the evaluation focused on participants in the project and was not able to assess views outside of those already engaged. Furthermore, the allocation of the evaluation resources was strongly skewed towards the initial phases of the Project which meant that although the evaluation could play a formative role, it limited the capacity to assess the longer-term impacts which accrued during the later stages of the Project.

Results and learning gained

Proof of concept

The development process underpinning the DSP activities was based on consultation and collaborative work with a range of sector representatives, first through getting buy-in at senior level, then through the hands-on development work with key stakeholders, including quality assurance professionals across a group of providers initially identified as 'early adopters', and working with subject-specialists. Careful piloting and refinement of the activities followed over the course of the Project (for further detail see Chapter 10). The pace and scale of the professional development activities was much faster and wider than the calibration strand activities, the former representing the main focus of the efforts in terms of resources and the wishes of the funders. The bottom-up development approach, and focus on institutional involvement, was designed to ensure acceptability to a sector that has traditionally resisted central direction. At the same time, it was important for the consistency and reliability of the provision that the content and mechanisms of professional development were agreed and controlled.

The DSP pilot was working in a contested field within a diverse sector of autonomous providers with differing national quality frameworks. Therefore, it was important to assess whether the developments for external examiners could be delivered and achieve the desired reach in practice. Monitoring of take-up, together with data collected at Level 1 (the reaction level) of the Kirkpatrick model, was useful to inform this question, specifically the feedback received about engagement in and satisfaction with the activities.

Figure 12.1 shows the evolution of professional development in 2016–2021 and the patterns in the activities over time. The challenges brought about by the COVID-19 pandemic made some shifts in delivery necessary. Due to social distancing measures, the face-to-face aspects of the blended delivery model were being undertaken remotely by the end of the funding period. However, the methods were sufficiently established to be able to translate relatively smoothly to remote delivery. Fluctuations in the patterns of take-up of professional development appeared to be most influenced by limitations of capacity within the delivery teams, which faced the challenge of driving forward multiple project strands and delivery methods simultaneously, including Develop the Developers (see Chapter 9). Overall, the numbers receiving professional development was impressive considering the Project was starting from a standing start. The fact that institutional courses represented the bulk of provision (see Figure 12.1) was testament to the effectiveness of the approach to develop institutional buy-in across the sector for professional development for external examiners.

Lessons learnt from the evaluation of the Degree Standards Project 153

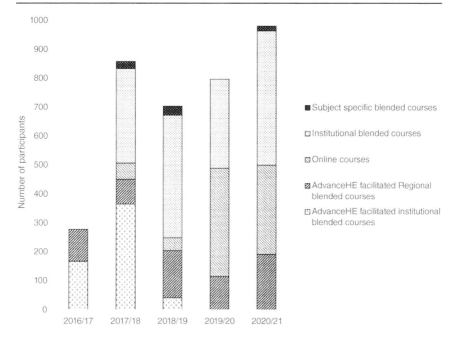

Figure 12.1 Numbers participating in professional development for external examiners by type of delivery and academic year.

A relatively wide range of individuals and institutions were engaged from across the higher education sector, and course completers represented varied institutional types as illustrated in Figure 12.2. The profile was underpinned by careful targeting and engagement of the institutional adopters by type and location. Most people consulted for the evaluation believed the PDC to be beneficial and relevant across a range of institutional settings and contexts. The online follow-up survey in July 2021 saw nine out of ten respondents agreeing or strongly agreeing that they would recommend the course to others. Respondents with no experience of external examining were slightly more likely to say they would recommend the PDC than those with experience. The grounding in the academic literature helped with credibility. Many participants said they had kept the course materials to hand as an ongoing reference source. Where negative views were expressed these tend to be coming from the perspective of cynicism regarding whether comparability of standards is practicably possible, differences in standards across institutional and course types being an inevitable consequence of a diverse HE sector.

Institutional roll-out of professional development

The size of institution and the emphasis placed on external examining appeared to be key factors in institutions' propensity to deliver the course. There was stronger engagement among larger post-92 institutions (i.e. more vocationally focused

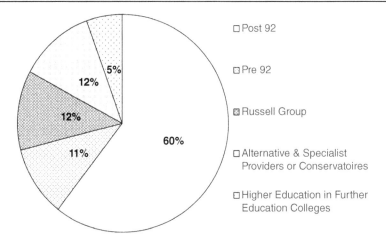

Figure 12.2 All PDC completers by institutional type.

former polytechnics), bound by the post-92 national agreement on contracts for academic staff, which encourages external examining and ways to demonstrate how staff members are engaging with developments in teaching and learning. The PDC potentially supported a range of different institutional objectives around assessment literacy or quality processes, which helped with 'selling' the course to senior staff in institutions. Institutions which were looking to strengthen their CPD offer appeared to be particularly strongly committed to the Project. In some institutions it took several years for the provision to get going and the support from senior leaders was important to kickstart institutional involvement in the Project and to keep it on the agenda over time. Much of the material was perceived as tricky even for experienced educational developers to facilitate. However, feedback indicated that facilitators became more comfortable with delivery over time. In general, there seemed to be demand in institutions, although there were limitations in terms of take-up, especially in small providers. Collaborative delivery arrangements, i.e. institutional developers offering delivery to examiners from outside their own institution or supporting delivery within other institutions, were starting to be seen from 2020. Such collaborations helped to share capacity to deliver and maximise the demand for places. Over three quarters of institutional colleagues who had delivered courses described the take-up as either 'good' or 'excellent'. Most people seemed highly motivated and keen to engage, regardless of the formal certification the course provided, although some participants said they were motivated by needing to demonstrate external examining credentials. Prospective examiners were looking for help to secure positions.

The case studies of adopter organisations strongly highlighted the risks that provider-led delivery posed to the vision of sector-wide professional development and the sustainability of the provision over time. The idiosyncrasies inherent in institutionally led delivery reflected the wide-ranging nature of the contexts and challenges. Workload issues, and changes in staff roles or turnover of staff, came out as the main threats to the ongoing sustainability of the course in the early adopter institutions. Continuing effort was required to refresh the pool of course facilitators due to staff turnover, with over half of adopter institutions needing to train more than two facilitators. An important outstanding question is whether institutional delivery would undermine the consistency and reliability of the course. In the longer term, the course developers felt that sustainability was linked to the continuation of centralised support for the materials and those who facilitate it. Most respondents wanted oversight of professional development for external examiners to remain on a supra-institutional basis, including the maintenance and development of the PDC course materials and the online learning platform.

Subject/discipline professional development and calibration

Most traditional external examiners in higher education operate within the boundaries of a subject discipline, and their practice is informed using practical skills and relevant subject knowledge. Overall, when thinking about the professional development delivered, most of the activities were 'generic' in the sense of not having a specific subject focus. However, having cross-subject groups did not seem to be a limitation in terms of the learning that participants took away. Participants with no external examining experience appeared to benefit most from enhanced understanding of the external examiner role and the nature of standards in the HE context.

The scale and reach of calibration activities for facilitating interaction at subject discipline level, remained relatively low compared to the large numbers going through the PDC. Three different 'models' of calibration were discerned: 'Stand-alone' calibration events (2017–2018); an 'integrated' PDC and calibration model (2018–2019); and a revised model (2020–2021) whereby participants who had completed the generic PDC were offered a separate remotely delivered subject-specific calibration event. Specific discipline-based individuals played a major role in taking forward the calibration events, in conjunction with AdvanceHE Associates/consultants. Existing regional networks and subject specialists with an interest in calibration were useful in instigating calibration. The main outcome was to highlight the variability between assessors in relation to marking. It seemed unlikely that participation in 'one-off' calibration activities would make much difference to practice or comparability of how standards were applied on the ground in institutions.

The PDC promoted the importance of calibration activities through including a focus on social moderation as a mechanism for ensuring comparability of standards. It stimulated a latent interest in calibrating, but there was no traction or clear direction of travel for it. Not everyone was convinced of the benefit. As well as issues to do with resourcing and lack of clear lead for cross-institutional calibration, one of the main barriers emerging from the research was the sheer scale of the task. Chapters 14 and 15 discuss the delivery and impacts of calibration activities in specific subject communities in detail. Further possibility also emerged from the pandemic in that virtual activities were tested and demonstrated how technology could potentially be used to mitigate the logistical and cost issues limiting the scope for face-to-face activities.

Learning from the PDC

Data were collected to assess the extent to which participants improved their knowledge and skills and changed their attitudes, representing Level 2 (learning) in the Kirkpatrick approach (Kirkpatrick, 2006). The contribution made to changes in individuals' knowledge about external examining, and underpinning aspects such as reference points for standards and knowledge of assessment were a prime consideration given the great responsibility that the UK quality system places on external examiners. Many of the existing external examiners, consulted at interview, also conceded to a 'novice' like status, despite being selected to be external examiners because of high professional status as perceived by their peers. Prior to the course, external examiners reported very little support or guidance on the knowledge and skills required for the job. Their judgements and actions traditionally appeared to be informed by 'learning by doing' rather than by a pertinent body of knowledge. While it was clear that many examiners felt they were already doing a good job, their role had developed as a skilled craft rather than an expert occupation. The evidence from the interviews reflected the conclusion of other researchers that guidelines and training from appointing institutions had traditionally been rather spasmodic and sketchy and had tended to focus on procedures (Bloxham, 2009).

Overall, the participants had increased their self-assessed knowledge and understanding as a result of the course. When comparing participants' pre- and post-course questionnaire scores against the formally stated PDC learning outcomes, the average scores for all outcomes rose (Table 12.1). The patterns did not suggest major differences for different types of delivery, but that the outcomes were greater for less experienced participants. A small minority rated themselves lower on the learning outcomes after the course. This may be due to the course bringing to light over-confidence or confusing some people. There was a sense that making explicit the challenges in the external examiner role could be off-putting; some participants indicated they would not be applying for external examining positions because of the complexities involved in the role. The results will now be discussed in more detail.

Learning about the external examiner role and academic standards

Some 84% of matched data respondents who had no or less than a year of external examining experience, recorded a positive change in their ability to explain the function of the external examiner role, compared to 64% of those with existing experience. Similar results applied to participants' self-reported ability to explain the nature of standards. Seven out of ten respondents indicated that it had improved (71% of those with no or little examining and 65% of experienced

Table 12.1 Perceived change in relation to the PDC learning outcomes based on pre- and post-course survey responses.

Learning outcome	Average rating pre-course	Average rating post-course	% who recorded a positive increase
Explain and discuss the nature and purpose of the external examiner role and its enhanced function in the new model for quality assessment in higher education	6.4	8.6	77%
Explain the nature of standards in the higher education context	6.7	8.4	70%
Draw on practical and scholarly knowledge of assessment as appropriate to the role	7.1	8.5	64%
Deal with the challenges to examiners representing the standards of their subject/discipline/professional community presented by the varied provenance and uniqueness of individuals' standards	5.9	8.5	82%
Explain the purpose and value of ongoing calibration activities in supporting the use of common 'discipline community' standards	6.5	8.5	66%

examiners), and well over half (60%) reported a change in their thinking on the academic standards in their subject/discipline area, with a further third (33%) reporting it had possibly changed. Around half (52%) identified a definite change in their views about the existence of shared academic standards in their discipline/subject professional area (and 34% possibly so), with those who took part in calibration and online activities being more likely to do so.

The survey results suggested the PDC had a considerable impact on participants' perceived ability to deal with the challenges to examiners presented by the varied provenance and uniqueness of individuals' standards. This aspect was rated particularly low on average in the pre-course questionnaire, so there was room for most improvement. Overall, eight out of ten (82%) recorded a positive increase in this aspect (85% of respondents with no experience of external examining or less than a year in post recorded an improvement, and 71% of experienced external examiners). However, perhaps a remaining difficulty that came out in the qualitative comments was associated with the challenges external examiners face in triangulating between external standards and reference points, the locally developed practices and institutional expectations, and their own personal standards and expectations.

Learning about assessment

The importance of knowledge and understanding of the assessment-related literature and research on marking and academic standards was strongly highlighted in the PDC, yet was generally implicit within descriptions of the external examiner role. On average, experienced external examiners rated their ability to draw on practical and scholarly knowledge of assessment only slightly higher following the course. Interviews with participants suggested that many saw the course as a useful refresher rather than offering new information. Matched respondents with no previous experience of external examining recorded a larger increase in how they rated their ability to draw on practical and scholarly knowledge of assessment (perhaps because these were more junior academics). Over half (53%) of follow-up survey respondents indicated that their attitudes towards different types of assessment had changed (and 33% possibly so). This differed by mode of delivery – proportionally more regional and online participants identified a definite change in their attitudes towards different types of assessment, and fewer participants in courses run in institutions.

Learning about reference points

Evidence was also sought to assess the extent to which the PDC was affecting understanding of the reference points underpinning professional judgement of the standards, i.e. national frameworks/benchmark statements and professional body standards. Just over half (51%) identified a greater awareness of the reference points for academic standards in their subject/discipline/professional area, and a further third (34%) said there had possibly been an increase in their awareness. Again, proportionally more online and regional course participants, compared to institutional course participants, indicated this and comments suggested that they had had exposure to a wider range of perspectives.

Impact on external examining practices

The follow-up surveys and interviews were designed to test whether the PDC led to changes in the practice of external examining. This is Level 3 (behaviour) of the Kirkpatrick model. While not all those consulted agreed or benefitted to the same degree, most identified some positive behavioural outcomes. Taken together, there were indications that the external examining role may be more effectively implemented as a result.

The qualitative comments suggested that PDC graduates were more mindful of academic standards and, in some cases, this played out in practice in terms of the degree of challenge or criticality that external examiners brought to the role. External examiners said that they felt more able to bring challenge in an appropriate way to programme teams and were able to appropriately balance being both 'critical' and 'friend'. There was the sense that examiners were not coming at the issue from the perspective of a deficit model. Indeed, most examiners perceived that they were already doing a good job, and participation in professional development seemed to have strengthened rather than changed judgements about the quality of students' work and how work should be viewed. Some interviewees spoke about a shift of focus away from processes and the minutia of student work/marking, and more towards a programme-wide approach. Encouragingly, participants said that the course had clarified what materials and insights they needed to access when they started an examining position. Such a finding is also evident in other studies with external examiners regarding the challenges of the role (Medland, 2015).

The primacy of relationships between external examiners and programme teams was foregrounded in comments which suggested that building more effective ongoing relationships with a programme team opened up potential for greater influence on quality enhancement. Most practitioners focused on informal influence through dialogue with the programme team rather than through the formal institutional structures of the external examiner report and examination board.

There was some evidence that changes in external examining practice were easier to implement from the start of a new examining position, rather than trying to adjust behaviours after a period of engagement. This echoes the findings of the review of external examining by UniversitiesUK, GuildHE and QAA (2010), which suggested that the degree of criticality could be affected by pre-existing ways of working with a programme team. Other limitations related to the time and resources that individual external examiners had to undertake the role (for example, time to scrutinise students' work). The low level of reward and recognition for external examiners was commented on frequently by interviewees, although many implied professional development for external examiners had raised perceptions of status. How the knowledge and learning was applied during the external examining process depended on the context and opportunities available to influence in practice. It was clear from the interviews that there were disparities with regard to the use of external examiners and their field of action, which need to be evaluated further if the influence of examiners on academic standards is to be fully understood.

Impact on participants' home institutions

A range of outcomes were found as course participants transferred what they had learnt back into their own academic practice in their home institution. Questions in the 2021 follow-up survey explored the implications for their own academic practice and dealings with external examiners on their courses internally. The responses suggested that such changes could be highly impactful, given they have direct control, unlike recommendations made in the role of external examiner which must be mediated through the institutional structures and processes for receiving and acting on external examiner feedback.

Most respondents (94%) in the post-course survey indicated that the course had given them ideas for changes within their home institution. It seemed to generate momentum for changes to institutional external examining practices (see Chapter 11) and affected the nature of the relationship between participants who were programme managers and the external examiners on their own courses. Participants commented that 'it's made me a more discerning receiver of external

Table 12.2 Outcomes of the PDC for development of internal academic practice within the institution.

Outcome	Results
Conversations among academic colleagues and institutional leaders about academic standards.	Three quarters (75%) said there had been changes in conversations among academic colleagues about academic standards, and 44% said that conversations with institutional leaders about academic standards had changed.
Attitudes towards assessment, marking and feedback.	Over half (53%) said the PDC had definitely changed their attitudes to assessment, and a third (33%) said it possibly had.
Feeling more confident that your judgements when marking work were consistent with others.	Eight out of ten (80%) said they felt more confident that their judgements when marking work are consistent with others (but only 75% of calibration activity participants said this).
Changes in how you worked with external examiners who examine your own provision.	Nearly two-thirds (65%) of respondents said there had been changes in how they work with external examiners who examine their own provision.

examining' and 'getting better value from the relationship' and noted various changes they had made when working with external examiners. The benefits of institutional courses in creating the conditions for discussion within teams of colleagues became clear from the interview data. Participants also commented that having senior staff involved in the PDC was of real benefit and more likely to lead to changes related to internal practices. The course also appeared to support innovations that were already taking place. Participants with an academic quality role spoke about changes to processes for appointing, inducting and working with external examiners, and systems for collecting and learning from external examiner reports. At the institutional level, maximising the role of the external examining system for the benefit of the institution was feeding through into engagement with the DSP. Some central quality assurance teams were attempting to improve the quality of the feedback from examiners and to tap into the richness of the informal conversations and learning that previously went on only at programme level. How institutions seek to maximise external examining relationships for the benefit of institutional practice is a crucial side of the equation which affects standards.

The PDC enhanced participants' understanding of the importance of calibration activity, and participants in subject specific calibration activities said that they had taken away learning that had been applied in their own discipline area. However, one of the main criticisms was that the DSP failed to provide a clear mechanism for it. The comments suggested that there might be appetite for cross-institutional calibration (see also Chapters 14 and 15) and that the calibration activities provided insights into practices in other institutions and networking, but individual academics were not in a position to put the work into setting up social moderation processes themselves. Lack of evidence on the effectiveness of social moderation processes as a mechanism for supporting comparability of academic standards was a further obstacle.

Long-term impact on external examining practices

The course appears to have had an impact on external examiners' practices over time. In the longitudinal follow-up survey (July 2021), three-quarters of respondents (75%) said their view of the external examining role had definitely changed, and 19% said their view had possibly changed. Interviewees who had taken part in the PDC before 2019 admitted that the details of the course were only sketchy, but there was a general sense that the key messages were retained over time. In addition, some respondents said that the course handbook was used as an ongoing reference source.

It was encouraging that the majority of respondents to the 2021 follow-up survey, who had gone on to do external examining, perceived that the PDC had made them more effective as an external examiner than they otherwise might have been (85%). Confidence in the role also stood out as a key component of effectiveness. 92% of respondents who had gone on to do external examining roles since the professional development agreed or strongly agree that they felt more confident in the role as an external examiner (60% strongly agreed). Comments highlighted that the course made experienced examiners feel validated in the role (e.g. one person said they had 'a firmer ground for engaging with the module team'). Not all respondents had changed their approach (or indeed saw the need to) but becoming more confident meant that participants were more likely to be pro-active in situations where this might be required. A fifth (22%) of respondents who had undertaken external examining said that academic standards (i.e. the quality of students' work) had improved on the course they were external examining, linked to improvements in practices in the assessment cycle or the strengthening of systems to assure academic standards. Other people tended to say that the standards were good in the first place. How exactly the knowledge and learning from the course was applied depended on the specific individual and institutional context for the external examining and the consequences of the COVID-19 pandemic, as in some cases there was less access to students work and less contact with the programme teams in 2020–2021.

Reasons for the effectiveness of the PDC

Feedback overall suggested that the approach taken to the PDC for external examiners was successful in stimulating new knowledge and understanding. The evaluation concluded that the reasons for this success was based on its credibility through the grounding in the academic literature and the alignment with other sector and institutional priorities. The rationale, philosophy and design of the course was strongly rooted in the experiential learning approach and peer learning. This was achieved by designing the professional development to include collective and collaborative learning activities. Reflection on real-life 'dilemmas' that examiners face stood out in comments from participants as a useful approach. This seemed to reveal to participants a new way of working by identifying and challenging individually constructed understandings that might otherwise limit practice. However, some participants, particularly prospective external examiners, were critical of the course and requested that the course team just 'tell them how to examine'.

The literature suggests that higher education professionals gain significant benefits from engaging in a critical, systematic reflection and examination of practice, especially when informed by scholarship (Evans et al., 2015). This was supported by comments from PDC participants, which suggested that the professional development had most meaningful impact where there was a process of professional critical reflection on values and practices, informed and developed with reference to the literature. One respondent said:

> [What stood out was] the opportunities for reflection and the support with the pre-prepared resources. I know a lot about internal and external standards and have vast experience of academic standards and quality work but I still learnt and gained new perspectives.

The DSP facilitated the development of communities of practice – in the sense of collaborative or collective learning processes – for both academic staff members and quality professionals. Kennedy (2005) categorised such communities of practice as 'transitional'. However, the evaluation highlighted the potential of such approaches to contribute to the transformation of local environments as well as the centrality of participatory and relational professional development. External examiner knowledge seemed to be developed through active reflection on experiential expertise, combined with discussion with peers. In qualitative feedback many people expressed demand for ongoing continuing professional development through collaborative and supportive peer group mechanisms, workshops, discussion forums and networking, aimed at active sharing and comparing of practices among colleagues with a range of perspectives.

PRACTICAL STRATEGY

Box 12.2 Effective design features of the PDC in the UK context

The evaluation showed that the PDC benefited from a number of design features:

- The professional development was grounded in the academic literature to support credibility and promote scholarship.
- The course included experiential and peer learning approaches involving peer discussion of real-life scenarios to facilitate peer learning and support engagement.

- The course was targeted at academics and quality professionals and both experienced and aspiring external examiners. This enabled the groups to draw on a range of perspectives, while also supporting the supply of new external examiners.
- The course included opportunities for critical reflection on participants' values and practices in order to deepen the learning, including for the most experienced external examiners.
- The PDC sought to align with institutional priorities for CPD within the adopter organisations to promote institutional buy-in.
- Collaborative opportunities within and between early adopter institutions helped to maximise the delivery and take-up of courses.

Conclusion

The evaluation of the PDC sought to understand how the developments for external examiners were received, and whether the interventions to improve knowledge and understanding could strengthen the role. The scale of the quality assurance task is immense and clearly the DSP alone will not assure the efficacy of external examining or the comparability of standards. Where the outcomes of the Project had been able to benefit examiners was in terms of:

- Addressing knowledge and skills gaps that affected the external examining system. Prior to taking part, external examiners reported very little support or guidance on the knowledge and skills required for the job.
- Highlighting the key elements of the role and its significance. This aspect was not only in relation to how external examiners approached the role but also in how programme teams received examiners (i.e. institutional practices on external examining).
- Promoting understanding of principles and theory of assessment practice. The PDC supported wider developments in the sector around assessment. While understanding of assessment should probably be part of good academic practice anyway, respondents seemed to value additional professional development in this respect due to the complexity of the issues involved. The professional development had the advantage of bringing together and facilitating active sharing and learning among colleagues with a range of perspectives.
- Highlighting the importance of the external examiners' contribution to safeguarding academic standards, engendering conversations on the nature of standards within institutions, and raising awareness of the reference points e.g. (subject benchmarks, national qualification framework) for academic standards.

Taken together these developments should help the external examining role, and this was seen in follow-up interviews and surveys with external examiners where a significant proportion identified changes in their practice and effectiveness on the ground. The PDC seemed to be beneficial for both existing external examiners, those who are aspiring and those at a distance from examining who are looking to improve their day-to-day assessment practice. Participation in professional development had promoted reflection on the nature of academic standards and the need to calibrate professional judgement along with the use of reference points for standards. Calibration was an area that most respondents said they had become more interested in. The scale of the task and logistical difficulties makes this an extremely tricky area to address effectively at a sector level without further significant resources and sustained commitment. Chapters 14 and 15, however, provide case studies in two different subject areas of how this was and might be delivered.

References

AdvanceHE. (2018). *Ensuring greater comparability of degree standards: the external examining project*. Presentation to AdvanceHE Teaching & Learning Conference 2018.

Arthur, W., Tubre, T.C., Paul, D.S. & Edens, P.S. (2010). Teaching effectiveness: The relationship between reaction and learning criteria. *Educational Psychology*, 23(3), 275–285. https://doi.org/10.1080/0144341032000060110.

Birks, M. & Mills, J. (2015). *Grounded Theory: A Practical Guide* (2nd edition). London: Sage.

Bloxham, S. (2009). Marking and moderation in the UK: false assumptions and wasted resources. *Assessment & Evaluation in Higher Education*, 34(2), 209–220. https://doi.org/10.1080/02602930801955978.

Bloxham, S., Boyd, P. & Orr, S. (2011). Mark my words: the role of assessment criteria in UK higher education grading practices. *Studies in Higher Education*, 36(6), 655–670. https://doi.org/10.1080/03075071003777716.

Bloxham, S. & Boyd, P. (2012). Accountability in grading student work: securing academic standards in a twenty-first century quality assurance context. *British Educational Research Journal*, 38(4), 615–634. https://doi.org/10.1080/01411926.2011.569007.

Bryant, A. & Charmaz, K. (2007). Grounded theory research: methods and practices. In A. Bryant & K. Charmaz (eds), *The Sage Handbook of Grounded Theory*, pp. 1–28. Thousand Oaks, CA: Sage.

Evans, C., Muijs, D. & Tomlinson, D. (2015). *Engaged Student Learning: High Impact Strategies to Enhance Student Achievement*. York: Higher Education Academy.

Haupt, G. & Blignaut, S. (2007). Uncovering learning outcomes: explicating obscurity in learning of aesthetics in design and technology education. *International Journal of Technology and Education*, 18(4), 361–374. http://dx.doi.org/10.1007/s10798-007-9029-1.

HEFCE. (2016). *Revised Operating Model for Quality Assessment*. Bristol: HEFCE.

Freeth, D., Hammick, M., Reeves, S., Koppel, I. & Barr, H. (2005). *Effective Interprofessional Education: Development, Delivery and Evaluation*. London: Blackwell.

Jarvis, D.S.L. (2014). Regulating higher education: Quality assurance and neo-liberal managerialism in higher education: a critical introduction. *Policy and Society*, 33(3), 155–166. http://dx.doi.org/10.1016/j.polsoc.2014.09.005.

Kennedy, A. (2005). Models of continuing professional development (CPD): a framework for analysis. *Journal of In-Service Education*, 21(2), 233–252. http://dx.doi.org/10.1080/13674580500200277.

Kirkpatrick, D.L. (2006). *Evaluating Training Programs: The Four Levels* (3rd ed.). San Francisco: Berrett-Koehler Publication.

Medland, E. (2015). Examining the assessment literacy of external examiners. *Review of Education*, 13(3), 21–33. https://doi.org/10.18546/LRE.13.3.04.

Sadler, D.R. (2016). Assuring academic achievement standards: from moderation to calibration. In V. Klenowski (ed.), *International Teacher Judgement Practices* (1st ed.). London: Routledge.

Shay, S. (2008). Researching assessment as social practice: implications for research methodology. *International Journal of Educational Research*, 47(3), 159–164. http://dx.doi.org/10.1016/j.ijer.2008.01.003.

Stowell, M., Falahee, M. & Woolf, H. (2016). Academic standards and regulatory frameworks: necessary compromises? *Assessment and Evaluation in Higher Education*, 41(4), 515–531. http://dx.doi.org/10.1080/02602938.2015.1028331.

Tamkin, P., Yarnall, J. & Kerrin, M. (2002). *Kirkpatrick and Beyond: A Review of Models of Training Evaluation*. Report no. 392. London: Institute for Employment Studies.

UniversitiesUK, GuildHE & QAA. (2010). *Review of External Examining Arrangements in the UK: A discussion paper*. Gloucester: The Quality Assurance Agency for Higher Education.

Part IIIB

Practical strategies for reducing variation in academic standards

Chapter 13

Working with rubrics

Codification plus dialogue in developing shared academic standards

Pete Boyd and Jennifer Hill

Introduction

A rubric is a framework using clear and concise language to support assessment of student work and includes three key features: evaluative criteria; quality definitions for those criteria at different grades; and an agreed approach to scoring (Brookhart, 2013). Rubrics have been widely adopted in higher education since the 1960s and they are used today in the UK, United States, Europe and Australasia, among other regions (Chan & Ho, 2019). A rubric is used to inform summative grading by tutors, but is also provided to students to inform their formative self-assessment during completion of assignments. A body of research, mainly consisting of relatively small-scale studies, indicates that rubrics are popular with academic staff and students (Bell et al., 2013; Brookhart, 2018; Chan & Ho, 2019) and may improve learning (Reddy & Andrade, 2010; Panadero & Jonsson, 2013; Jonsson, 2014). However, their use as a tool to maintain standards has been contested: rubrics should not be viewed as a magic bullet that will resolve assessment issues and lead to more consistency when marking student work (Bloxham et al., 2016a).

This chapter will argue that carefully designing and implementing rubrics, in ways that promote dialogue between academic staff and across staff and students, is essential if they are to contribute positively to shared academic standards. Only then will rubrics support more accurate and consistent tutor grading and student self-assessment, thus contributing towards the development of sustainable assessment practices (Boud, 2000). The chapter will therefore offer practical advice for designing rubrics and for complementing their use with dialogue.

PRACTICAL STRATEGY

Box 13.1 Key questions to ask about your use of rubrics

As you read this chapter, and consider the design and use of rubrics, we ask you to keep the following practical questions in mind:

1   (How) does the design and use of rubrics in your programme help to provoke dialogue between tutors and students around learning, quality and academic standards in the subject discipline?
2   How does the design and use of rubrics in your programme help to avoid student dependence on overly detailed assessment guidance and develop students as self-assessors and self-regulated learners, with a capacity for evaluative judgement within the subject discipline?

Why rubrics are used

In higher education, students are commonly assessed against learning outcomes in their taught units as part of constructive alignment (Biggs, 2003). In an aligned learning environment, it should be clear to students where they are going (learning outcomes), how they will get there (learning activities) and what is expected of them (marking rubrics). As such, rubrics present explicit expectations for students and other stakeholders about assessment standards and provide a means for tutors to assure their students can meet the learning outcomes (Brookhart, 2013; Chan & Ho, 2019). This is the concept of 'transparency' in assessment, where grading decisions (judgments of quality) are made against published written criteria (Price, 2005; Sadler, 2009a), aimed at facilitating more consistent and fairer evaluation. Rubrics thereby provide a basis for assessment and grading by the academic tutor and self-assessment by the student. Rubrics are an important element in quality assurance in evaluating both student learning and educational curricula.

Benefits of using rubrics

Rubrics are popular with both academics and students. Price & Rust (1999) found greater consistency in marking and easier moderation for staff through use of assessment grids across a university business department. Use of rubrics can clarify expectations, reduce anxiety, aid the feedback process, and improve self-efficacy and self-regulation in learners (Reddy & Andrade, 2010; Jonsson, 2014; Panadero & Jonsson, 2013, 2020). Student learning was improved significantly through the provision of explicit guidance to first year business students and this improvement was shown to last over time and be transferable within similar contexts (Rust et al., 2003). More recently, Bell et al. (2013) examined first-year accounting students' perceptions of the usefulness of marking guides, grade descriptors and annotated exemplars and discovered the vast majority of students found them useful in providing direction and establishing an idea of standards. Likewise, in a study of nursing students and staff in Hong Kong (Chan & Ho, 2019), respondents generally believed that good rubrics established more objective and standardised evaluation methods, offered students clear direction about what they were expected to include in their work, and demonstrated the nature of high-quality work.

Another strand of research focuses on students co-constructing rubrics. In this process, students and tutors work together to express the criteria against which work will be judged (Fraile et al., 2017; Kilgour et al., 2020). Co-construction of criteria, devised and developed through consensus and discussion, has been shown to broaden students' understanding of rubrics and assessment, and allow them to make their own meanings about work, promoting more personalised understanding and meta-cognition (Bearman & Ajjawi, 2018).

Challenges of using rubrics

Rubrics have also been shown to suffer from a number of important limitations. Codifications, even when written carefully, are incapable of defining academic standards consistently because their terms tend to be interpreted differently by individual students and academics (O'Donovan et al., 2004; Sadler, 2007, 2014). When rubrics are used to grade student work, it is assumed that breaking down the judgment into more manageable parts may increase objectivity. However, markers bring with them different provenance of their standards. They may hold different values, beliefs and specialist knowledge, meaning they will read and apply standards in different ways, drawing upon tacit knowledge learnt 'on the job' (O'Donovan et al., 2008; Bloxham & Boyd, 2012; Bloxham et al., 2016a; Bloxham et al., 2016b; Liao, 2024). From this perspective, written criteria/standards only take on meaning once tutors apply their personal and contextual 'standards framework' to them.

Using rubrics does not acknowledge the complexity of judging open-ended university assignments and can distort grading decisions by simplifying the complex nature of work (Sadler, 2009b). In these instances, tutors can struggle to articulate their expectations for the work, and students find it difficult to understand their tutors' expectations (O'Donovan et al., 2004; Bloxham et al., 2016a). The concise language used in rubrics to keep them manageable in length (often one or two sides of A4 paper), such as 'generally good critical analysis', cannot communicate exact meaning and requires interpretation. As such, standards are socially constructed, developing meaning in use through involvement in academic communities (Bloxham & Boyd, 2012) and the ways of thinking and practising of a discipline (McCune & Hounsell, 2005). This can lead to differential interpretation of standards among academic staff and students (Zhao, 2023), and to students experiencing tensions between their own and their tutors' expectations of standards (Andrade & Du, 2007).

It is important to consider critically the metaphor of 'transparency' with respect to how tutors may think about, develop, and work with rubrics (Bearman & Ajjawi, 2018). There is a risk that heightened transparency may lead to increasingly detailed and reductionist assessment guidance (O'Donovan et al., 2004; Sadler, 2007), such that students may become dependent on that guidance, instrumentally seeking to use rubrics to pass assessment rather than learn (Torrance, 2007). Bell et al. (2013), for example, distinguished differential first year student responses in engaging with marking guides. Almost half the surveyed students, having engaged with a rubric, continued to seek out precise guidance by asking tutors for more detailed information. By contrast, learning through development as a self-assessor is strongly linked to the concept of students developing evaluative judgment of the quality of multiple pieces of work (Tai et al., 2018), and is crucial for sustainable assessment (Boud, 2000). The capacity to self-assess does not develop through the use of criteria and rubrics alone, but through their active use in repeatedly making judgements about pieces of work of varying quality, such as through peer review activities (Nicol et al., 2014).

The design and use of rubrics can counteract students' development as self-regulated and autonomous learners (Zimmerman, 2002). There is a danger that creating rubrics results in tightly defined and 'measurable' outcomes that might constrain creative responses by students to assessment tasks. It is therefore important that assessment criteria and rubrics are not used in ways that encourage conformity and compliance to deliver what is expected (Torrance, 2007) and counteract independence and liberatory learning (Freire, 1998). It has been argued that, through using rubrics, power relations are insidiously shaping student subjectivities as the expert assessor rewards learners for 'engaging' and (re)presenting themselves according to the neoliberal and hegemonic norms of higher education (Torrance, 2017). The assessment criteria contained in rubrics can thereby legitimise and delegitimise particular forms of knowledge, and can be said to facilitate managerialism and governance (Carson, 2019; McKnight et al., 2020).

Despite these criticisms, rubrics have become commonplace in higher education and many academics are obliged to use them. In this chapter, we argue that both staff and students can benefit from them if they are used in ways that enable the development of evaluative judgement and generate dialogue. We therefore provide some advice on how effective rubrics can be created and on different ways in which dialogue can be incorporated into their use.

Characteristics of an effective rubric

When judging a piece of work, tutors and students tend to juggle at least four different sources of information (Sadler, 2010):

- *Learning outcomes*: published for a course or module and shared with students.
- *Written assessment guidance*: Briefing for the students as text and often supplemented with oral sessions.
- *Assessment criteria*: published and strongly reflecting the learning outcomes, often including one or more task or format related criteria.
- *Level and grade descriptors*: provided by the institution, describing requirements for each grade at different levels of study (sometimes also called 'standards').

An advantage of using a rubric for an assignment is that it brings together assessment criteria with descriptions of different levels of performance. The assessment criteria within a rubric should reflect the learning outcomes of the module or

Table 13.1 A basic outline for an analytical rubric for use in the UK, with no weighting of assessment criteria.

Module Summative Assessment Rubric	F (FAIL) 0–39%	D (PASS) 40–49%	C 50–59%	B 60–69%	A 70–79%	AA (OUTSTANDING) 80–100%
Assessment criterion 1	Quality descriptor	Quality descriptor	Quality descriptor	Quality descriptor	Quality descriptor	Quality descriptor
Assessment criterion 2	Quality descriptor	Quality descriptor	Quality descriptor	Quality descriptor	Quality descriptor	Quality descriptor
Assessment criterion 3	Quality descriptor	Quality descriptor	Quality descriptor	Quality descriptor	Quality descriptor	Quality descriptor
Assessment criterion 4	Quality descriptor	Quality descriptor	Quality descriptor	Quality descriptor	Quality descriptor	Quality descriptor
Assessment criterion 5	Quality descriptor	Quality descriptor	Quality descriptor	Quality descriptor	Quality descriptor	Quality descriptor
Assessment criterion 6	Quality descriptor	Quality descriptor	Quality descriptor	Quality descriptor	Quality descriptor	Quality descriptor

course. A typical outline framework for the rubrics used most widely across higher education is shown in Table 13.1, and consists of Popham's (1997) three essential features: assessment criteria; quality definitions for those criteria at particular levels, which the student should demonstrate to achieve different grades against each criterion; and an agreed approach to scoring (e.g. analytic versus holistic). A final possible element of a rubric is a 'weighting' of the assessment criteria.

Analytic versus holistic judgement

The rubric shown in Table 13.1 implies that the tutor will use a criterion-based approach to assessment and grade the work 'analytically' by judging its quality against each of the assessment criteria separately (Brookhart, 2018). However, there is no weighting given to the different criteria. This leaves reasonable scope for holistic evaluative judgment by the tutor on the overall grade to be awarded, reflecting the level reached across each of the criteria. It allows the tutor to treat the criteria as thresholds, so to gain an overall pass the student must at least demonstrate all of the quality definitions in the 'pass grade' column. Beyond gaining a pass, the student may be graded very highly on some criteria and not on others.

In a 'think-aloud' study of English university tutors grading student work, Bloxham et al. (2011) found tutors made holistic rather than analytical judgements, with many only referring to the criteria as a check on their overall decision. It can be argued that this kind of analytical grading, which limits itself to the pre-ordained criteria, cannot take into account the many nuances of expert judging

(Sadler, 2009b). Criteria often merge in assessors' minds or interact with each other and this 'fuller' process of judgement might generate a 'truer' representation of the quality of work. Equally, a student might take an innovative and even original stance in completing the assessment task. If that approach demonstrates excellence within the subject discipline then the tutor may face a dilemma; do they award excellence or in effect punish the student for not complying with the expected response to the task?

Weighting of assessment criteria

It is quite common for tutors who are using rubrics to add weightings to each of the criteria. A percentage figure of the overall grade marks would be added to each criterion in Table 13.1. For example, criterion one might be 10%, criterion two 10%, criterion three 30%, criterion four 30%, criterion five 10% and criterion six 10%. Adding weightings to a rubric is contested. It can be viewed as increasing the transparency and making the grading more consistent. There is a danger, however, that it is a techno-rational solution to what is a sociocultural problem (see Chapter 3 for a more in-depth discussion). A 'simplistic combination rule' cannot capture the complex ways in which criteria are actually being used by an expert judge (Sadler, 2009b). It seems more 'transparent', and even 'scientific' and objectively 'mathematical' to use the weightings, but their use may not allow sufficient flexibility for holistic judgment or merely distort the process of making such an evaluative judgment. Some programme leaders reach a compromise by avoiding applying percentage weightings to criteria, instead allowing the teaching team to add a note as part of the rubric which might signal to students, for example, that: 'learning outcome 4 is considered to be particularly significant in the overall judgment of this task'.

Creating effective rubrics

It is helpful to consider six steps in creating an effective rubric, and these are summarised in Box 13.2.

PRACTICAL STRATEGY

Box 13.2 Six steps in creating an effective rubric

Step 1: Checking your starting point

- You are likely to need one rubric per assessment type within your module (e.g. essay, laboratory report, presentation).
- Do your assessment criteria capture the module learning outcomes and the assessment task format? Are they sufficiently clear to support action, but also creative interpretation, by the students?

Step 2: Confirm your approach to scoring

- Do any of your assessment criteria represent 'red lines', i.e. a threshold that must be passed? For example, in Nursing, 'failure to ensure patient safety' might be considered as an overall fail, no matter the standards in other learning outcomes.
- Is there a criterion that is fundamental, which carries more weight within an overall judgment? You might point this out to students as a footnote to your rubric.
- Do you allocate a percentage weighting to your criteria, even though this might be pseudo-scientific? Programme or institutional policy might require or prevent this.

Step 3: Identify the relevant grade descriptor (if available)

- Do you have an institutional 'grade descriptor' for the level of your chosen module? If not, then you need to capture the progression of a grade descriptor within your rubric.
- In England, grade descriptors are provided at different academic levels, i.e. years one, two and three of undergraduate study, or Masters' level.

Step 4: Completing the 'pass' grade column

- Set up a blank rubric template (and insert grade labels from your institutional policy, if there is one).
- Write clear and concise 'quality descriptors' for a 'pass' grade against each criterion.

Step 5: Completing the top-grade column

- Now work on the top-grade column, imagining what you might expect from the highest performing students at this academic level (informed by your institutional grade descriptor, if there is one).

Step 6: Completing, reviewing and monitoring your rubric

- Complete the quality definitions for each criterion and grade. Avoid describing levels using terms such as 'excellent – good – moderate – weak'. Instead, describe the different qualities of each level.

Continually review and monitor your rubric, considering the appropriateness of the criteria and language.

In developing and refining rubrics, tutors will benefit from considering exemplars within their own subject discipline or field, so that the knowledge and ways of knowing content is familiar. Here, an example is provided of a first-year undergraduate module from an Education Studies degree programme in the UK. The example includes learning outcomes and assessment criteria (Table 13.2). The

Table 13.2 Exemplar module assessment instructions, including learning outcomes and assessment criteria.

Exemplar module: Education studies year one undergraduate
'Introduction to application of theory in education'
Learning outcomes:
On successful completion of the module, you should be able to:

1 Position contemporary issues within a broad overview of the development of education in the UK.
2 Describe the basics of identity theory and how this is linked to educational opportunities.
3 Apply sociological concepts of field and different forms of capital to educational experiences and cultural reproduction.
4 Articulate a basic understanding of social justice and its links to education.

Summative assessment task:
Individual essay (2,500 words): How do some of your own experiences in school relate to history, identity formation, cultural reproduction and social justice?

---

crucial first step in creating a full rubric is then shown in Table 13.3 with threshold 'pass' quality descriptors completed. As the teaching team develop the complete rubric, this initial column of threshold quality descriptors is likely to be further revised. In this exemplar module, the first four assessment criteria in the rubric capture the four module learning outcomes. Two additional assessment criteria are included in the rubric to capture requirements of the essay assessment format.

Developing shared academic standards using rubrics plus dialogue

In terms of increasing the understanding of assessment standards for students and staff, rubrics are useful but not sufficient in themselves. It is important to consider rubrics as elements of communication and to consider how, in practice, with effective design and use, they can be part of a social process to drive learning. Research shows that to make meaning of rubrics, tutors and students need to use them to judge and debate exemplars or draft writing and to develop a shared understanding of academic standards (Rust et al., 2003, 2005; Bloxham & Boyd, 2007, 2012; Bearman & Ajjawi, 2018). Ideally, dialogue will achieve transfer of knowledge, both explicit and tacit, in the form of agreeing the standard of a piece of student work. To this end, Zhao (2023) argues for a process-oriented dialogic approach to use of rubrics with students, informing them about what they need to improve in future. This also applies to dialogue between members of university staff.

The learning power of dialogue is explained in social constructivist learning theory (Vygotsky, 1978), which argues that social interaction plays a crucial role in developing higher mental functions. However, it is important to note that dialogue involves knowledge power negotiations, especially when it involves university

Table 13.3 The crucial first step of completing the 'pass' column for an education studies module rubric.

Assessment criteria	F 35–49	D (pass) 40–49	C 50–59	B 60–69	A 70–79	AA 80–100
Your chosen educational issue is positioned within an historical perspective		Links current and past practice and policy				
You explain clearly how the identity formation of learners is related to your chosen issue		Connects identity formation to the issue				
You apply concepts of field and different forms of capital to analysis of some of your experiences of school		Analysis includes application of field and capital				
*You define social justice and build an argument about how it relates to your chosen issue and experiences		A basic definition and connection to the issue				
You present complex educational issues in clear plain English, while making effective use of relevant technical terms		Explains complex ideas in plain English				
You support your argument by citing and evaluating selected, relevant academic texts using a consistent citation and referencing style		Selects relevant texts and uses consistent citation style				

*Note: This criterion carries considerable weight in this assessment.

tutors working with each other and with students. Power relations and differentials have a considerable impact on the ways in which teaching teams interact with each other. Marking teams, in particular of large modules, can comprise both experienced and novice markers, the module leader as well as colleagues who may be more peripherally involved in the module, academics who have more and less expertise in the specific area that is assessed, academics on permanent contracts alongside those in temporary positions or on casual contracts, and postgraduate students employed as markers. This generates a complex web of power relations that needs to be carefully negotiated.

When working with students, a tutor might position themselves as 'all knowing' and adopt a teaching strategy of 'telling' but, in fact, students can use their power by ignoring much of what the teacher tells them. Alternatively, students might push power towards their tutors by becoming dependent on the expert and thus not developing as self-regulated learners. It is helpful to think of power as distributed evenly within the field and everyone negotiating through dialogue within that field. Northedge picks up this idea, based in a sociocultural 'academic literacies' perspective (Lillis & Scott, 2007):

> Students need practice at participating both vicariously, as listeners and readers, and generatively, as speakers and writers, so that they can develop identities as members of the knowledge community and move from peripheral forums to more active, competent engagement with the community's central debates.
>
> (Northedge, 2003, p. 31)

In contemplating the design and use of rubrics, it is useful to consider how to generate genuine dialogue. You might continually negotiate rules for dialogue and coach colleagues and students in their contributions, for example to listen, to seek clarification, to challenge ideas and to offer alternatives. You might consider how you present the rubric as a contested and partial indicator of the problem of judging academic standards related to complex higher education assignment responses. A rubric arguably should be considered as a material object whose agency and voice forms part of the 'entanglement' (Barad, 2007) of student learning through assessment.

Using rubrics effectively

As outlined above, written criteria and rubrics are interpreted differently by individuals (see Chapter 3). Therefore, the practical application and debate of a rubric, in a low-stakes dialogic activity with good levels of trust between participants, is helpful in developing a shared understanding of academic standards. The rounded, holistic judgment of the quality of a piece of student work, influenced by criteria but also involving tacit knowledge and reflective awareness, is referred to as 'evaluative judgment' (Tai et al., 2018). Both tutors and students need to develop evaluative judgment and they might achieve this by assessing student work against the rubric and then debating their decision on grading with others. These types of activities are helpful in developing a shared understanding of standards and have the potential to lead to more consistency in marking. There is some overlap here with the idea of social moderation and calibration that is explored further in Chapter 8.

Using rubrics with tutors

Rubrics do not have to be created by one individual only. In fact, if they are created collaboratively, e.g. by members of a given teaching team, the discussion which takes place to achieve agreement on criteria and level descriptors helps develop a shared understanding and generates ownership of the rubric by all (prospective) markers. Such a discussion could be initiated by brainstorming criteria for an assessed task or by marking one or two exemplar assignments from the past without criteria and then identifying the characteristics that influenced markers' judgements about their quality. Alternatively, an existing rubric or an initial draft by the module leader could be used as a starting point and then amended in discussion. Considering a rubric in conjunction with exemplars, i.e. actual pieces of student work, is strongly recommended.

In addition to collaboratively crafting rubrics, it is useful to engage teaching teams in developing a shared understanding of the quality descriptors of rubrics and how these relate to the levels of performance at which these quality attributes are enacted in student work. As such, module or programme leaders can organise a social moderation exercise for their teams, following a dialogic process of peer review where the programme team mark and then discuss exemplars of student work against the rubric. The basic 'rules' for moderation dialogue include: an agreement to seek consensus; confidentiality beyond the group present; and contributions to discussion that either offer an idea or, in response to someone else's idea, build on the idea or diplomatically challenge it. The facilitator should introduce and reinforce these rules during the discussion as well as inviting quieter colleagues to contribute at appropriate moments. The process is similar to that of cross-institutional calibration (see Chapters 8, 14 and 15), but carried out internally only within a specific teaching team at one university.

Working with the teaching team, discussions should focus on how the rubric will be used within an agreed approach to grading student work and could be extended to include decisions upon a framework or template for written tutor feedback to students. Tutors might decide to refer explicitly to the rubric in written comments, or to include a copy of the rubric with particular quality descriptors highlighted to indicate to the student what level they were judged to have reached for each of the criteria. Remember, the more the rubric can become a jointly owned object, the more influence it will have on teacher grading behaviours.

Using rubrics with students

While this book focuses on the notion of academic standards that academic staff hold, it is useful to briefly consider how rubrics can help students to better understand what quality looks like in their discipline. A review of research studies in higher education from 2005 to 2017 (Brookhart, 2018) found that only 56% reported using rubrics with students. This is problematic as research findings also indicate that rubrics have the potential to influence student learning positively (Jonsson & Svingby, 2007; Panadero & Jonsson, 2013). Positive outcomes of rubrics can be strengthened by inviting students to 'work with' them to make meaning with respect to holistic, dynamic and highly tacit concepts that are poorly captured in writing (Bearman & Ajjawi, 2018, 2021). Tightly defined concrete terms such as 'include at least three relevant citations' support transparency of assessment criteria but tend to close down student autonomy. By contrast, terms such as 'present a coherent argument' are open-ended but are perhaps too vague to be of much help to students. Brookhart (2018) refers to 'true descriptive rubrics' and argues that clear and substantive criteria (for example: 'states a compelling thesis') are essential for an effective rubric. It is not easy to find this balance between concrete suggestions for student action while inviting creative responses in a language that is comprehensible to students.

During the delivery of a module teachers might therefore run student workshops using their rubric to judge exemplars of assignments and then facilitate debate about academic standards, allowing students to contribute their own thinking and practice towards the development of high-quality work (Rust et al., 2003; O'Donovan et al., 2004; Panadero & Jonsson, 2013). These workshops would broadly follow the format:

- Students pre-read three pieces of exemplar student work, which may be extracts and are similar to the module assessment task.
- Students work in small groups to debate the strengths and weaknesses of each exemplar and the grade to be awarded, seeking consensus.
- Mini-presentations are made by each group and the tutor collates students' judgments.
- The tutor models and coaches to promote dialogue and negotiation for consensus.
- The tutor may either reveal the 'actual' tutor grade and feedback or leave it more open.
- The plenary of the workshop includes key points on assessment literacy, including how to use the rubric as well as its limitations.

(Carless & Chan, 2017)

Alternatively, or in addition, teachers might plan for student peer review of draft work using the rubric, as part of a taught session or online activity (Nicol et al., 2014). Students need to understand that it is the judgment and giving of feedback to their peer that is the key learning activity and that by applying the rubric in this practical task they will gain a deeper understanding of academic standards.

Teachers might require students to use the rubric to self-assess their draft coursework prior to a tutorial and be prepared to discuss the strengths and weaknesses against the rubric with their tutor. Additionally, teachers might work together with their students to co-create rubrics, helping them to express the quality of work using their own language and to internalise the descriptors of the rubric (Fraile et al., 2017).

CRITICAL PERSPECTIVE

Box 13.3 Key points on rubrics

In considering the research on rubrics, key points to note are:

1. A majority of students and many tutors across numerous studies think rubrics are useful, but their use has also been contested.
2. Rubrics are effective for instructional leverage as well as a guide to grading; if designed and used wisely, they can support student learning.
3. Language use in rubrics is a critical issue and is culturally situated, so this is a key challenge in writing and using rubrics. Rubrics will be interpreted differently by individual staff and students, and they cannot explicitly articulate the standards of complex, open-ended assessment tasks.
4. Rubrics on their own do not increase consistency when grading student work. Their use needs to be complemented with training based on dialogue and the principles of social moderation.
5. It is important to consider how rubrics, with effective design and use, can be part of a social process to drive student learning.
6. Rubrics should be designed in a way that allows students to make their own meanings about work in relation to standards, rather than offering reductionist guidance.
7. Further research is needed on rubrics and their impact on staff understanding of academic standards and the development of self-regulated learners.

Leading change in practice with rubrics

Demonstrating a rigorous approach to assessment, grading and the award of degrees is a key strategic ambition for universities. While we celebrate student successes, we also need to defend academic standards. Introducing and refining well designed rubrics is a useful and explicit step and, if it is backed up by practical and dialogic work by tutors and students working with exemplars, then it can become one potential advance in establishing shared academic standards at module and programme level.

Introducing rubrics via top-down managerial imposition is likely to meet considerable resistance from some tutors, leading to limited impact and even unintended consequences. Developing and implementing rubrics requires a teaching team to debate the academic standards of exemplars of student work. This activity requires good levels of trust between academics and a workplace learning culture in which managers allocate time to it, actively include all members of staff who are involved in assessing student work regardless of their position, and welcome critical thinking and challenge to current ways of working and policy.

The development and dialogic implementation of rubrics lends itself to a distributed leadership approach, where all stakeholders contribute to collective leadership in different ways and at different times during a change project. A distributed leadership approach requires managers to build social identity with academics in the teaching team and, through that identification and group formation, achieve sharing of power and ultimately control of resources (Turner, 2005; Haslam et al., 2020). Desirable change is most likely achieved through collaboration, which means that positive development is contingent and contextualised (Knight & Trowler, 2000). A professional enquiry approach to developing rubrics would be helpful here and involve module and programme teaching teams analysing sources of data that are likely to include: the current rubrics; tutor written feedback; student grades; a sample of student work; student perspectives; tutor perspectives; and external examiner perspectives. Framing the academic development project as a collaborative inquiry aligns with a distributed leadership approach and is likely to lead to effective implementation and embedding of rubrics with maximum fidelity and impact on student learning.

Conclusion

Engaging in dialogue in designing, using and reviewing rubrics in relation to exemplar student work is a powerful approach to overcome the criticisms of rubrics and to build a learning community with shared academic standards across teaching teams and student cohorts. Making evaluative judgments about the quality of work within the subject discipline is a core academic practice. Students can be viewed as 'legitimate peripheral participants' learning to make judgments about the quality of their work and gaining full membership of the community of practice alongside academics who are established members (Wenger, 1998).

Universities should consider a strategic leadership focus on academic standards, rather than the current emphasis on quality of processes in teaching, learning and assessment. This strategic approach, adopting an academic literacies approach and using rubrics as one element, will help institutions to foreground academic challenge and high expectations for all students, deliver fairness in assessment and grading, and secure social justice for a diversity of students as key elements of their student experience.

References

Andrade, H. & Du, Y. (2007). Student responses to criteria-referenced self-assessment. *Assessment & Evaluation in Higher Education*, 32(2), 159–181. https://doi.org/10.1080/02602930600801928.

Barad, K. (2007). *Meeting the Universe Half-Way: Quantum Physics and the Entanglement of Matter and Meaning.* Durham: Duke University Press. https://doi.org/10.2307/j.ctv12101zq.

Bearman, M. & Ajjawi, R. (2018). From "seeing through" to "seeing with": assessment criteria and the myths of transparency. *Frontiers in Education*, 3, article 96, 1–8. https://doi.org/10.3389/feduc.2018.00096.

Bearman, M. & Ajjawi, R. (2021). Can a rubric do more than be transparent? Invitation as a new metaphor for assessment criteria. *Studies in Higher Education*, 46(2), 359–368. https://doi.org/10.1080/03075079.2019.1637842.

Bell, A., Mladenovic, R. & Price, M. (2013). Student perceptions of the usefulness of marking guides, grade descriptors and annotated exemplars. *Assessment and Evaluation in Higher Education*, 38(7), 769–788. https://doi.org/10.1080/02602938.2012.714738.

Biggs, J. (2003). Constructing learning by aligning teaching: constructive alignment. In Teaching for quality learning at university. 2nd ed., 11–33. Buckingham: The Society for Research into Higher Education & Open University Press.

Bloxham, S. & Boyd, P. (2007). *Developing Effective Assessment in Higher Education: a practical guide*. London: Mc Graw Hill / Open University Press.

Bloxham, S. & Boyd, P. (2012). Accountability in grading student work: securing academic standards in a twenty-first century quality assurance context. *British Educational Research Journal*, 38(4), 615–634. https://doi.org/10.1080/01411926.2011.569007.

Bloxham, S., Boyd, P. & Orr, S. (2011). Mark my words: the role of assessment criteria in UK higher education grading practices. *Studies in Higher Education*, 36(6), 655–670. https://doi.org/10.1080/03075071003777716.

Bloxham, S., den-Outer, B., Hudson, J. & Price, M. (2016a). Let's stop the pretence of consistent marking: exploring the multiple limitations of assessment criteria. *Assessment & Evaluation in Higher Education*, 41(3), 466–481. https://doi.org/10.1080/02602938.2015.1024607.

Bloxham, S., Hughes, C. & Adie, L. (2016b). What's the point of moderation? A discussion of the purposes achieved through contemporary moderation practices. *Assessment and Evaluation in Higher Education*, 41(4), 638–653. https://doi.org/10.1080/02602938.2015.1039932.

Boud, D. (2000). Sustainable assessment: rethinking assessment for the learning society. *Studies in Continuing Education*, 22(2), 151–167. https://doi.org/10.1080/713695728.

Brookhart, S.M. (2013). *How to Create and Use Rubrics for Formative Assessment and Grading*. Alexandria, VA: ASCD.

Brookhart, S.M. (2018). Appropriate criteria: key to effective rubrics. *Frontiers in Education*, 3, article 22, 1–12. https://doi.org/10.3389/feduc.2018.00022.

Carless, D. & Chan, K.K.H. (2017). Managing dialogic use of exemplars. *Assessment & Evaluation in Higher Education*, 42(6), 930–941. https://doi.org/10.1080/02602938.2016.1211246.

Carson, J.T. (2019). Blueprints of distress? Why quality assurance frameworks and disciplinary education cannot sustain a 21st-century education. *Teaching in Higher Education*, 24(8), 1014–1023. https://doi.org/10.1080/13562517.2019.1602762.

Chan, Z. & Ho, S. (2019). Good and bad practices in rubrics: the perspectives of students and educators. *Assessment & Evaluation in Higher Education*, 44(4), 533–545. https://doi.org/10.1080/02602938.2018.1522528.

Fraile, J., Panadero, E. & Pardo, R. (2017). Co-creating rubrics: the effects on self-regulated learning, self-efficacy and performance of establishing assessment criteria with students. *Studies in Educational Evaluation*, 53, 69–76. https://doi.org/10.1016/j.stueduc.2017.03.003.

Freire, P. (1998). *Pedagogy of Freedom: Ethics, Democracy and Civic Courage*. Lanham, MD: Rowman and Littlefield.

Haslam, S.A., Reicher, S.D. & Platow, M.J. (2020). *The New Psychology of Leadership: Identity, Influence and Power*. Second edition. New York: Psychology Press.

Jonsson, A. (2014). Rubrics as a way of providing transparency in assessment. *Assessment & Evaluation in Higher Education*, 39(7), 840–852. https://doi.org/10.1080/02602938.2013.875117.

Jonsson, A. & Svingby, G. (2007). The use of scoring rubrics: reliability, validity, and educational consequences. *Educational Research Review*, 2(2), 130–144. https://doi.org/10.1016/j.edurev.2007.05.002.

Kilgour, P., Northcote, M., Williams, A. & Kilgour, A. (2020). A plan for the co-construction and collaborative use of rubrics for student learning. *Assessment & Evaluation in Higher Education*, 45(1), 140–153. https://doi.org/10.1080/02602938.2019.1614523.

Knight, P.T. & Trowler, P.R. (2000). Department-level cultures and the improvement of learning and teaching. *Studies in Higher Education*, 25(1), 69–83. https://doi.org/10.1080/030750700116028.

Liao, L. (2024). Dancing with explicit criteria or marginalizing them: the complexity of grading student work and the reconstruction of the meaning of criterion-referenced assessment. *Teaching in Higher Education*, 29(5), 1181–1196. https://doi.org/10.1080/13562517.2022.2119076.

Lillis, T. & Scott, M. (2007). Defining academic literacies research: issues of epistemology, ideology and strategy. *Journal of Applied Linguistics*, 4(1), 5–32. https://doi.org/10.1558/japl.v4i1.5.

McCune, V. & Hounsell, D. (2005). The development of students' ways of thinking and practising in three final-year biology courses. *Higher Education*, 49, 255–289. https://doi.org/10.1007/s10734-004-6666-0.

McKnight, L., Bennett, S. & Webster, S. (2020). Quality and tyranny: competing discourses around a compulsory rubric. *Assessment & Evaluation in Higher Education*, 45(8), 1192–1204. https://doi.org/10.1080/02602938.2020.1730764.

Nicol, D., Thomson, A. & Breslin, C. (2014). Rethinking feedback practices in higher education: a peer review perspective. *Assessment & Evaluation in Higher Education*, 39(1), 102–122. https://doi.org/10.1080/02602938.2013.795518.

Northedge, A. (2003). Enabling participation in academic discourse. *Teaching in Higher Education*, 8(2), 169–180. https://doi.org/10.1080/1356251032000052429.

O'Donovan, B., Price, M. & Rust, C. (2004). Know what I mean? Enhancing student understanding of assessment standards and criteria. *Teaching in Higher Education*, 9(3), 325–335. https://doi.org/10.1080/1356251042000216642.

O'Donovan, B., Price, M. & Rust, C. (2008). Developing student understanding of assessment standards: A nested hierarchy of approaches. *Teaching in Higher Education*, 13(2), 205–217. https://doi.org/10.1080/13562510801923344.

Panadero, E. & Jonsson, A. (2013). The use of scoring rubrics for formative assessment purposes revisited: a review. *Educational Research Review*, 9, 129–144. https://doi.org/10.1016/j.edurev.2013.01.002.

Panadero, E. & Jonsson, A. (2020). A critical review of the arguments against the use of rubrics. *Educational Research Review* 30, 100329. https://doi.org/10.1016/j.edurev.2020.100329.

Popham, W.J. (1997). What's wrong – and what's right – with rubrics. *Educational Leadership*, 55(2), 72–75.

Price, M. (2005). Assessment standards: the role of communities of practice and the scholarship of assessment. *Assessment & Evaluation in Higher Education*, 30(3), 215–230. https://doi.org/10.1080/02602930500063793.

Price, M. & Rust, C. (1999). The experience of introducing a common criteria assessment grid across an academic department. *Quality in Higher Education*, 5(2), 133–144. https://doi.org/10.1080/1353832990050204.

Reddy, Y.M. & Andrade, H. (2010). A review of rubric use in higher education. *Assessment & Evaluation in Higher Education*, 35(4), 435–448. https://doi.org/10.1080/02602930902862859.

Rust, C., Price, M. & O'Donovan, B. (2003). Improving students' learning by developing their understanding of assessment criteria and processes. *Assessment & Evaluation in Higher Education*, 28(2), 147–164. https://doi.org/10.1080/02602930301671.

Rust, C., O'Donovan, B. & Price, M. (2005). A social constructivist assessment process model: how the research literature shows us this could be best practice. *Assessment & Evaluation in Higher Education*, 30(3), 231-240. https://doi.org/10.1080/02602930500063819.

Sadler, D.R. (2007). Perils in the meticulous specification of goals and assessment criteria. *Assessment in Education: Principles, Policy & Practice*, 14(3), 387–392. https://doi.org/10.1080/09695940701592097.

Sadler, D.R. (2009a). Grade integrity and the representation of academic achievement. *Studies in Higher Education*, 34(7), 807–826. https://doi.org/10.1080/03075070802706553.

Sadler, D.R. (2009b). Indeterminancy in the use of preset criteria for assessment and grading. *Assessment and Evaluation in Higher Education*, 34(2), 159–179. https://doi.org/10.1080/02602930801956059.

Sadler, D.R. (2010). Beyond feedback: developing student capability in complex appraisal. *Assessment & Evaluation in Higher Education*, 35(5), 535–550. https://doi.org/10.1080/02602930903541015.

Sadler, D.R. (2014). The futility of attempting to codify academic achievement standards. *Higher Education*, 67, 273–288. https://doi.org/10.1007/s10734-013-9649-1.

Tai, J., Ajjawi, R., Boud, D., Dawson, P. & Panadero, E. (2018). Developing evaluative judgement: enabling students to make decisions about the quality of work. *Higher Education*, 76, 467–481. https://doi.org/10.1007/s10734-017-0220-3.

Torrance, H. (2007). Assessment *as* learning? How the use of explicit learning objectives, assessment criteria and feedback in post-secondary education and training can come to dominate learning. *Assessment in Education: Principles, Policy & Practice*, 14(3), 281–294. https://doi.org/10.1080/09695940701591867.

Torrance, H. (2017). Blaming the victim: assessment, examinations, and the responsibilisation of students and teachers in neo-liberal governance. *Discourse: Studies in the Cultural Politics of Education*, 38(1), 83–96. https://doi.org/10.1080/01596306.2015.1104854.

Turner, J.C. (2005). Explaining the nature of power: a three-process theory. *European Journal of Social Psychology*, 35(1), 1–22. https://doi.org/10.1002/ejsp.244.

Vygotsky, L.S. (1978). *Mind in Society*. Cambridge, MA: Harvard University Press.

Wenger, E. (1998). *Communities of Practice: Learning, meaning, and identity*. Cambridge: Cambridge University Press.

Zhao, H. (2024). Promoting accessibility of assessment criteria: shifting from a product- to a process- and future-oriented approach. *Teaching in Higher Education*, 29(5), 1283–1301. https://doi.org/10.1080/13562517.2022.2129964.

Zimmerman, B.J. (2002). Becoming a self-regulated learner: an overview. *Theory into Practice*, 41(2), 64–70. https://doi.org/10.1207/s15430421tip4102_2.

Chapter 14

The need for calibration in the disciplines
A case study from sport and exercise science
Ian Sadler and Matthew A. Timmis

Introduction

This chapter will focus upon sport and exercise science as a specific case in order to examine the critical role that the discipline plays within calibration. Firstly, it will provide an insight into the aspects of the discipline that have implications for academic standards and calibration. Secondly, it will outline an approach to calibration that has been trialled as part of the UK Degree Standards Project and consider the consequences that this may have for calibration in sport science and beyond. The aim is to provide an insight of calibration for someone in the same or a different discipline and to outline the practicalities, considerations and potential outcomes/benefits of undertaking calibration in a specific discipline.

Within the degree of sport and exercise science, three distinct sub-disciplines exist:

- biomechanics;
- (exercise) physiology; and
- (sport and exercise) psychology.

Biomechanics is understood as the analysis of human movement; investigating how and why the body moves in the manner that it does (BASES, 2023a). Physiology explores how the body responds to exercise and training; investigating the responses and adaptations to muscular activity. Aspects of nutrition and diet also comprise this sub-discipline (BASES, 2023b). Psychology contains two distinct areas. Sport psychology helps athletes to improve performance, be more consistent, and improve the quality of experience of participation in sport. Exercise psychology helps people to become more active, more often. Here, the goal is not performance, but health and wellbeing (BASES, 2023c).

Disciplinary characteristics in sport and exercise science

Sport is one of the largest areas of academic interest across the UK and, because of this popularity, considerable differences in the emphasis in content and approach to learning have arisen across the subject (QAA, 2019). In addition to the variation

DOI: 10.4324/9781003379768-18

driven by the breadth of provision in this subject area, sport and exercise science has its own idiosyncrasies and characteristics that shape what it is to study or practise in the area. Within sport and exercise science, the sub-disciplines (i.e. exercise physiology, biomechanics, sport and exercise psychology) themselves can be considered quite different. Although, based on the Biglan (1973) categorisation, it could be argued that they are all hard-applied disciplines, in reality it is far more nuanced than this. The inter-disciplinary nature of sport and exercise science itself, along with the softer sides of the discipline within psychology, coaching and athlete support, means that there is overlap, complexity and ambiguity in definition. These disciplinary cultures have implications for assessment culture and variability (Ylonen et al., 2018). Within this section, it will be argued that these disciplinary characteristics are apparent within the academics making judgments about the work (*people*), the disciplinary points of reference that help to guide judgements (*tools*) and the type of assessments that students are required to do in the discipline (*tasks*). These three sources of variation (people, tools and tasks), outlined in Chapter 10, are critical inter-related factors, which impact upon academic standards in higher education. Finally, this section will recognise how higher education institution themselves, based upon their entry profile, can be a source of variation (*institutional*).

People as a source of variation in sport and exercise science

The academics making judgements about student work are likely to all be from a broadly similar sport science related background, but the sub-discipline within the subject area, and the standards within each, tend to play a significant role. Based upon how the discipline is structured, both from an academic and professional point of view, the sub-divisions between the disciplines are exacerbated. The division between people based on sub-discipline is commonplace in higher education due to how programmes are designed and structured, often into sub-disciplinary modules and module teams. Also, in the professional body, the British Association for Sport and Exercise Sciences (BASES), activities such as annual conferences, special interest groups and accreditation are based on the sub-disciplines. Therefore, although from the same broad subject community of sport and exercise science, many of the teaching and assessment conversations, which help to shape the academic standards of an individual, tend to happen in separate sub-discipline groupings. Although across a wider range of disciplines and based on marks as opposed to standards, in a case study from a single university, Ylonen et al. (2018) demonstrated variability of mark profiles across disciplines and suggested that this is likely to be a consequence of different assessment cultures. Hence, there are likely to be differences in the academic standards of people based upon their sub-disciplinary backgrounds.

Tools relevant to sport and exercise science

The UK Framework for Higher Education Qualifications (FHEQ) provides the generic points of reference in higher education. Additionally, it is important to be aware of discipline-specific tools that can be used to inform the judgements made about the academic standards of undergraduate and postgraduate performance. Although the limitations of these tools has been outlined in Chapter 10, some of them can help to reduce variability in judgements of standards. However, quite often the link between these points of reference and the academic standards that reside within the student work is tenuous to say the least. The tools in sport and exercise science are no different in that they are relatively implicit in the assessment and marking of student work. Therefore, the extent to which these guide the standards of individuals is likely to be variable and inform the judgements of just a few.

As with other subjects, there are Quality Assurance Agency (QAA) benchmark statements that describe the nature of study and the academic standards expected of UK graduates in specific subject areas. For sport science, the relevant subject benchmark statements are within the broader 'events, hospitality, leisure, sport and tourism' document (QAA, 2019). The 'subject specific benchmark standards' for sport science relate to human response to sport and exercise (6.17), performance of sport and its enhancement, monitoring and analysis (6.18) and the health-related and disease management aspects of exercise and physical activity (6.19). These benchmark statements are written as learning outcomes and therefore can help to guide the development of the curriculum content but are relatively detached in terms of the academic standards of specific pieces of assessed work.

A more specific influence upon standards of sport and exercise science is the UK professional body (BASES), the key mission of which is to support the professional development of practitioners. The point of reference within the professional body that is most closely related to undergraduate programmes is a set of criteria that has been introduced, in 2005, as part of the BASES Undergraduate Endorsement Scheme (BUES). In order for an undergraduate degree to be eligible for endorsement it is required to develop specific scientific knowledge and applied technical skills across the three sub-disciplines, which are considered essential to enter into the profession. Currently, there are 75 sport related degrees across 48 higher education institutions with BUES accreditation (BASES, 2023d). Generally, in a similar way to the benchmark statement, these criteria for knowledge and skills on a sport and exercise science programme are used to support the design of teaching, learning and assessment on programmes. However, these tend not to guide the academic standards of student work or even the development of assessment criteria or grade descriptors for specific assessment tasks.

In other words, the level of connect between the tools in the form of outcome statements (FHEQ, Subject Benchmark, BUES criteria) and assessment criteria (grade descriptors, marking rubrics), and the academic standards (judgement made about a performance), is extremely fuzzy. These reference points also represent multiple layers of descriptors or criteria about what a student should be able to do and therefore the assessment should demonstrate their ability to meet the criteria. These layers go from broad sector level, national subject level, institutional level, module and then assessment task level (Figure 14.1). When each of the descriptors within the different layers is taken in turn and unpicked in relation to academic

Framework for Higher Education Qualifications
FHEQ Level 4 Outcomes

Student who have demonstrated:
- knowledge of the underlying concepts and principles associated with their area(s) of study, and an ability to evaluate and interpret these within the context of that area of study
- an ability to present, evaluate and interpret qualitative and quantitative data, in order to develop lines of argument and make sound judgements in accordance with basic theories and concepts of their subject

Students will be able to:
- communicate the results of their study/work accurately and reliably, and with structured and coherent argument

Subject Benchmark Statement
Sport Courses– human response to sport and exercise

Understand and explain human responses to sport and exercise, including being able to:
i. make effective use of knowledge and understanding of the disciplines underpinning human structure and function
ii. critically appraise and evaluate the effects of sport and exercise intervention on the participant
iii. demonstrate the skills required to monitor and evaluate human responses to sport, exercise and/or rehabilitation
iv. critically appreciate the relationship between sport and exercise activity and intervention in a variety of participant groups.

BASES Undergraduate Endorsement Scheme criteria
Scientific Knowledge: Physiology

Be able to demonstrate an understanding of the key bodies of knowledge relevant to Sport & Exercise Sciences (Physiology): Structure and function of the human body; Energy systems & metabolic cost

Technical Skills: Development & Application – Physiology

Be able to demonstrate the development and application of relevant scientific and practical techniques relevant to Sport & Exercise Sciences (Physiology): Cardiovascular function; Respiratory function; Submaximal and maximal exercise tests

University Grade descriptors
Level 4 written work: Exceptional Pass- 90-100

- Exceptional knowledge of the underlying concepts and principles associated with the subject.
- Offers an exhaustive exploration of the literature and evidence base.
- The material covered is accurate and relevant. The argument is highly sophisticated.
- There are no spelling errors.
- Grammar and punctuation appear to be accurate and consistent.
- It facilitates the reader's engagement with, and understanding of, the work.
- No errors in the use of the specified referencing system.
- Well-presented and organised in an appropriate academic style.

Learning Outcomes
Level 4 – Exercise Physiology module

- Describe the basic structure and function of key physiological systems and metabolic processes
- Describe how physiological systems and metabolic processes respond to feeding/acute exercise

Criteria for the Specific Assessment Task
Level 4 – Exercise Physiology Scientific Laboratory Report: A comparison of aerobic capacity in males and females

- Ability to accurately describe and present methodological information in an appropriate scientific format
- Ability to present clear and concise results of analysed data using written sections, figures and tables
- Ability to compare the findings to those of previous research and demonstrate an understanding of the physiological mechanisms that help to explain the results

Figure 14.1 Relevant descriptors for a Level 4 Exercise Physiology Laboratory Report to show the multi-layered nature of reference points and criteria that guide academic standards and marking judgements (using the example of one particular university course, module and assessment task).

standards it is highly complex and often problematic. For example, what does the ability to evaluate and interpret underlying concepts and principles in the area of study (FHEQ Level 4) look like when it is done well, satisfactorily or unsatisfactorily? Similarly, what does comparing the findings to those of previous research and demonstrate an understanding of the physiological mechanisms that help to explain the results (Level 4 Exercise Physiology Report specific assessment criterion) look like at different levels of performance? Therefore, the level of connect, the multi-layered nature, and problems with translation into judgements, mean these tools to guide academic standards are by no means without their problems.

Tasks specific to sport and exercise science

Another consideration in terms of sources of variability in academic standards is the assessment tasks that students complete and about which academics make judgements. Hounsell and McCune (2005) introduced the idea of 'ways of thinking and practising' (WTPs) within the subject as a way of referring to outcomes in terms of subject-specific knowledge and skills from the study of a discipline. The assessment tasks need to be reflective of the WTPs and therefore the discipline plays a significant role in terms of the task design. This can be observed in the different types of assessments in different disciplines. Neumann (2001) reported that the hard disciplines tend to use exams and tests, while soft disciplines rely more on essays, both of which assess different types of outcomes. In applied fields the focus is upon 'real world' and professional problems (Neumann et al., 2002). Jessop and Maleckar (2016) also found similar variations in assessment tasks across humanities, professional and science courses.

The expectation for graduates of sport and exercise science to have developed the knowledge and skills essential to enter into the profession results in a diverse portfolio of learning and teaching methods. This often includes combinations of the following: lectures, workshops and seminars, group and individual tutorials, laboratory practicals, real-time practical activities, live performance and events, casestudies, field studies, placements, internships, consultancy, working in small groups, independent study and research, and technology-enhanced and blended learning (QAA, 2019).

Within sport and exercise science, particularly in the physiology and biomechanics sub-disciplines, the use of laboratory reports to assess scientific communication is commonplace. However, there are some slight variations in convention between these sub-disciplines that can impact on judgements of academic standards of a laboratory report. Within the sub-discipline of psychology, assessment methods are slightly different, with more reliance upon case studies, essays and client reports. More recently, potentially due to increased student numbers and a desire to reduce marking time, research posters have additionally become a typical form of assessment. In itself, this slight shift in task has significant implications for academic standards. For a poster, presentation and aesthetics might be considered important attributes of quality, while this is less likely to be the case for a laboratory report or an essay. Again, this provides an insight into the complex interactions between the (sub)discipline, assessment task and academic standards.

Institutions delivering sport and exercise science

Sport and exercise science is a subject that provides opportunities for a diverse range of students, enabling study across the spectrum of entry qualifications. This diversification is highlighted for students seeking to enter UK higher education in September 2023 based on the 878 sport science related courses available at 161 different higher education institutions (UCAS, 2023). The prior educational achievement requirement of these courses ranged considerably from 144 tariff points (i.e. grade A in three different subjects in A-level school-leaving qualifications) to 72 UCAS tariff points (i.e. grade D in three different subjects in A-level school-leaving qualifications). There are fewer courses at the higher entry tariff ($n = 160$) that the lower ($n = 407$), but this demonstrates the significant variation in prior educational attainment of students entering a similar degree programme with the same national standards. The sheer volume of sport and exercise courses, in a large range of different institutions, along with this variation in entry tariff needs to be considered in relation to grade attainment.

For the past decade, graduate attainment rates have shown a steady increase for all subjects across the UK higher education sector. Between 2010–2011 and 2020–2021, the proportion of full-time first-degree graduates attaining a first-class honours degree has more than doubled, from 16% in 2010–2011 to 38% in 2020–2021 (OfS, 2022); 84% of students achieved a first or upper second-class degree in 2020–2021, increased from 67% in 2010–2011. This is accompanied by a reduction in the number of students achieving a lower second-class degree, which in 2010–2011 was 33%, and 16% in 2020–2021. This trend has brought with it the persistent use of the term 'grade inflation', which may reflect falling standards in UK higher education (Bachan, 2017) and indicate a gradual lowering of the expectations for attainment in each grade boundary.

The issue of grade inflation is of particular interest to sport and exercise science when considering the change in grade attainment across the past decade in relation to entry qualification. Data shows that across the higher education sector, between 2010–2011 and 2020–2021 disproportionally more 'good degrees' (first class honours and upper second class) were awarded to those with lower entry qualification; 38% increase in number of students achieving a good degree when entering higher education with three A-levels with grades D or below, in comparison to 5% increase when entering higher education with three A-levels with grades A and above (OfS, 2022). A similar profile is also observed when considering the equivalent but more vocational entry qualifications (i.e. BTEC qualifications). Based upon the disproportionate awarding of 'good degrees' to those students with lower entry qualification, and the discipline of sport and exercise science recruiting students from across the entry tariff spectrum, this suggests that the standards applied at some institutions could be very different to those at another institution and highlights the importance of ensuring national standards.

Calibration event in sport and exercise science

Overview of the event

Based on the considerations outlined above, this section considers the practical experience of delivering a calibration event in sport and exercise science. A total of 27 academics from the sport science discipline in 21 different UK higher education institutions signed up to the event. Twenty-three participants completed all elements of the calibration event. A North West Consortium, formed as part of the wider AdvanceHE Degree Standards Project, was initially used as a way to convene academics from the same subject area from institutions within a similar geographical area. This approach was designed to reduce travel time and build a more sustainable approach to calibration. The event was also supported by BASES who helped to advertise the event more widely within their monthly newsletter.

Prior to the calibration workshop, the participants were required to undertake an online task to mark and make judgements on the quality of three student assignments. The calibration workshop was a full-day, in-person event. This day aimed to calibrate the marking judgements of the three pieces of work considered by participants in the pre-workshop activity and then, based on this, to mark two further assignments.

The calibration workshop had three key design features. The first was the selection of the three assignments that were the foundation to the workshop. Key consideration in the selection of the assignments were that they:

a   should be a typical or defining assessment of the subject area, which in this instance was a scientific laboratory report;
b   where possible should not require overly specialist knowledge to make a judgement;
c   should not be too long and should be easy to access and navigate; and
d   should provide a range of quality but potentially have two that cluster around a point of interest (i.e. pass/fail or upper second class borderline).

The second design feature was a focus upon how the standards could be exemplified. In order to do this, there had to be a consideration of what it was that assessors valued, labelled as Key Influential Characteristics (KIC), and also the perceived quality of the KIC. In order to communicate the quality, it was important to go beyond a descriptor and to provide an exemplification, which was an extract from an individual assignment that illustrated the quality of a specific KIC. The third point of design was the progressive way in which the calibration conversations were developed. This was both in terms of the number of people involved (i.e. individual, small group, whole group) and also the point of focus (i.e. mark; mark and KIC; mark, KIC and exemplification).

The workshop began by sharing the range and standard deviation of the marks awarded by the participants for each assignment. This was proceeded by small group discussion to start the consensus reaching process. Each of the three assignments were taken in turn and, in a progressive way, the calibration conversations were developed in small groups starting with a focus on the mark (Stage 1; Assignment 1), to a focus on the mark and key influential characteristics (Stage 2; Assignment 2), to a focus on the mark, the characteristics and exemplifications of these (Stage 3; Assignment 3). After each stage, there was a period of whole group discussion where the group marks were discussed and defended. The outcome was broad group agreement of a mark, albeit across a range, for each piece of work. An electronic shared file was used to manage the tasks and collate outcomes from small group calibration discussions. One outcome from this was the shared development of a number of characteristics and associated exemplifications to create benchmark annotated assignments that could be used with other groups to support calibration discussion.

The next stage of the workshop (Stage 4) required the groups to defend their choice of characteristics and associated exemplifications. We used a carousel approach with one member of each group staying at their initial table to explain the exemplifications and the rest going to look at other group's choices (moving table). This generated plenty of discussion but when we tried to firm these up as a whole group, there was a concern that the resultant list became too broad and abstract in order to guide more consistent judgements.

The final stage (Stage 5) was to get the participants to work with the shared characteristics (although exemplifications were not explicitly used at this stage) to mark two new assignments. Participants seemed to move through this activity rather swiftly and anonymously submitted their judgements to the facilitators. Participants were then asked to discuss this in pairs and then the group marks were analysed and broadly discussed.

Variation in the marks and calibration

There was a high level of variation in the marks for the three assignments that the participants marked prior to the workshop (see Figure 14.2). The home institution was a post-1992 higher education institution. For Assignment 1 (moderated mark from home institution was 2:1/2:2 borderline) the size of the range was 40% marks from 30 to 70%, for Assignment 2 (moderated mark from home institution was a borderline pass) the range was 35% marks between 30 and 65%, and marks for Assignment 3 (moderated mark from home institution was First class) ranged by 18% marks between 62 and 80%. Although the broad ranking between the original marks and the mark of the group were relatively similar, the range of marks for each assignment was extremely high. However, there seemed to be much smaller variation in relation to high quality work compared to that in the middle range and at the threshold standard. This

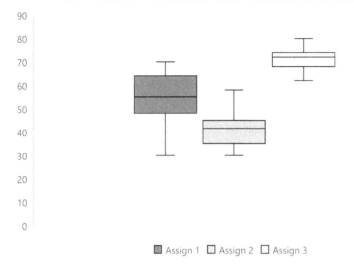

Figure 14.2 Mark variation for three assignments graded prior to a sport and exercise science calibration workshop (n = 23).

Table 14.1 Difference in mark from the mean based on the institution type of the assessor.

HE Institutional Type	Difference in mark awarded from the mean		
	Assign 1	Assign 2	Assign 3
Pre-1992 (n = 4)	+6.2	+3.1	−1.0
Post-1992 (n = 9)	−3.6	−3.8	+0.9
Post-2002 (n = 4)	+7.2	+1.6	+3.0
HE in FE (n = 6)	−3.4	+2.6	−2.7

potentially helps in terms of ensuring there is work selected for calibration that represents these standards where there appears to be greater variation.

Marks were also analysed for any trend in judgements made about the same pieces of work from participants at different institution types. Although numbers in each group are modest and not evenly spread, the data do not support the perception that standards are higher in the traditional, pre-1992 universities in comparison to the post-1992 and further education institutions delivering degree level qualifications. On average, the marks awarded for each of the assignments were lower from participants at post-1992 higher education institutions and those teaching higher education in further education (HE in FE) (Table 14.1).

As far as we are aware, beyond the two subject-specific calibration events run as part of the Degree Standards Project (see also Chapter 15), in higher education, the effectiveness of calibration discussions in reducing variation in academic standards has not been tested by marking a new set of assignments. In the Sport and Exercise event, the participants were required to mark two further assignments from the same set of work, where they were asked to apply their calibrated standards. Although slightly reduced, the variation in marks remained high. The size of the range was 30 marks (35–65) for Assignment 4 and 23 marks (42–65) for Assignment 5. This was disappointing, but it is important to be realistic about the extent that a 1-day calibration event can impact on the academic standards that have been developed tacitly and through social interactions over an extended period of time. As such, it is not unreasonable to expect that there is a need for multiple calibration interactions over a period of time. In addition, and following the accountancy example from Australia (Watty et al., 2014), it may be more feasible to calibrate specific aspects of assignments, for example, scientific writing or critical evaluation, than all the criteria combined as in the overall assignment mark.

Despite the high variation in marks, the key influential characteristics identified by markers did seem to have some greater consistency and, in particular, focussed upon: use/evaluation of evidence; structure and written style; and clarity of the method and results. Therefore, although the participants were now seemingly looking for very similar characteristics within assignments, their perception of the standard to which this was being achieved was a likely source of variation in the marks awarded. This is the issue that calibration needs to focus upon and is related to the methodology that should be used to deliver calibration workshops in the future.

Methodology for the calibration workshop

The design and management of calibration workshops is highly complex. This complexity is at a conceptual level, in terms of approaches that may work best to encourage participants to make their tacit marking judgement explicit, and then potentially re-frame these standards to reach greater consistency with their peers. There is also complexity in the practicalities, such as how best to distribute and collate the necessary materials and how to facilitate the whole group calibration discussion at the right level of detail to remain meaningful. A range of different methodologies are possible and it is important to be able to identify the key features of these designs, how they differ from one another, and to test which seems to be the most effective. The main features of the sport and exercise science calibration workshop have been identified (see Table 14.2). These categories are intended to help in the design and articulation of different methodologies for calibration events in the future.

A key focus for the design of the sport and exercise workshop was to identify and use exemplifications. It is within exemplifications that standards are visible and therefore they have a critical role in calibration discussions. It was for this reason that there was a progressive focus in the calibration discussions, which culminated in the drawing out of exemplification from the third assignment. The selected exemplifications could productively be used alongside the consensus judgements to create a resource (i.e. annotated exemplar assignment) to support further

Table 14.2 Considerations to make explicit in the design of a calibration workshop.

Subject	Sub-discipline	Assessment Type	Methodology				
			Focus of marking judgements	Interactions	Instantiation	Focus of agreement	Post calibration activity
Sport and Exercise Science	Physiology	Scientific Laboratory Report	How well the learning outcomes had been achieved	Small to whole group calibration discussions for each assignment	Three assignments considered separately in turn	Progressive focus upon mark, KICs and exemplifications	Mark two new assignments

calibration in sport and exercise science. However, a number of issues with the exemplification approach remain and these include:

- The practical difficulty of sharing detailed exemplifications in the whole group discussion of standards. This means conversations revert back to the key influential characteristics, which are too broad and abstract to share standards.
- The number of key influential characteristics and associated exemplifications quickly becomes too bulky and goes beyond the scope of what is realistic in the timeframe. Therefore calibration needs to be focussed on a specific standard (e.g. scientific writing style).
- Different standards across different pieces of work need to be shown through the identification of contrasting exemplifications of the same key influential characteristic. However, equivalent exemplifications that are short-hand enough to share are not always easy to access in contrasting pieces of work.

Reflections and outcomes

Several months after delivery of the calibration event, two attendees of the event were approached to write a reflective account of their experience of attending and how this had impacted their practice. One was an early career academic and new to external examining and the other was a mid-career academic and a more experienced external examiner. A sufficient period of time was left to allow anything adopted from the event to have been implemented into practice. In addition, a written reflection was also obtained from one of the workshop facilitators.

When writing their reflection, individuals were asked to reflect on the following 3 questions.

1 What made you participate / engage in the event?
2 Were there any critical incidents during the event, a memory (or memories) that stand out from the event? Why did it leave an impact on you?
3 Can you explain how your practice has changed since the event?

From initially reviewing each written account, it became apparent that there were commonalities in the reflections provided. Rather than present each participant separately, the key reflections were grouped and are illustrated through the inclusion of quotes (Table 14.3).

Table 14.3 Key reflections on a calibration workshop with example quotes to support.

Key reflections	*Quotes/examples to support*
The specific discipline expertise may cause potential variation and a power dynamic during calibration conversations.	A key point I do remember is the variation in specific topics within sport science, i.e. I may have a better understanding in physiological-related work, as opposed to psychology. However, this happens within HE, especially when assessing/marking/moderation and/or double marking dissertations where the topic may not be within my area of so-called 'expertise'. (New External Examiner) A key memory of the event was when a fellow academic on the course explained their judgement of the physiology script we had all reviewed pre-event: 'I'm a physiologist at X institution and I notice they are missing Y from the reference list.' I was sitting there, as a biomechanist and felt the need to just accept their point as correct. I'm not the expert at the table and therefore don't have a voice. (Experienced External Examiner) What did help is a sense that it was my subject discipline and the specific assignment that I knew well that was under consideration and therefore I did have a level of expertise and ownership. On reflection, subject expertise and familiarity with the assessment item between the facilitation team (I would recommend having at least two people) is critical to be able to answer specific queries, moderate discussion and be empathetic. (Workshop Facilitator)
The large time-cost to the development of calibrated academics needs to result in perceived benefit from engaging.	I found it hard finding/making the time to do these types of tasks before the day. This was, however, completed and took at least two hours to do, so considering the time-cost of the pre-tasks and then the day spent at the event (regardless of the 6-hour return trip), there was a large time-cost of the total event. (New External Examiner) If the event hadn't been subject-specific, I probably wouldn't have made the effort to travel across the country. (Experienced External Examiner)

Key reflections	Quotes/examples to support
	This was one of the most complex academic development sessions I have facilitated. As a relatively new member of the degree standards team and still getting to grips with some of the ideas within the Degree Standards Professional Development Course, I felt a little out of my depth. What exacerbated this was that the calibration event had relatively limited pre-prepared input and yet the in-situ guidance and facilitation of the small and whole group discussion is central. (Workshop Facilitator)
	A particularly difficult part of the day was half-way through the calibration discussions where all we seem to have got to was a list of Key Influential Characteristics (KICs), which seemed very similar to a set of assessment criteria that we could probably have got to without careful consideration and discussion of the pieces of student work. (Workshop Facilitator)
Impact of calibration on personal and local assessment practice.	My own practice has changed with regard to calibration exercises for level 6 project. I also took it upon myself as a course leader, to utilise the need for calibration and parity between assessors within our distance learning course, where we have numerous external tutors that teach and mark across different levels/modules/courses. We began with focus on marking criteria and language used for certain grade boundaries. (New External Examiner)
	I have also undertaken some local level social moderation activity. During the summer period, I attempted to replicate the social moderation activity I experienced at the calibration event ... At the very least, it provided an opportunity for staff to consider why they mark the way they do and hear the perspectives from others and reflect on the variety of elements that influence the judgements about the quality of the work, some that are less explicit than others. (Experienced External Examiner)
Facilitation of calibration, importance of exemplifications/artefacts as an outcome.	This is where constant reference back to the student work itself is vital. However, this in itself is not straightforward ... for example, exemplification of the structure of an argument requires sight of large parts of the work as opposed to manageable extracts. (Workshop Facilitator)
	I would recommend that events try to focus upon: points of adjustment or recalibration of standards; specific areas of disagreement/contention; developing a socially constructed artefact that attempt to capture aspects of the calibration in quotes from conversations and extracts from the work; and consider the variation in the process of moving from the standard to the award of a mark. (Workshop Facilitator)

Conclusion: challenges and implications for calibration in the disciplines

As outlined at the beginning of the chapter, key sources of variation in academic standards reside within the *people, tools* and *tasks* that are inherent within the judgements being made. Therefore it is important that calibration activities attend to these three different aspects. The fundamental outcome of calibration is to develop a greater shared understanding of the academic standards as a result of the discussions. Despite this seeming relatively straightforward, there are significant challenges that have important implications for undertaking calibration of academic standards.

It is *people* that are at the heart of calibration, therefore the conversations with others to share implicit marking judgements regarding specific pieces of student assessments are fundamental. The role and importance of specific disciplinary variation and the expertise of the individuals also needs to be taken into account. This is particularly the case for multi-disciplinary subjects such as sport and exercise science where the differences between the WTPs of the sub-disciplines of psychology and biomechanics, for example, are quite stark. However, again, this needs to be balanced with the reality that those marking and moderating the work will have quite different levels of expertise in relation to the specific assessment in hand. It is important to be aware of the implications expertise has for judgements (i.e. are experts more likely to be critical and therefore have higher expectations or standards?) and the power dynamic that this may create within calibration activities.

What individuals take from the calibration activities, and the extent to which they influence future independent judgements, is also a significant issue and relatively unknown. The idea of 'conceding ground' and 'moving towards' the standards of others is an important message during the event. The development of artefacts to capture the agreed standards and support this movement to shared standards is important. However, the key influential characteristics (KICs) in themselves are not a sufficient *tool* in the calibration process. This is where it is vital that the facilitator encourages or requires the participants to constantly make reference back to the quality of these KICs as depicted in the work itself (i.e. exemplification).

The selection of the assessment *task* for the calibration event requires much thought. Key issues are that the assignment is not overly long but does require higher order skills to be demonstrated. It should be a single assessment item or type (e.g. report, presentation or essay) and usually in a specific topic area within a particular subject or sub-discipline within the subject area. The level of study and the original marks awarded all need considering in terms of any particular areas of focus for the calibration. For example, if there are issues in relation to the pass/fail boundary for first year students this would influence the work selected. As a facilitator, it is important to know the student work extremely well and the broader concepts and ideas regarding academic standards and calibration (e.g. Sadler, 2013, 2014; Bloxham et al., 2016). During calibration events, this background knowledge allows for 'real time' reflection and planning of what needs to be done to help the participants come to a shared understanding of the standards. The paradox here is the desire to develop broadly 'calibrated academics' (Sadler, 2013), when continuous calibration for different topics and assessments is unrealistic. Therefore, how academics translate calibrated standards from one context or task to another is a significant consideration.

In summary, calibration is not easy and has significant challenges in terms of: the translation to different subjects and assessment contexts; managing the role of discipline and expertise in the variation in judgements; the extent to which the calibration will influence future judgements of individuals; and the complexity in the facilitation and development of artefacts to capture shared standards. Despite this, we would argue that developing calibration is worthwhile. The participants who attend calibration workshops appear to be highly engaged and appreciative of the event as it is grounded in a significant and challenging aspect of their academic role for which they seem to have had little support or conversation with others. Although the evidence base for calibration improving shared standards is limited, social interaction with others can only help.

References

Bachan, R. (2017). Grade inflation in UK higher education. *Studies in Higher Education*, 42(8), 1580–1600. https://doi.org/10.1080/03075079.2015.1019450.

BASES. (2023a). Biomechanics and motor behaviour division. Accessed November 2022. www.bases.org.uk/spage-divisions-biomechanics_and_motor_behaviour.html.

BASES. (2023b). Physiology and nutrition division. Accessed November 2022. www.bases.org.uk/spage-divisions-physiology_and_nutrition.html.

BASES. (2023c). Psychology division. Accessed November 2022. www.bases.org.uk/spage-divisions-psychology.html.

BASES. (2023d). BASES course finder. Accessed November 2022. www.bases.org.uk/courses.php?endorsed=1.

Biglan, A. (1973). The characteristics of subject matter in different scientific areas. *Journal of Applied Psychology*, 57(3), 195–203. http://dx.doi.org/10.1037/h0034701.

Bloxham, S., Hughes, C. & Adie, L. (2016). What's the point of moderation? A discussion of the purposes achieved through contemporary moderation practices. *Assessment & Evaluation in Higher Education*, 41(4), 638–653. http://dx.doi.org/10.1080/02602938.2015.1039932.

Hounsell, D. & McCune, V. (2005). The development of students' ways of thinking and practising in three final-year biology courses. *Higher Education*, 49, 255–289. http://dx.doi.org/10.1007/s10734-004-6666-0.

Jessop, T. & Maleckar, B. (2016). The influence of disciplinary assessment patterns on student learning: a comparative study. *Studies in Higher Education*, 41(4), 696–711. https://doi.org/10.1080/03075079.2014.943170.

Neumann, R. (2001). Disciplinary differences and university teaching. *Studies in Higher Education*, 26(2), 135–146. http://dx.doi.org/10.1080/03075070120052071.

Neumann, R., Parry, S. & Becher, T. (2002). Teaching and learning in their disciplinary contexts: a conceptual analysis. *Studies in Higher Education*, 27(4), 405–417. http://dx.doi.org/10.1080/0307507022000011525.

OfS. (2022). Analysis of degree classifications over time changes in graduate attainment from 2010–11 to 2020–21. www.officeforstudents.org.uk/media/cd778d76-5810-488b-b1e6-6e57797fe755/ofs-202222.pdf (accessed June 2022).

QAA. (2019). Subject benchmark statement: events, hospitality, leisure, sport tourism. www.qaa.ac.uk/docs/qaa/subject-benchmark-statements/subject-benchmark-statement-events-leisure-sport-tourism.pdf?sfvrsn = c339c881_11 (accessed 19 October 2022).

Sadler, D.R. (2013). Assuring academic achievement standards: from moderation to calibration. *Assessment in Education: Principles, Policy & Practice*, 20(1), 5–19. http://dx.doi.org/10.1080/0969594X.2012.714742.

Sadler, D.R. (2014). The futility of attempting to codify academic achievement standards. *Higher Education*, 67, 273–288. https://doi.org/10.1007/s10734-013-9649-1.

UCAS. (2023). Search courses, apprenticeships, information guides and more. https://digital.ucas.com/coursedisplay/results/courses?searchTerm=sport%20science&studyYear=2023&destination = Undergraduate&postcodeDistanceSystem=imperial&startDates=09%2F2023&pageNumber=1&sort=MostRelevant&clearingPreference=None (accessed January 2023).

Watty, K., Freeman, M., Howieson, B., Hancock, P., O'Connell, B., de Lange, P. & Abraham, A. (2014). Social moderation, assessment and assuring standards for accounting graduates. *Assessment & Evaluation in Higher Education*, 39(4), 461–478. http://dx.doi.org/10.1080/02602938.2013.848336.

Ylonen, A., Gillespie, H. & Green, A. (2018). Disciplinary differences and other variations in assessment cultures in higher education: exploring variability and inconsistencies in one university in England. *Assessment & Evaluation in Higher Education*, 43(6), 1009–1017. http://dx.doi.org/10.1080/02602938.2018.1425369.

Chapter 15

The need for calibration in the disciplines
A case study from geography

Jennifer Hill, Helen Walkington, Ben Page and Stephanie Wyse

Introduction

Ensuring consistency in the marking (grading) of student work, to achieve comparability of academic standards across a range of markers and over time, is important to assure the credibility, value and reliability of the qualifications awarded by higher education institutions. Students, their families, employers and other stakeholders want to feel confident that a degree classification is a reliable measure of student performance. Indeed, there is a formal requirement of comparability of awards in the UK, at least at the level of threshold academic standards (QAA, 2012). In England, the Office for Students (OfS), which acts as the sector regulator, has introduced a condition requiring universities to assess students effectively, and to award qualifications that are credible compared to those granted previously, and that are based on the knowledge and skills of students. If this condition is deemed to be breached, an institution can be fined a proportion of its income, suspended from the register, or face de-registration.

Much of the academic, political and media attention focused on the comparability of standards is set against the backdrop of a steady rise in higher education degree outcomes for more than two decades across many countries (see, for example, Bagues et al., 2008; Rojstaczer, 2016; Bachan, 2017; Baird et al., 2019; Müller-Benedict & Gaens, 2020; Jephcote et al., 2021). In England, the OfS published a recent analysis of degree classifications between 2010–2011 and 2020–2021. The report highlighted that the proportion of UK-domiciled, full-time, first degree graduates attaining a first-class honours degree (graded 70% and above and considered exceptional academic performance) from an English higher education provider more than doubled, from 15.7% in 2010–2011 to 37.9% in 2020–2021 (OfS, 2022a). In terms of 'good' degrees (first and upper second class, the latter graded 60% to 70% and considered a strong academic performance), 84.4% of students achieved such a classification, increasing from 67.0% in 2010–2011. Assessment practices in 2019–2020 were atypical as a response to 'no detriment' policies, which were introduced during the Covid-19 pandemic to ensure students were not unfairly disadvantaged by changes to their courses. Many of these changes continued into 2020–2021 and this may have impacted degree

DOI: 10.4324/9781003379768-19

outcomes. The OfS report noted that over half of the 37.9% of first-class honours degrees in 2020–2021 (22.4%) could not be explained when accounting for a range of explanatory variables including provider, year, subject, entry qualification and a range of demographic factors. The OfS stated that 'the sustained increase in unexplained firsts awarded continues to pose regulatory concerns' (OfS, 2022b). In response, members of Universities UK in England have committed to reviewing classifications against pre-pandemic levels, working to return to these levels as soon as possible.

In the subject of geography, Wyse et al. (2020) have highlighted that the percentage of 'good' geography degrees awarded to first degree qualifiers in the UK has risen from 40% in the early 1970s to 71% in 2010 (Thornes, 2012), and rising sharply to approximately 80% by 2016 (Wyse et al., 2020). Geography has had a higher proportion of 'good' degrees than the average for all subjects since 2010. It is particularly important, therefore, for geography assessors to understand and endeavour to apply academic standards consistently to ensure comparability of awards.

Degree outcomes are influenced by a plethora of factors including: inputs of student attributes; throughputs of teaching, learning and assessment environments and processes; and output influences such as degree algorithms and labour market requirements (Wyse et al., 2020). Positive explanations for a rise in degree outcomes over time include higher student entry qualifications, improvements in teaching (linked with enhanced staff development, reward and recognition), student engagement as partners in learning, increased modular and assessment choice, increased formative feedback, outcomes-based curricula with marking criteria, higher proportions of coursework, enhanced skills guidance, improved reasonable adjustment and mitigating circumstances procedures, investment in services, facilities and technology, and increased student motivation due to fee increase (Thornes, 2012; Richards, 2012; Hefce, 2015; Wyse et al., 2020; Jephcote et al., 2021). A recent study in the UK (Jephcote et al., 2021) concluded that rising grades over the period 2009–2010 to 2018–2019 represent a complex and contextual, but positive and proactive picture of a higher education system that is engaged in a process of continuous enhancement.

There is a counter-argument, however, often evoked in the popular media, which quotes national league tables putting pressure on academics to award more good degrees, and changes to degree classification algorithms, enabling students to gain a good degree with lower mean marks compared with the past (see also HEFCE, 2015). Critics suggest that grades have been 'inflated' internationally in response to the marketisation of the sector, with the need to improve enrolments on courses, and the transparency and accountability of student evaluation of teaching (SET) scores and league tables providing incentive to universities around the world to increase the proportion of good degrees awarded without a corresponding increase in learning or performance (Berezvai et al., 2021).

In this chapter, we address two key themes. Firstly, we open a discussion about assurance of academic standards in relation to ideas put forward as part of the UK-based AdvanceHE Degree Standards Project (see Chapter 9). AdvanceHE is a member-led, sector-owned charity that works with institutions and higher education across the world to improve higher education for staff, students and society. Secondly, we describe calibration activities undertaken by the geography subject community, run through the Royal Geographical Society (with Institute of British Geographers) (RGS-IBG), as part of and moving beyond the Degree Standards Project, as a means of providing transparent assurance about the high quality and consistency of assessment.

Assuring academic standards: what works?

Consistent marking between assessors, which reflects national standards, is vital for the reputation of the geography discipline in higher education, fairness to students and confidence amongst graduates and employers. But, ensuring consistency in marking is challenging and research over many years has found considerable discrepancy in the grades accorded to the same student work (Price, 2005; Bloxham, 2009; Bloxham et al., 2015, 2016b). Variations in marking occur due to markers' differential understanding of the standards against which student work is appraised (Sadler, 2013), their tacit knowledge (Bloxham 2009), expertise and experience (Bloxham et al., 2016b) and individual biases (Orr & Bloxham, 2013). We cannot rely on written codifications (particularly to describe standards applied to complex, open-ended tasks) or on our informal learning about standards to ensure that we share standards with the rest of our subject community. As such, a variety of approaches have been developed within the sector to help reduce variation in academic standards within and across modules, courses, and institutions (Table 15.1) (see also Chapters 5 and 8).

Some of the approaches in Table 15.1 are directly related to maintaining academic standards, such as second marking, moderation and use of external examiners. Others are more indirect processes, such as markers being members of a subject association or professional body. As Chapter 5 noted, the table demonstrates a predominance of approaches concerned with internal consistency compared to external or sector-wide consistency. Equally, many approaches occur after teaching rather than before, when they might be more beneficial to staff and students. As such, many of the approaches offer a public image of systematic checking of standards, but they do not necessarily guarantee appropriate 'output' or performance standards (Alderman, 2009). We might, therefore, question the benefit of many widely accepted approaches in contributing significantly to the assurance of higher education standards (Bloxham et al., 2016a).

The key to achieving greater success is to support moderation, which focuses on agreeing marks post-teaching (Chapter 5), with calibration. Calibration concerns sharing knowledge of standards, ideally prior to course delivery and therefore detached from summative marking decisions, based on intentional reflection and discussion of examples of student work as concrete referents, and preferably drawing on relevant external reference points (see Chapters 8 and 15 for more

Table 15.1 Common approaches that aim to reduce variation in the judgement of academic standards.

Approach	Internal/ external	Pre-/ post-teaching
Peer scrutiny of module assessment	Internal	Pre-teaching
Briefing to module team on assessment expectations	Internal	Pre-teaching
Module team marks and discusses exemplar assignments	Internal	Pre-teaching
Markers mark and discuss a common sample of work immediately prior to full marking	Internal	Post-teaching
Use of a detailed marking scheme	Internal	Post-teaching
Provision of a model answer	Internal	Post-teaching
Second marking of work, resolving differences by discussion	Internal	Post teaching
Moderation discussion after first marking, involving all markers on a module	Internal	Post-teaching
Moderation by comparing averages and distribution of marks by each marker in team	Internal	Post-teaching
Examination board consideration of means and standard deviations of module marks	Internal	Post-teaching
External examining	External	Post-teaching
Markers having experience as external examiners at other institutions	External	Pre- and post-teaching
Markers being members of a learned society or professional body	External	Pre- and post-teaching
Markers being familiar with national reference points	External	Pre- and post-teaching

Source: information adapted from the Professional Development Course for External Examiners

detail). Calibration aims to enable academic staff to make consistent marking decisions that are: commensurate with the respective levels of academic achievement they represent; are comparable across course and institutional boundaries at any one point and over time; and are consistent with disciplinary and societal expectations of higher education graduates (Sadler, 2009). Hence, calibrated academics are able to make judgements about assessed work that are consistent with those made by other, similarly calibrated colleagues (Sadler, 2013).

To promote a shared understanding of what constitutes quality in student work, we cannot rely on codified standards alone to assure consistency (for example, assessment criteria, qualification descriptors and benchmarking statements). This is because it is impossible to explicitly state most academic standards such that they are interpreted similarly by different academics (Sadler, 2007, 2014). While codifications can provide a useful basis of discussion about standards (see Chapter 13), they do not offer an unambiguous description of standards. Adopting such a sociocultural view, academic standards are viewed as socially constructed, subjective, contextual and contested (Ajjawi et al., 2021). Individuals construct their own standards frameworks, co-creating standards through local assessment practices and communities, mobilising tacit knowledge learnt 'on the job' in addition to explicit knowledge (Bloxham et al., 2016a, 2016b; see also Chapters 3 and 8).

Personal standards frameworks mean that assessors' understanding of terms differs due to their previous experiences and current values and hence they interpret criteria differently. They focus on diverse aspects of importance in student work, they value aspects not reflected in assessment criteria and they make limited use of external reference points (Bloxham & Price, 2015). Furthermore, criterion-based marking is influenced by norm referencing, where a piece of work is referenced against other students in a cohort rather than against the criteria (Bloxham et al., 2011). Tackling these issues, calibration, involving dialogue, provides a means through which assessors can establish a common vocabulary and set of meanings in relation to the criteria they are using to judge the academic standards of pieces of work (Sadler, 2013; Bloxham & Price, 2015). The intent with such calibration discussions is to share the rationales for making judgements about quality, identifying meanings-in-use for the principal explanatory terms, increasing marker confidence, and resulting in greater consistency in understanding and application of academic standards (Bloxham, 2009; Crimmins et al., 2016; O'Connell et al., 2016; Beutel et al., 2017).

Calibration has the potential to offer quality assurance for academic standards and to support professional development, as markers learn from more experienced colleagues taking part in shared conversations (Crimmins et al., 2016). There are, however, complexities when endeavouring to apply consistent standards through calibration activities (Mason & Roberts, 2024). Seniority may impact the consensus moderation process, as markers may defer to those in power or with more experience (Watty et al., 2013; Boyd & Bloxham, 2014; Grainger et al., 2016; Mason & Roberts, 2024). The increasing use of part-time sessional academics to deliver teaching and undertake marking can exacerbate this process (Crimmins et al., 2016). Markers need to be socialised into teaching teams to understand marking requirements and this is difficult to achieve when teams are extensive and dislocated over space and time, and where staff mobility between institutions (including different country contexts) brings in different expectations and perspectives (Adie et al., 2013, Grainger et al., 2016). Shared understandings are more closely aligned within stable teaching teams, where understandings are built over time and through interrogation in differing circumstances; where calibration processes are strategically sequenced so that understanding can be built over the teaching period; and where new teaching staff are purposefully inducted and provided with clear written guidelines (Beutel et al., 2017).

Additionally, in an expansive subject such as geography, which straddles the physical and social sciences, academic staff have expertise in sub-domains of the discipline, drawing upon diverse epistemologies, methodologies, concepts, language and viewpoints. Agreeing with the authors of Chapter 14, this diversity means that standards are likely to be judged differently by academics across the discipline. Also mirroring Chapter 14, student assignments are varied across geography courses, but are usually complex and open-ended in nature. These two aspects can result in lengthy discussions about student work during calibration and to divergent opinions about the standards displayed by particular assignments that can be hard to resolve.

There is consequently a need for professional development in calibration, including how to be collaborative across a diversity of staff types, how to deal with sub-disciplinary expertise, and how to manage inherent power differentials (Mason et al., 2022; Beutel et al., 2017; Mason & Roberts, 2024). Indeed, professional learning should be established as a goal rather than a by-product of calibration (Mason & Roberts, 2024; Bloxham et al., 2016a). Embedding calibration into the assessment process thereby requires academic administrators to recognise its value and to allocate workload to academic staff so that they can take part in truly collaborative, developmental and sustainable calibration activities, learning from one another across the full assessment cycle (Sadler, 2013; Bloxham et al., 2016a).

Calibration in geography: process and outcomes

The RGS-IBG was involved in the Degree Standards Project (Chapter 9) from its inception, helping to shape the nature of the calibration programme through enthusiastic participation of the subject community. The Society co-developed with AdvanceHE and academic colleagues a geography calibration toolkit for use across the sector (see www.advance-he.ac.uk/geography-calibration-toolkit), and developed two types of workshops. One was a subject-specific calibration workshop and the other an integrated calibration version of the Professional Development Course (PDC) for geography academics.

Working with PDC team members, the RGS-IBG hosted two subject-specific events at the Society in the summer and winter of 2017 to deepen knowledge about academic standards and to pilot approaches to calibration. Across both events, geographers from a range of types of institutions interrogated disciplinary data on degree outcomes, and explored a social moderation approach that aimed to foster the same marking judgements *for the same reasons* among a group of disciplinary peers (Sadler, 2013; Watty et al., 2013). Following these sector-level exploratory workshops, a third departmental-level workshop was held by one participating institution.

Subject-specific society and departmental workshops

Across the subject-specific society workshops, participants were provided with a small set (3–5 pieces) of anonymised final year student work from an undisclosed institution (with the module/unit descriptor). These assignments were marked by participants in advance of the workshops, referring to their knowledge of appropriate academic standards in geography rather than their localised assessment rubrics. The marks and comments to justify the marks were submitted to the convenor. In the workshops, participants were shown the wide range of marks they awarded for each piece of work along with the mark awarded by the parent institution. Participants were then divided into small groups and, based on an understanding that discussion should be open and constructive, each participant justified to their group the marks they had awarded the work, clarifying key criteria used in their decision-making. In the process of agreeing a mark in the small team, individuals worked through any sticking points to achieve consensus over the criteria and how they were employed. The small teams then reconvened into the larger workshop group, which went through a second iteration of facilitated discussion over the marks awarded. Although time was constrained in these workshops, meaning that not all assignments were discussed, groups did reach a consensus on marks from a wide initial range for the assignments discussed. For some groups, the process seemed to be more about agreeing a mark rather than discussing the standard and forming a consensus on what comprised a good or bad piece of work. This was perhaps because the institutional mark was shown before the calibration activity took place, affording this mark a credence it did not necessarily warrant. Overall, more time was required to create calibrated academics in terms of generating a detailed understanding of appropriate standards across a range of marks.

In qualitative evaluation surveys, all of the society participants reported that the workshops afforded them greater confidence in their understanding of academic standards to be applied in the subject community. They recognised that variation in marking exists, with a concomitant need to calibrate their standards beyond their immediate context:

> The calibration activity highlighted to me how much your own context influences the mark you award.
> (Participant, Society workshop)

> I found it immensely useful to consider how our socialised community of practice might 'sway' our judgement of standards. You must have your eyes opened to looking into your community and to challenge your established norms ... to encounter, talk about and address variation head-on.
> (Participant, Society workshop)

Participants rated highly how well the course had enabled them to: articulate the nature of standards in the higher education context; and to explain the purpose and value of ongoing calibration activities in supporting the use of common 'discipline community' standards.

Some participants recognised the need to adjust their marking, and even that of their colleagues, to bring them in line with academics from beyond their department:

> It did make me think that I'm actually marking too generously at the bottom end of the scale ... it is possible that the sheer volume of average work is moving our internal marking goal posts.
> (Participant, Society workshop)

In the departmental workshops (run in the same way as the society workshops but with participants marking according to their local rubric), participants had to identify a common assessment language to clarify what specific criteria meant and how these criteria articulated quality. This is demonstrated by a participant from the departmental workshop:

> It was illuminating to see how our [department] approached the task quite differently and valued different aspects of the assignment. It was encouraging to discuss this together and eventually reach a consensus that made sense to us all.
>
> (Participant, Departmental workshop)

Calibration brought to light differential interpretation of criteria within rubrics by academics, even within the same localised community, highlighting the need to reflect upon and achieve common understanding:

> Despite giving pretty consistent marks, people interpreted the criteria quite differently. Critical evaluation meant critique of the literature for one marker, whereas for another they expected the student to critique their own research design.
>
> (Participant, Departmental workshop)

Working across institutions lengthened the calibration process. Initially, participants had to 'translate' criteria in relation to their own institution's assessment culture, before cross-checking with other participants against their standards. The act of translation, in forming a shared language of academic standards before rather than after marking, meant that some participants gained extra perspectives to take back to their institutions:

> The notion that we can calibrate 'marking' rather than moderate 'marks' with focus on input and not output is not one that I had come across before. The fact there is research suggesting this is an effective method has really encouraged me to implement a calibration exercise in my department.
>
> (Participant, Society workshop)

Almost all of the participants at the Society's workshops agreed that the events afforded them ideas for change that they would follow up in their own institutions. By far the most popular action was to engage their teams in social moderation before teaching commenced, especially with respect to the capstone independent research project. Participants also identified the need to promote the PDC course more widely and to take part in ongoing calibration activities at the subject level to help build a stronger, more networked subject community, and to maintain academic standards across the geography community.

Regional integrated Professional Development Course

In the autumn of 2018, the RGS-IBG and members of the PDC team ran a two-day regional integrated Professional Development Course for geography external examiners in the north-west of England, which, once again built in calibration of geography assignments (day 2) with established PDC course content (day 1). This was a select gathering of nine staff drawn from eight institutions across a diversity of mission groups. Initial marking of three final year coursework essays ahead of the calibration day, with participants applying what they viewed as appropriate academic standards for the stage of study and module learning outcomes, revealed considerable variation in marks (Table 15.2). It was notable that variation existed between individuals rather than between types of institution. There were examples of strong (high and low) outliers, whose marks were consistently away from the norms of the group.

During the calibration workshop, participants worked together, in small groups and then via whole-group facilitated discussion, to calibrate their judgement of the essays, one at a time, aiming to arrive at a consensus regarding the marks and iteratively building common influential characteristics that most determined the marks awarded. Despite initial variation, the outcome of the calibration was commonly agreed marks for all three essays (Table 15.2), based on shared views about key characteristics in the work and, finally, drawing on relevant external reference points (the UK Quality Code Geography Subject Benchmark Statement Standards and Levels of Achievement and the descriptor for a higher education qualification at level 6 i.e. final year of an undergrate programme). Prior to the workshop, the three essays had been marked by a panel of 14 experienced geography examiners drawn from different university mission groups in order to provide 'expert' grades for the work. Grade descriptors for the essays, produced by the experienced examiners, were supplied to the workshop participants after their discussions, along with a summary explanation of the key reasons the grades were awarded. The consensus marks derived from the workshop participants were very close to or directly in line with expert grade descriptors.

In the afternoon of the calibration workshop, a different 'institutional' calibration activity was trialled. The aim was to extend the personal calibration experience to new student work from a variety of institutions to ascertain if the earlier calibration had resulted in greater consistency of judgement. Participants marked

Table 15.2 Marks awarded to final year geography coursework essays pre- and post-calibration.

Pre-calibration:	Essay 1	Essay 2	Essay 3
Marks awarded (%)	52–68	38–58	68–82
Range (%)	16	20	14
Mean (%)	62.0	47.0	73.1
Final resolution:	Mid 2:1 (64%)	High 3rd (48%)	Mid 1st (75%)

two anonymised second- or third-year essay exam answers at the borderline between first class and second class performance, which had been from a core subject, brought in by their peers attending the workshop. Participants were provided with information about the level of study, the subject area and the question with each answer. Participants made a judgement based on their sense of appropriate standards and the influential characteristics derived from the earlier calibration exercise.

The exercise did not particularly reduce variability across markers. It was somewhat rushed at the end of the day and participants noted they had to read the essays and make decisions quickly, not having sufficient time to reflect upon and apply their recently developed influential characteristics with due consideration. Moving from coursework to exam answers also raised issues of different expectations of quality and how it is judged in exam essays versus coursework contexts. The constraints and context of exams resulted in different criteria being brought into play by the participants. The activity illustrated and enabled a discussion about the need for criteria to be thought through for different assignment types. Additionally, a minority of participants commented that they were marking beyond their comfort zone, beyond their sub-discipline (physical or human geography) or even their area of research expertise. The exercise demonstrated that calibration requires appropriate time and alignment to assessment task/expertise in order for academics to feel confident in delivering calibrated judgements.

Feedback from the regional course demonstrated, once again, increased confidence in participants with respect to judging standards. Some participants openly acknowledged a need to revise their personal standards frameworks to bring them more consistently in line with their disciplinary peers. Participants were able to see that others had clear but different views about how to decide the quality of work, which can impact on standards. Fundamental questions were also raised and discussed about what should be valued in student work, such as a synoptic view versus particular aspects such as use of references. All participants agreed the course had given them ideas for changes to follow up in their own institutions. They also expressed considerable interest in following up on the calibration activities periodically at the national level through further activity of the RGS-IBG, valuing the professional development associated with calibration.

Assessment literacy and standards workshop

In the summer of 2019, academic and RGS-IBG staff facilitated a half day workshop ahead of the Society's Annual International Conference. The workshop aimed to develop participants' understanding of assessment and feedback literacy, the nature of academic standards and the role of professional judgement in assuring standards within the discipline. The workshop identified key principles of effective assessment and feedback design to support students to achieve good degree outcomes whilst safeguarding academic standards. It did not include a calibration exercise, but it introduced staff to the nature and causes of variability in judging standards and the need for calibration.

The workshop brought to light two key issues. Firstly, it made academic staff question the alignment of their learning outcomes with the rubrics used to guide their judgement of academic standards. Some participants realised their rubrics were too generalised to effectively direct discussions to reach shared meaning of the most important influential characteristics of student work. Feedback after the event demonstrated participants committing to revise their rubrics to align more specifically with the learning outcomes of their modules and to national reference points (such as the UK Quality Code Subject Benchmark Statement and Frameworks for Higher Education Qualifications). Secondly, the workshop highlighted the importance of collective learning about different departmental assessment practices, such that best practice could be shared and disseminated. In short, the participants came to recognise that robust standards are a combination of establishing appropriate assessment tasks, criteria and rubrics, and more consistently judging student performance via calibration.

Implications of the workshops for disciplinary academic standards

There is clearly potential for calibration workshops to have notable impact in highlighting academic standards issues among subject communities and generating enthusiasm for calibration activities to continue within existing networks. The social moderation approach revealed that calibration can work at a disciplinary scale, particularly by consistently relating student work to the Geography Subject Benchmark Statement, which describes the nature of study and the academic standards expected of graduates in the discipline (QAA, 2022). Calibration can also help to maintain departmental autonomy with respect to forms of assessment, learning outcomes and marking rubrics, rather than resorting to nationalised assessment systems. However, more sustained activities, achieving greater reach and incorporating a clear evaluation strategy, are needed in order to test the efficacy of calibration for strengthening comparability at geographical scales beyond individual institutions and over the longer term. Agreeing with the authors of Chapter 14, calibration decisions need to focus on *who* to involve (from external examiners, departments, course teams, to module teams), *when* the calibration should take place (before or after assessment, ongoing across the teaching life cycle), and *at what scale* (national benchmark standards, inter-institutional degree outcomes, course or module level).

CRITICAL PERSPECTIVE

Box 15.1 The opportunities and challenges of undertaking calibration in geography

Disciplinary opportunities

- Calibration has the potential to enable geographers to develop shared understanding of academic standards and to make more consistent marking decisions over space and time.

- Calibration offers an opportunity for professional development, increasing marker confidence, building stronger communities of practice, and enhancing fairness for students.
- Through collective sharing of best practice, calibration improves the assessment literacy of academics, leading to enhanced assessment materials and processes.
- Ongoing calibration activities at the subject-level can help to build a strong subject community, and to maintain academic standards across the geography community.
- Calibration can take place effectively across scales, iterating between teaching teams, departments and the national disciplinary community, supporting external examining.
- Calibration offers external quality assurance for academic standards, supporting the credibility, value and reliability of geography degrees.

Disciplinary challenges

- Power relations might bias calibration discussions, leading senior staff to dictate standards.
- Calibration discussions can become difficult when assessment tasks reach beyond markers' sub-discipline / area of expertise, or cover different assignment types, leading to divergent opinions about standards.
- There is a need for professional development in calibration, which requires the input of assessment literate staff developers and workload allocation for participants.
- Truly collaborative developmental and sustainable calibration takes time. Administrators need to value and allocate workload to academic staff to take part in such activities.
- Sustainable subject-level calibration requires ongoing support at national level from government, the RGS-IBG, and higher education institutions.

Conclusion

In light of the rise in proportion of good degrees awarded in geography in the UK, we make a case in this chapter for an assessor-centred collaborative approach to achieve acceptable comparability of academic standards in the discipline, controlled by professional geographers as custodians of standards knowledge. This is optimally achieved through regular calibration activities that centre on face-to-face dialogue about standards pre-assessment, within disciplinary – and perhaps more ideally sub-disciplinary – communities of practice. Such activities will help to develop shared understanding of academic standards based on identifying key influential characteristics of assessed work that evidence these standards. We recommend the adoption of calibration within our subject community at a variety of scales, and over space and time, in order to strive for a sustainable process that can iterate between teaching teams, departments, external examiners, and the national disciplinary community. This would represent a more robust and granular approach to the existing external examiner system and would link departmental and national-level calibrations, but it does require support at national level from government, the RGS-IBG, and higher education institutions. A relevant commitment, and positive intent, is for further workshops to take place to (re-)calibrate geography academics periodically.

While moderation after assessment might appear sufficient for internal institutional quality assurance, it is ineffective for calibration at the scale of degree outcomes externally across departments. Calibration activities should be built into the whole teaching and assessment process (Mason & Roberts, 2024), with a particular focus on pre-teaching calibration that references external benchmarks. The ultimate goal is to more closely align the judgement of academic standards within and across institutions and with those standards expected by relevant discipline associations, accreditation agencies, professional bodies and/or employers (Sadler, 2011). Such activities, supported by professional bodies, carry considerable weight with educational practitioners (Watty et al., 2013; O'Connell et al., 2016). Through calibration, standards are understood and enacted by geographers in complex social arrangements, dynamic to a certain extent, but coordinated across space and time. In this way, calibration across a range of scales can help to reassure higher education stakeholders that degree outcomes are assessed with appropriate consistency across institutions and over time, and that 'good' degree outcomes in geography represent improved teaching and student learning.

References

Adie, L., Lloyd, M. & Beutel, D. (2013). Identifying discourses of moderation in higher education. *Assessment & Evaluation in Higher Education*, 38(8), 968–977. https://doi.org/10.1080/02602938.2013.769200.

Ajjawi, R., Bearman, M. & Boud, D. (2021). Performing standards: a critical perspective on the contemporary use of standards in assessment. *Teaching in Higher Education*, 26(5), 728–741. https://doi.org/10.1080/13562517.2019.1678579.

Alderman, G. (2009). Defining and measuring academic standards: a British perspective. *Higher Education Management and Policy*, 21(3), 11–22. https://doi.org/10.1787/hemp-21-5ksf24ssz1wc.

Bachan, R. (2017). Grade inflation in UK higher education. *Studies in Higher Education*, 42(8), 1580–1600. https://doi.org/10.1080/03075079.2015.1019450.

Bagues, M., Sylos Labini, M. & Zinovyevaz, N. (2008). Differential grading standards and university funding: evidence from Italy. *CESifo Economic Studies*, 54(2), 149–176. DOI:10.2139/ssrn.1089653.

Baird, A.F., Carter, J.S. & Roos, J.M. (2019). Seeking evidence of grade inflation at for-profit colleges and universities. *Sociological Focus*, 52(4), 343–358. https://doi.org/10.1080/00380237.2019.1668321.

Berezvai, Z., Lukáts, G.D. & Molontay, R. (2021). Can professors buy better evaluation with lenient grading? The effect of grade inflation on student evaluation of teaching. *Assessment & Evaluation in Higher Education*, 46(5), 793–808. https://doi.org/10.1080/02602938.2020.1821866.

Beutel, D., Adie, L. & Lloyd. M. (2017). Assessment moderation in an Australian context: processes, practices, and challenges. *Teaching in Higher Education*, 22(1), 1–14. https://doi.org/10.1080/13562517.2016.1213232.

Bloxham, S. (2009). Marking and moderation in the UK: false assumptions and wasted resources. *Assessment and Evaluation in Higher Education*, 34(2), 209–220. https://doi.org/10.1080/02602930801955978.

Bloxham, S. & Price, M. (2015). External examining: fit for purpose? *Studies in Higher Education*, 40(2), 195–211. https://doi.org/10.1080/03075079.2013.823931.

Bloxham, S., Boyd, P. & Orr, S. (2011). Mark my words: the role of assessment criteria in UK higher execution grading practices. *Studies in Higher Education*, 36(6), 655–670. https://doi.org/10.1080/03075071003777716.

Bloxham, S., Hughes, C. & Adie, L. (2016a). What's the point of moderation? Discussion of the purposes achieved through contemporary moderation practices. *Assessment & Evaluation in Higher Education*, 41(4), 638–653. https://doi.org/10.1080/02602938.2015.1039932.

Bloxham, S., den-Outer, B., Hudson, J. & Price, M. 2016b. Let's stop the pretence of consistent marking: exploring the multiple limitations of assessment criteria. *Assessment & Evaluation in Higher Education*, 41(3), 466–481. https://doi.org/10.1080/02602938.2015.1024607.

Bloxham, S., with Hudson, J., den-Outer, B. & Price, M. (2015). External peer review of assessment: an effective approach to verifying standards? *Higher Education Research and Development*, 34(6), 1069–1082. https://doi.org/10.1080/07294360.2015.1024629.

Boyd, P. & Bloxham, S. (2014). A situative metaphor for teacher learning: the case of university tutors learning to grade student coursework. *British Educational Research Journal*, 40(2), 337–352. https://doi.org/10.1002/berj.3082.

Crimmins, G., Nash, G., Oprescu, F., Alla, K., Brock, G., Hickson-Jamieson, B. & Noakes, C. (2016). Can a systematic assessment moderation process assure the quality and integrity of assessment practice while supporting the professional development of casual academics? *Assessment & Evaluation in Higher Education*, 41(3), 427–441. https://doi.org/10.1080/02602938.2015.1017754.

Grainger, P., Adie, L. & Weir, K. (2016). Quality assurance of assessment and moderation discourses involving sessional staff. *Assessment & Evaluation in Higher Education*, 41(4), 548–559. https://doi.org/10.1080/02602938.2015.1030333.

Hefce (2015). *A Review of External Examining Arrangements across the UK*. Report to the UK higher education funding bodes by the Higher Education Academy. Available at: http://www.hefce.ac.uk/media/HEFCE,2014/Content/Pubs/Independentresearch/2015/Review,of, external,examining,arrangements/2015_externalexam.pdf. Last accessed 30/01/2024.

Jephcote, C., Medland, E. & Lygo-Baker, S. (2021). Grade inflation versus grade improvement: are our students getting more intelligent? *Assessment & Evaluation in Higher Education*, 46(4), 547–571. https://doi.org/10.1080/02602938.2020.1795617.

Mason, J. & Roberts, L.D. (2024). Consensus moderation: the voices of expert academics. *Assessment & Evaluation in Higher Education*, 48(7), 926–937. https://doi.org/10.1080/02602938.2022.2161999.

Mason, J., Roberts, L. & Flavell, H. (2022). A Foucauldian discourse analysis of unit coordinators' experiences of consensus moderation in an Australian university. *Assessment & Evaluation in Higher Education*, 47(8), 1289–1300. https://doi.org/10.1080/02602938.2022.2064970.

Müller-Benedict, V. & Gaens, T. (2020). A new explanation for grade inflation: the long-term development of German university grades. *European Journal of Higher Education*, 10(2), 181–201. https://doi.org/10.1080/21568235.2020.1718516.

O'Connell, B., De Lange, P., Freeman, M., Hancock, P., Abraham, A., Howieson, B. & Watty, K. (2016). Does calibration reduce variability in the assessment of accounting learning outcomes? *Assessment and Evaluation in Higher Education*, 41(3), 331–349. https://doi.org/10.1080/02602938.2015.1008398.

OfS (2022a). *Analysis of Degree Classifications over Time: Changes in graduate attainment from 2010–11 to 2020–21*. OfS, London. Available at: https://www.officeforstudents.org.uk/publications/analysis-of-degree-classifications-over-time-changes-in-graduate-attainment-from-2010-11-to-2020-21/. Last accessed 30/01/2024.

OfS (2022b). Universities must not allow a 'decade of grade inflation to be baked into the system'. Available at: https://www.officeforstudents.org.uk/news-blog-and-events/press-and-media/universities-must-not-allow-a-decade-of-grade-inflation-to-be-baked-into-the-system/. Last accessed 30/01/2024.

Orr, S. & Bloxham, S. (2013). Making judgements about students making work: lecturers' assessment practices in art and design. *Arts and Humanities in Higher Education*, 12(2-3), 234–253. https://doi.org/10.1177/1474022212467605.

Price, M. (2005). Assessment standards: the role of communities of practice and the scholarship of assessment. *Assessment & Evaluation in Higher Education*, 30(3), 215–230. https://doi.org/10.1080/02602930500063793.

QAA (2012). *UK Quality Code for Higher Education*. Available at: https://www.qaa.ac.uk/the-quality-code. Last accessed 30/01/2024.

QAA (2022). *Subject Benchmark Statement: Geography*. Available from: https://www.qaa.ac.uk/the-quality-code/subject-benchmark-statements/geography. Last accessed 30/01/2024.

Richards, K. (2012). Comment on 'External examiners and the continuing inflation of UK undergraduate geography degree results'. *Area*, 44(3), 379–381. https://doi.org/10.1111/j.1475-4762.2012.01090.x.

Rojstaczer, S. (2016). Grade inflation at American colleges and universities. http://www.gradeinflation.com/. Last accessed 30/01/2024.

Sadler, D.R. (2007). Perils in the meticulous specification of goals and assessment criteria. *Assessment in Education: Principles, Policy & Practice*, 14(3), 387–392. https://doi.org/10.1080/09695940701592097.

Sadler, D.R. (2009). Grade integrity and the representation of academic achievement. *Studies in Higher Education*, 34(7), 807–826. https://doi.org/10.1080/03075070802706553.

Sadler, D.R. (2011). Academic freedom, achievement standards and professional identity. *Quality in Higher Education*, 17(1), 103–118. https://doi.org/10.1080/13538322.2011.554639.

Sadler, D.R. (2013). Assuring academic achievement standards: from moderation to calibration. *Assessment in Education: Principles, Policy & Practice*, 20(1), 5–19. https://doi.org/10.1080/0969594X.2012.714742.

Sadler, D.R. (2014). The futility of attempting to codify academic achievement standards. *Higher Education*, 67(3), 273–288. DOI 10.1007/s10734-013-9649-1.

Thornes, J.E. (2012). External examiners and the continuing inflation of UK undergraduate geography degree results. *Area*, 44(2), 178–185. https://doi.org/10.1111/j.1475-4762.2011.01077.x.

Watty, K., Freeman, M., Howieson, B., Hancock, P., O'Connell, B., de Lange, P. and Abraham, A. (2013). Social moderation, assessment and assuring standards for accounting graduates. *Assessment & Evaluation in Higher Education*, 39(4), 461–478. https://doi.org/10.1080/02602938.2013.848336.

Wyse, S., Page, B., Walkington, H. & Hill, J. (2020). Degree outcomes and national calibration: debating academic standards in UK Geography. *Area*, 52(2), 376–385. https://doi.org/10.1111/area.12571.

Chapter 16

Making holistic pairwise judgements
Comparative judgement

Ian Jones

Introduction

Comparative judgement methods run counter to trends towards increasingly detailed and precise assessment criteria by doing away with rubrics entirely. Instead, assessors make holistic pairwise judgements of student work and the resultant decisions are statistically modelled to produce a unique score for each piece of work. The application of comparative judgement methods in higher education contexts is rare bar studies into their use in peer assessment contexts in which students comparatively judge one another's work.

This chapter starts by describing the origins and rationale of comparative judgement, and how it has been applied to the study of education and standards. It discusses the underpinning theoretical assumptions of comparative judgement. Perhaps problematically, the statistical models that underpin comparative judgement methods are derived from techno-rationalist testing theories that assume every student has a stable and true 'value' of educational achievement, if only we could accurately obtain it. Conversely, the holism and reliability of comparative judgement methods means they might be ripe for addressing issues arising from the social constructedness and tacit nature of academic standards. In this sense ideas of techno-rationalism allow us to identify paradoxes related to comparative judgement's lack of rubrics, measurement models and dependence on holistic judgement.

Throughout, the chapter draws on studies that have used comparative judgement methods in higher education, and considers such methods' potential for enhancing professional development in the context of assessment and moderation. To conclude, it outlines how comparative judgement methods might be applied specifically to the study and development of academic standards in higher education.

Comparative judgement

Comparative judgement (CJ) is commonly attributed to the work of the psychologist L.L. Thurstone in the early twentieth century. Thurstone (1927) developed a method for constructing scales based on 'stimuli' such as the perception of the heaviness of a weight, or the neatness of a child's handwriting. His method involved presenting a laboratory subject with a pair of objects (weights, pieces of handwriting) and asking them which of the two had more of a given property (heaviness, neatness). Thurstone found that by collecting numerous such pairwise judgements from a group of subjects he could produce measurement scales that could be reliably replicated by different groups of subjects. He also applied CJ to more subjective phenomena such as social attitudes (Thurstone, 1928).

The principle underpinning Thurstone's method is the law of comparative judgement, which holds that human beings are more consistent when judging one object relative to another than when judging a single object in absolute terms. For example, people tend to agree which object is heavier than the other, but disagree how much a single object weighs. In educational contexts the judges tend be educators, or sometimes their students, and the objects are usually student responses to complex, open-ended assessment tasks (essays, portfolios and so on).

The law of comparative judgement can be theorised in terms of discriminal dispersion (Bramley, 2007). When we hold a weight there will be a 'psychological impact' (Bramley, 2007, p. 249) of heaviness. But on different occasions the same weight will feel heavier or lighter to us. This variation is called discriminal dispersion and it follows a normal distribution. When we hold two weights the discriminal dispersions might overlap. Figure 16.1 shows an example where we would mostly declare B heavier than A, but the overlap means occasionally we will declare A heaviest. In this sense CJ is probabilistic rather than deterministic, a point we shall return to later.

A pairwise decision produces only a single binary data point. It tells us nothing about *how much* heavier B is than A, only that it probably is heavier. Accordingly, many decisions are collected from a group of judges in order to construct a measurement scale. A mathematical model, called the Bradley–Terry model (Bradley & Terry, 1952), is then fitted to the binary decision data to produce a score, along with a standard error, for each object. These scores can be interpreted as estimates of 'quality' according to a specified criterion (heaviness, neatness), and taken together the scores form a linear measurement scale. Typically, two reliability statistics are commonly reported. One is called Scale Separation Reliability (SSR),

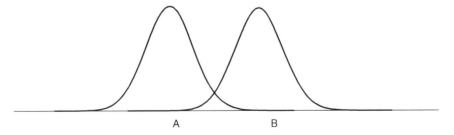

Figure 16.1 An illustration of discriminal dispersion (in this example most often B would be chosen over A).

and reflects the extent to which judges were consistent in their pairwise decisions (Pollitt, 2012). The other statistic is a form of inter-rater reliability, and reflects the extent to which an independent group of judges would have produced the same measurement scale (Bisson et al., 2016).

In Thurstone's day, CJ methods were limited to constructing measurement scales of just a handful of objects in laboratory settings. These days the internet and more tractable mathematical models mean we can construct measurement scales of hundreds or thousands of objects (Wheadon et al., 2020). CJ methods are now accessible to many researchers due to the continuous emergence of research programmes, online platforms, and guidance (see Box 16.1). Contemporary applications of CJ in academic research range from physics (e.g. Jones et al., 2020) to philosophy (e.g. Mejía Ramos et al., 2021), but perhaps the most common field of application is education.

PRACTICAL STRATEGY

Box 16.1 Reflecting upon comparative judgement in your subject area

You might reflect on what type of student work lends itself to being comparatively judged within your own subject specialism. Consider extended writing, portfolios, performance pieces, oral exams and digital artefacts. Think about who would do the judging, an appropriate high-level criterion for making pairwise decisions, and how doing judging might benefit judges' learning. You might select a few samples of student work and try making pairwise decisions yourself to see how it feels, or do so with a colleagues and see what types of discussion it stimulates.

Applications to education and standards

One of the earliest and most widespread applications of CJ to education research has been the evaluation of qualification standards over time (Bramley et al., 1998). For example, Jones et al. (2016) obtained a historic archive of mathematics A-level (a terminal school qualification in parts of the UK) examination scripts ranging from the 1960s to the 2010s. Expert judges (mathematics PhD students) were presented with pairs of scripts via an internet browser and asked to decide, for each pairing, 'which student you think is the better mathematician' (Jones et al., 2016, p. 550). The resultant measurement scale enabled the authors to conclude that standards had declined between the 1960s and 1990s (a grade B in the 1990s was judged as equivalent to a grade E in the 1960s), but they found no evidence of a change in standards between the 1990s and the 2010s. A key methodological point is that judges were asked to compare pairs of student scripts that were based on two different examinations. The construction of measurement scales of unlike objects is a powerful feature that sets CJ apart from rubric-based methods (as discussed in Chapter 13).

Other studies have investigated the potential of CJ for summative assessment as an alternative to rubrics and marking. For example, Jones and Alcock (2014) investigated the potential of CJ to assess undergraduate's conceptual understanding of mathematics. They administered an open-ended task that required students to communicate their understanding of differential calculus using words, formal notation and diagrams. Others have conducted analogous studies in subjects ranging from essay writing (van Daal et al., 2019) to design (Bartholomew et al., 2019). These and other researchers have demonstrated that across subjects, age ranges and countries, CJ offers great promise for validly and reliably assessing complex, open-ended assessment tasks that are resistant to rubric-based approaches. Moreover, moderation and assessor learning are readily harnessed as part CJ-based assessments, and I expand on this later.

Paradoxes of comparative judgement

Some scholars have described debates and practices around standards in higher education as predominantly techno-rationalist (Bloxham & Boyd, 2012). O'Connell et al. (2016, p. 337) define techno-rationalism as the view that 'standards can be made explicit via a criterion-referenced approach, and thereby interpreted in an objective manner'. It has been argued that techno-rationalist assumptions reduce the agency of those involved in education and assessment, and instead privilege 'explicitness and clarity' (Orr, 2007, p. 646) without 'sufficient flexibility for holistic judgement' (see Chapter 13). Some (e.g. Gipps, 1999) contrast techno-rationalism against a sociocultural paradigm, which privileges the agency of lecturers as members of an assessment community. The techno-rational/sociocultural dichotomy brings into view interesting and productive paradoxes about CJ. Here I will focus on three features of CJ: the lack of rubrics; the underpinning measurement model; and holistic judgement.

The lack of rubrics

It could be argued that CJ is not inherently techno-rationalist because there is no ready place for rubrics or detailed criteria. Instead, CJ harnesses the collective judgements of a community of assessors, and therefore a case can be made that CJ is inherently sociocultural. Moreover, each judgement made by an assessor is an act of interpretation, with no right or wrong answer, and there is no pretence of objectivity. CJ means we can avoid what Sadler (2009) identified as assessors' dissatisfaction between holistic judgements and rubric-determined grades. Some educators have told me they have always made internal relative judgements when assessing, and that CJ merely formalises this process. Consistent with this, Bloxham et al. studied the thinking processes underlying marking and reported that higher education tutors explicitly used comparison to help them make their final grading decision. For example, one tutor consistently mentions the poor quality of the second assignment in comparison with the first. At the end, he decided that the mark he had awarded for the first was too low given the grade awarded to the second, and manipulated the marks to create greater differentiation.

(Bloxham et al., 2011, p. 665)

Through formalising and legitimising the holistic judgement that is implicit in much existing assessment practice, CJ methods can return agency to educators and assessors. For example, in the context of moderating primary students' writing, Ofqual (2018, p. 13) reported that in an effort to maximise standardisation across teachers, moderation training was 'delivered according to a script, and attendees were not allowed to ask any questions'. In response, Wheadon et al. (2020) demonstrated how CJ can enable moderation to be hardwired into assessment processes without such straightjacketing of assessors. In a large-scale study, teachers were involved in assessing the writing of over 55,000 primary students in England. Every teacher made pairwise decisions about the (anonymised) writing of students from their own school, and of those from other schools. Wheadon et al. (2020) found that CJ scores were valid and reliable, and that the exercise enabled the direct comparison of students' writing quality across primary schools. In Australia, Heldsinger and Humphry (2013) took an alternative approach, using CJ to identify a set of calibrated exemplars of students' writing, and these exemplars were distributed to teachers for use as comparators against their own students' writing.

Some researchers have argued that educators engaging with pairwise judgements is a form of professional development, helping them to understand what it means for students to understand a topic (van Daal et al., 2019; Fitzgerald et al., 2021). Others have investigated how CJ can support peer assessment, whereby undergraduates make pairwise decisions about one another's work. Across subjects, the evidence shows that peers can produce reasonably reliable and valid CJ scores, and that judging peers' work can be a valuable learning activity (Jones & Alcock, 2014; Bouwer et al., 2018; Bartholomew et al., 2022).

The measurement model

The mathematical model used to convert binary judgement data into student scores (Bradley & Terry, 1952) is perhaps implicitly techno-rationalist because it assumes every student has a 'true' score and any failure to capture that true score is due to measurement error. The concept of true-score-plus-measurement-error is an analogy to the physical sciences, and is not specific to CJ but an assumption underlying any assessment process that quantifies students or their work. Nevertheless, the analogy with measurement in the physical sciences is brought to the fore by CJ, as every student score is accompanied by a standard error that reflects how 'accurately' the 'true' score has been captured (Pollitt, 2012).

Importantly, CJ scores are only meaningful relative to other scores in the same scale. It is meaningless to compare a score from one CJ-based measurement scale with a score from another, independently constructed CJ-based scale. But within a single scale the scores are meaningful in that they are probabilistic: if we know the scores of two objects then we can plug them into the Bradley–Terry model and find the probability that a 'typical' judge would choose one object over the other. In this sense the Bradley–Terry model is all backwards: it assumes we know the scores, and that we want to find out which pairwise decisions the judges are likely to make. In practice we have already collected the pairwise decisions, and we want to know which set of scores would have been likely to produce those decisions.

Here the analogy to measurement in the physical sciences starts to break down. We can now perceive the scores not as static quantities we have discovered, but numerical estimates we have constructed to best match the pattern of holistic judgement decisions we have collected. As such the scores are context-dependent, which explains why it is meaningless to compare scores from independent scales. Contrast this with rubric-based assessments, where grades are assumed or desired to represent the same academic standards across examinations, and even across qualifications. It may be that CJ brings to the fore paradoxes that are inherent to all assessment approaches, and these paradoxes are simply less obvious to us when it comes to marking and rubrics.

Holistic judgement

One criticism of applying CJ to educational assessment is that Thurstone's (1927) theory assumes the stimuli are simple and immediate, such as heaviness. Perhaps this assumption does not hold for relatively lengthy and complex scenarios such as comparing two essays (Bramley, 2007). Moreover, judges are reported to make their decisions remarkably quickly, in a matter of minutes or even seconds (e.g. Jones et al., 2014). In my own standards research, I have also found that some judges claim to internally assign grades and compare those, rather than directly compare students' work (Marshall et al., 2020). Sometimes judges express discomfort when making binary judgements about multifaceted, complex student work (Jones et al., 2014). However, despite such concerns, there is overwhelming evidence that CJ methods produce valid and reliable outcomes across a range of educational contexts and study designs (Jones & Davies, 2023).

This may be another example of CJ bringing relief to those paradoxes that also apply to marking and rubrics. Rubrics fragment student achievement into bite-sized criteria, and then aggregate part marks to produce a final score or grade. Rubrics perhaps, then, can comfort us that a complex, multifaceted process has been applied to a multifaceted, complex object. But both approaches result in a unidimensional quantification of student work, even if CJ's more direct route can feel a little unnerving at first. Nevertheless, the evidence shows that CJ's more direct route avoids the reductionism of rubrics, and more readily produces reliable outcomes.

Conclusion: application to higher education

CJ has been used in higher education for summative and peer assessment purposes, as exemplified above, but not to my knowledge to investigate academic standards. There are proven CJ-based methods for investigating school-level standards, but care will be needed adapting them to university subjects. One challenge will be identifying what to judge. Universities teach much common content but courses and assessments are created in-house. For example, if we want to investigate standards across, say, physics undergraduate programmes at different universities, we might collect pairwise judgements of students' entire degree work (cf. Jones et al., 2016 for the case of A-level qualifications), or only selected work, or administer an additional and specially designed assessment tasks (cf. Wheadon et al., 2020, for the case of primary English). Another challenge will be identifying suitable judges. Relative to teachers, university lecturers' subject knowledge can be closer to that of their students. Accordingly, lecturers' discriminal dispersion (Figure 16.1) for a 'typical' pairing of student work can overlap more, reducing judging consistency. We could recruit further judges to compensate, but this leads to a second, related challenge. Some university modules are highly specialised – such as some final year modules –and there simply might not be many people qualified to make judgements.

PRACTICAL STRATEGY

Box 16.2 Your first comparative judgement assessment

Have a go at CJ, starting with an informal pilot. Gather a few complex, open-ended student artefacts (say, 10 to 20), and try comparatively judging them with one or more friendly colleagues.

There are several online CJ platforms available, and I mostly use nomoremarking.com. It is free to use and has no limits on numbers of student work uploads or judges, although it only supports PDF documents. Other options include a Moodle plug-in I have developed (https://tinyurl.com/3t225bof), which supports a range of media types including video-files, although it was designed with peer assessment rather than standards research in mind.

For practical guidance, Jones & Davies (2023) provides a general overview of using CJ methods for educational research. I have also written nomoremarking-specific guidance for researchers (https://tinyurl.com/NMM4researchers). Keep an eye-out for online and in-person training and events, such as run by the National Centre for Research Methods (www.ncrm.ac.uk/training/show.php?article=12040).

Finally, readers wishing to use CJ are welcome and encouraged to contact myself at l.Jones@lboro.ac.uk. I am very happy to offer informal support and advice.

I suggest that when considering the role of CJ for researching issues around standards in higher education we are informed but not restricted by the methods that have been developed in school-level contexts. CJ is, at heart, a simple idea that enables flexible and creative approaches. For example, CJ could be used to stimulate dialogue between higher education lecturers about standards, with the aim of achieving a more shared understanding, complementing the collaborative construction of rubrics discussed in Chapter 13. This could be achieved through lecturers making and discussing pairwise decisions within supportive and facilitated in-person sessions. There is also scope for including others, such as external examiners and students, in judging and discussions. More generally, the CJ-based approaches I have described, and others I have not, might productively complement and contrast with other methods considered in this volume.

References

Bartholomew, S.R., Mentzer, N., Jones, M., Sherman, D. & Baniya, S. (2022). Learning by evaluating (LbE) through adaptive comparative judgment. *International Journal of Technology and Design Education*, 32, 1191–1205. https://doi.org/10.1007/s10798-020-09639-1.

Bartholomew, S.R., Strimel, G.J. & Yoshikawa, E. (2019). Using adaptive comparative judgment for student formative feedback and learning during a middle school design project. *International Journal of Technology and Design Education*, 29(2), 363–385. https://doi.org/10.1007/s10798-018-9442-7.

Bisson, M.-J., Gilmore, C., Inglis, M. & Jones, I. (2016). Measuring conceptual understanding using comparative judgement. *International Journal of Research in Undergraduate Mathematics Education*, 2(2), 141–164. https://doi.org/10.1007/s40753-016-0024-3.

Bloxham, S. & Boyd, P. (2012). Accountability in grading student work: securing academic standards in a twenty-first century quality assurance context. *British Educational Research Journal*, 38(4), 615–634. https://doi.org/10.1080/01411926.2011.569007.

Bloxham, S., Boyd, P. & Orr, S. (2011). Mark my words: the role of assessment criteria in UK higher education grading practices. *Studies in Higher Education*, 36(6), 655–670. https://doi.org/10.1080/03075071003777716.

Bouwer, R., Lesterhuis, M., Bonne, P. & De Maeyer, S. (2018). Applying criteria to examples or learning by comparison: effects on students' evaluative judgment and performance in writing. *Frontiers in Education*, 3, 86. https://doi.org/10.3389/feduc.2018.00086.

Bradley, R.A. & Terry, M.E. (1952). Rank analysis of incomplete block designs: I. The method of paired comparisons. *Biometrika*, 39(3/4), 324–345. https://doi.org/10.2307/2334029.

Bramley, T. (2007). Paired comparison methods. In P. Newton, J.-A. Baird, H. Goldstein, H. Patrick & P. Tymms (eds), *Techniques for Monitoring the Comparability of Examination Standards*, pp. 264–294. QCA.

Bramley, T., Bell, J. & Pollitt, A. (1998). Assessing changes in standards over time using Thurstone paired comparisons. *Education Research and Perspectives*, 25, 1–24.

Fitzgerald, L., Hunter, J. & Hunter, R. (2021). Shifting teacher practices in relation to grouping: gap gazing or strengths focused approaches. *Mathematics Teacher Education and Development*, 23(3), 97–110.

Gipps, C. (1999). Chapter 10: Socio-cultural aspects of assessment. *Review of Research in Education*, 24(1), 355–392.

Heldsinger, S.A. & Humphry, S.M. (2013). Using calibrated exemplars in the teacher-assessment of writing: an empirical study. *Educational Research*, 55(3), 219–235. https://doi.org/10.1080/00131881.2013.825159.

Jones, I. & Alcock, L. (2014). Peer assessment without assessment criteria. *Studies in Higher Education*, 39(10), 1774–1787. https://doi.org/10.1080/03075079.2013.821974.

Jones, I. & Davies, B. (2023). Comparative judgement in education research. *International Journal of Research & Method in Education*. https://doi.org/10.1080/1743727X.2023.2242273.

Jones, I., Swan, M. & Pollitt, A. (2014). Assessing mathematical problem solving using comparative judgement. *International Journal of Science and Mathematics Education*, 13(1), 151–177. https://doi.org/10.1007/s10763-013-9497-6.

Jones, I., Wheadon, C., Humphries, S. & Inglis, M. (2016). Fifty years of A-level mathematics: have standards changed? *British Educational Research Journal*, 42(4), 543–560. https://doi.org/10.1002/berj.3224.

Jones, S. R., Scott, C.J., Barnard, L.A., Highfield, R., Lintott, C.J. & Baeten, E. (2020). The visual complexity of coronal mass ejections follows the solar cycle. *Space Weather*, 18(10), e2020SW002556. https://doi.org/10.1029/2020SW002556.

Marshall, N., Shaw, K., Hunter, J. & Jones, I. (2020). Assessment by comparative judgement: An application to secondary statistics and English in New Zealand. *New Zealand Journal of Educational Studies*, 55(1), 49–71. https://doi.org/10.1007/s40841-020-00163-3.

Mejía Ramos, J.P., Evans, T., Rittberg, C. & Inglis, M. (2021). Mathematicians' assessments of the explanatory value of proofs. *Axiomathes*, 31(5), 575–599. https://doi.org/10.1007/s10516-021-09545-8.

O'Connell, B., De Lange, P., Freeman, M., Hancock, P., Abraham, A., Howieson, B. & Watty, K. (2016). Does calibration reduce variability in the assessment of accounting learning outcomes? *Assessment & Evaluation in Higher Education*, 41(3), 331–349. https://doi.org/10.1080/02602938.2015.1008398.

Ofqual. (2018). *Key Stage 2 Writing Moderation Observations on the Consistency of Moderator Judgements*. Open Government License, Office of Qualifications and Examinations Regulation Report. https://assets.publishing.service.gov.uk/media/5abcc726ed915d44eb7e68b9/New_KS2_writing_moderation_research_-_FINAL.pdf (accessed December 2023).

Orr, S. (2007). Assessment moderation: constructing the marks and constructing the students. *Assessment & Evaluation in Higher Education*, 32(6), 645–656. https://doi.org/10.1080/02602930601117068.

Pollitt, A. (2012). The method of adaptive comparative judgement. *Assessment in Education: Principles, Policy & Practice*, 19(3), 281–300. https://doi.org/10.1080/0969594X.2012.665354.

Sadler, D.R. (2009). Indeterminacy in the use of preset criteria for assessment and grading. *Assessment & Evaluation in Higher Education*, 34(2), 159–179. https://doi.org/10.1080/02602930801956059.

Thurstone, L.L. (1927). A law of comparative judgment. *Psychological Review*, 34, 273–286. https://doi.org/10.1037/h0070288.

Thurstone, L.L. (1928). Attitudes can be measured. *American Journal of Sociology*, 33(4), 529–554.

van Daal, T., Lesterhuis, M., Coertjens, L., Donche, V. & De Maeyer, S. (2019). Validity of comparative judgement to assess academic writing: examining implications of its holistic character and building on a shared consensus. *Assessment in Education: Principles, Policy & Practice*, 26(1), 59–74. https://doi.org/10.1080/0969594X.2016.1253542.

Wheadon, C., Barmby, P., Christodoulou, D. & Henderson, B. (2020). A comparative judgement approach to the large-scale assessment of primary writing in England. *Assessment in Education: Principles, Policy & Practice*, 27(1), 46–64. https://doi.org/10.1080/0969594X.2019.1700212.

Chapter 17

Taking stock and looking ahead

Jennifer Hill, Nicola Reimann and Ian Sadler

The current higher education standards landscape

As has been highlighted from the outset of the book, academic standards are central, complex, ubiquitous and under significant scrutiny within the higher education system globally. The changing landscape, from an elite to a mass system, has raised concern about the quality and standards of higher education as outcomes are seemingly improving in many countries despite a larger and more varied intake of students (Jephcote et al., 2021). This counter-intuitive situation has consequently led to allegations by politicians and journalists of grade 'inflation': the upward shifting of grades without a corresponding increase in learning (Rosovsky & Hartley, 2002) (Chapter 2). It is important, therefore, to ensure, as far as is practical, that grades truly reflect the learning achievement of students in order to assure the credibility and comparability of higher education qualifications (Ajjawi et al., 2021) and the academic standards that underpin them.

Currently, universities operate systems that treat grades as if they are simply numbers, rather than symbolic representations of a range of different judgements. As numbers, grades can be added and combined. Yet if grades are seen as representing assessment judgements, aggregation is nonsensical. For example, adding a mark for a laboratory report to that of an exam obscures their underlying differences. These assessments have evaluated two distinct types of learning achievement. Essentially, grades are much more than numerical codes. They take on meaning depending on their use and how they fit into social and organisational praxis (Chapter 3). In addition, percentage grades, as used in many UK institutions, suggest a level of precision that is not humanly possible for a single criterion, let alone multiple criteria. Moving away from detailed numerical grades to broader pass/fail or pass/merit/distinction judgements, i.e. gradeless marking (Rust, 2011), might allow for more meaningful measurement of academic standards.

Research has also demonstrated distorting effects on standards of university systems that treat all marks the same regardless of the assessment type or the discipline/area of practice (Yorke et al., 2008). Students, for example, tend to score consistently better on coursework tasks compared with examinations, and in more numerate disciplines such as mathematics and engineering compared with the arts and humanities or social sciences (Yorke et al., 2000; Bridges et al., 2002; Simonite, 2003). Programme-focused assessment where knowledge, skills and understanding are assessed more synoptically through capstone work against programme learning outcomes (Hartley & Whitfield, 2011) may also be an important alternative to approaches where achievement in assignments, in modules, in years and finally in the entire programme are simply aggregated.

Additionally, the rules that determine how a final degree outcome is calculated, the specific way in which marks across a programme are aggregated, and whether and in what way certain fail or low grades can be compensated or condoned can vary considerably between institution or country (Stowell, 2004). For instance, given an identical set of assessment results, it has been shown that students at different institutions in the UK can secure different degree classifications due to the nature of the algorithms used (Yorke et al., 2008; Richmond, 2018; Allen, 2020) (see Chapter 2). In short, local and contextual assessment practices inform grade distribution and render it difficult to assure academic standards absolutely over space and time. However, in this book we have not argued in favour of developing standardised algorithms or statistical approaches to standardising degree outcomes. Rather, we have conceived academic standards as being socially constructed, less durable and more representative of tacit and implicit knowledge held by academic communities (Ajjawi et al., 2021) and manifested differently for different assessment tasks, courses and disciplines (Sadler, 2009). This chapter summarises explicitly how the sector, comprised of the subject communities, institutions and individuals within it, might act to maintain and assure academic standards for the diversity of its stakeholders, while foregrounding that standards are socially constructed in use.

The future for standards policy

As Chapter 5 notes, internationally, countries have more easily developed systems for the oversight of quality standards (inputs into and processes to ensure the quality of the educational provision) compared with academic standards (output measures of actual student achievement). We assert that the sector and higher education institutions within it would do well to interrogate their regulatory frameworks and policies to determine their effectiveness in developing shared understanding and monitoring of academic standards. Without national and institutional policies explicitly requiring that academics engage in social moderation and calibration activities, it is difficult for programme teams to make time for them as they will continue to be perceived as additional extras rather than essential for awarding fair and consistent higher education qualifications. Anecdotally, we know that much time is spent on processes that are less effective than social moderation, such as independent second marking (see Chapter 5) or the development of more intricate codifications (see Chapter 13).

One promising way forward is the recent UK sector-level 'Statement of Intent' (UKSCQA, 2019), which affirms the responsibility of institutions for the standards of their awarded degrees based on shared, consistent and comparable practices (Chapter 2). The Statement calls for higher education institutions in the UK to meet specific commitments and explicitly refers to professional development for external examiners and subject-specific calibration. The momentum gained from publication of the 'Statement of Intent' needs to continue across the UK sector and its key principles could well be mirrored across the globe.

Future directions to protect academic standards in practice

What practices then might help the higher education sector protect and assure academic standards? We recommend three developmental activities that are assessor-centred, and sector-owned and led:

1 support the assessment literacy of academic staff;
2 develop social moderation and calibration; and
3 professionalise the external examiner role.

We recommend these activities based on the socio-constructivist understanding of standards that the authors in this book have presented. It is important to acknowledge, however, that alternative methods for protecting academic standards have been proposed in the literature (Jephcote et al., 2021). These methods comprise introducing nationalised assessments (Richmond, 2018), reviewing and standardising the way in which degree outcomes are calculated, leading to national degree marks and grades (Allen, 2020), synthesising norm and criterion-referenced approaches (Lok et al., 2016), and abandoning the degree classification system (first to third class degrees) as used in the UK in favour of a Grade Point Average system as adopted in the USA (Higher Education Academy, 2012). However, if the root of the problem lies in the fact that standards are socially constructed, we suggest that social approaches to solving the problem are likely to be much more effective.

Support the assessment literacy of academic staff

We advocate the need to develop the assessment literacy (Price et al., 2012; Medland, 2015, 2019) of all staff involved in assessment in higher education, regardless of which system or country it exists within. To date, considerations of assessment literacy have tended to focus on enhancement of assessment design and processes and have been less focused on standards. But, in order to effectively enact their roles in the maintenance of standards, academic staff need to understand grading as an act of professional judgement and appreciate the complexities and variables that influence grading decisions. Staff need to articulate and interrogate their own underpinning personal standards frameworks and the way in which these are conceived and enacted in a variety of contexts and communities of practice. They also need to become aware of the evidence concerning the limitations of codifications and understand that there are alternatives to handing out ever more detailed descriptors of standards to their colleagues and students. This could be achieved through development of a 'shared language' of assessment literacy that will empower those involved to question their role in the assessment process (see Chapter 7). Additionally, we agree that assessment literacy is a particular obligation for external examiners (Bloxham & Boyd, 2012; QAA, 2022).

We espouse particular aspects of assessment literacy as defined by Price et al. (2012, p. 10), notably 'an appreciation of the purpose and processes of assessment, which enables one to engage deeply with assessment standards ... [enabling] one to go beyond a grasp of basic principles towards a deeper understanding and engagement.' Academic staff should thus engage in critical enquiry of their assessment practices, collaboratively questioning their understandings of standards and associated practices. The UK Degree Standards Project, through the Professional Development Course for External Examiners (PDC), initiates staff into such developmental activities (see Chapters 9 and 10), and the course is therefore relevant to all academic staff, not just to aspiring or experienced external examiners. In our experience as facilitators, course participants have found the course transformational since it invites critical enquiry, engages them with the research evidence, and challenges taken-for-granted beliefs and ingrained practices.

Develop social moderation and calibration

Our chapters have demonstrated that a common trend in contemporary higher education is the establishment of written codifications at various levels, from national benchmarks and qualification frameworks (see Chapters 2, 4 and 5) to more localised assessment criteria and rubrics (see Chapters 2 and 13), as the typical approach to establishing greater consistency in assessors' judgements. This is the techno-rationalist perspective, where standards are viewed as independent of the individuals who have created them or are their custodians (Bloxham, 2012). However, we have tried to show in this book that we cannot rely on written codification alone to produce consistent judgements of standards, particularly for the complex, open-ended tasks that are frequently encountered in higher education. This is due to the language used in these codifications, which requires personal interpretation and internalisation of meaning (Bloxham & Boyd, 2012; Sadler, 2017; see also Chapter 3). Additionally, the meaning of any written codification is prone to drift over time and across cohorts, assessment tasks and curriculum stages (Stewart et al., 2005). In other words, academic standards cannot be codified using specifiers that are unambiguous and stable over time (Sadler, 2014).

As such, the key to achieving greater success in securing comparability of standards lies in social moderation and calibration. This involves consensus seeking dialogue where assessors share knowledge of standards, discuss exemplars of student work, and draw on relevant external reference points to agree the rationale for their judgements (see Chapters, 2, 3, 8, 13, 14 and 15). Through this process the multiple influences affecting judgements are made explicit, as well as exemplified, and this facilitates the joint negotiation of standards. As Sadler (2017, p. 93) states, standards are 'grasped and communicated not through definitions but by inductive processes based on concrete cases'. We have shown in this book that these processes can be carried out in several different ways.

We advocate, in particular, regular social moderation and calibration activities that centre on face-to-face dialogue about standards, ideally detached from the assessment of student work, and taking place within disciplinary communities of assessment practice in order to acknowledge the specific complexities that disciplines offer the process (see Rust, 2009) (Chapters 14 and 15). Disciplinary calibration will develop a shared understanding of academic standards and of performances that meet those standards, which is owned by academic communities. As Dill & Beerkens (2013, p. 351) note: 'It is after all at the subject level that academic standards are best assured and improved.'

The Degree Standards Project in the UK was implemented in part to pilot methods for calibrating academic standards, particularly within subject-based communities of assessment practice (see Chapter 9). This was predicated on academic standards being set and understood by consensus, adequately externalised, and held as shared knowledge among academics in a discipline, field or profession (Sadler, 2013). In partnership with a number of professional bodies and subject associations, the viability and effectiveness of different models for subject-based calibration were explored (see Chapters 8, 14 and 15). But wider social moderation of academic standards can take place across scales, iterating between teaching teams, departments, and national disciplinary communities (including external examiners) (Chapter 8), offering progressive quality assurance for academic standards, and supporting overall credibility, value and reliability of higher education degrees (Chapter 15).

There are, however, challenges inherent in social moderation and calibration (see Chapters 8, 14 and 15 for detail). In particular, these processes require time and a shift in culture to a) seeing assessment as collaborative and reciprocal, not independent and isolationist, and b) the construction of shared academic standards becoming an integral part of the professional development of an individual (Beutel et al., 2017) (see Chapter 15). A culture will need to be adopted within institutions in which calibration dialogue can be held in a robust and respectful way, collectively taking on board the views of all participants (Chapters 8 and 15). Embedding calibration effectively into institutional assessment processes requires administrators to recognise the value of and allocate workload to academic staff so that they can train for and take part in truly collaborative, developmental and sustainable calibration activities (Bloxham et al., 2016; Mason & Roberts, 2024). At national level, achieving sustainable subject-level calibration requires ongoing support from government, learned societies, and higher education institutions (Wyse et al., 2020).

The sector and its various stakeholders should appreciate that academic standards are best set and understood by consensus, adequately externalised, and held as shared knowledge among academics in a discipline, field or profession (Sadler, 2013). This perspective acknowledges the socially constructed, subjective and emergent nature of standards (Hudson et al., 2016; Stowell et al., 2016; Ajjawi et al., 2021), recognising that they cannot be established independently from the individuals who are using them. Put simply, the fixed and durable notions of academic standards as portrayed in public debate are too simplistic, denying their intrinsically elusive and dynamic nature as they are continuously co-constructed by academic communities through local assessment practices (Bloxham, 2012; Bloxham & Boyd, 2012) (Chapter 3).

Professionalise the external examiner role

In the UK, the external examining system has been held up as the gold standard for the professional self-regulation of academic standards and quality assurance (Watson, 2006; Finch Review, 2011). It is not a system that is restricted to the UK, having equivalency in countries such as Ireland, Denmark, New Zealand, India, Hong Kong and South Africa (Bloxham & Price, 2015). Chapters 5–7 of this book, however, have shown that external examining, while making an important contribution to the maintenance of academic standards, has considerable limitations (see also Coates, 2010; Bloxham & Boyd, 2012; Bloxham & Price, 2015). This is largely because external examiners' assessment literacy varies (Medland, 2015), they can focus too much on the consistency and equivalence of procedures over the academic standards visible in the quality of student work (Bloxham, 2009), their knowledge of sector standards is actually limited (QAA, 2007), and they have usually experienced little opportunity to calibrate their standards within their disciplinary community, thus relying upon their personal standards frameworks (Sadler, 2011). We suggest that these limitations can be overcome, at least partially, by professionalising the external examiner role.

The sector has an obligation to ensure that examiners are sufficiently trained and experienced, alert to the vagaries of professional judgement and conscious of developments in good assessment scholarship and practice (Bloxham & Boyd, 2012). If the external examining system is to function effectively in a diversified sector, and reach its full potential to support national academic standards, it must acknowledge the role of assessment literacy as equally important to disciplinary expertise (Price et al., 2012; Medland, 2015, 2019) (Chapter 7). The UK Degree Standards Project PDC has made a start on advancing assessment literacy and in particular standards literacy, developing capacity within the sector to make it more sustainable (Chapters 9 and 10). The PDC worked to professionalise external examiners via centralised and also devolved training that enabled institutions to offer the course in-house, leading to entry for course completers onto a register of external examiners trained and accredited by AdvanceHE (Chapter 9).

Evaluation of the Degree Standards Project suggests that the external examining role may now be more effectively implemented by its participants (Chapter 12). External examiners who have taken part in the PDC have integrated their enhanced assessment literacy not just within programme teams they have worked with as part of their role, but additionally within their home institutions across varied types of institutions, transforming local environments (Chapters 11 and 12). Equally, through participation in the PDC, significant momentum has been generated within institutions for the development of staff with respect to assessment and feedback literacy, more widely impacting on their regulatory processes and documentation, and more meaningfully building relationships with external examiners (Chapter 11).

There are, however, challenges to sustaining the capacity of individual institutions to deliver the course via their own trained developers (Chapters 11 and 12). It has been shown that a way to overcome this weakness might be for universities who are proximate geographically to work together reciprocally as a consortium that is supported centrally. Maintaining centralised support is a key element to continuation of courses like the PDC and its recommended calibration activities, and so is buy-in from the disciplines and their disciplinary associations. A national organisation that supports and coordinates institutional and disciplinary efforts, like AdvanceHE in the UK, is needed to turn a course and calibration activities into a sustainable sector-wide and sector-led process of professional development. The scale of the task and logistical difficulties makes this a demanding area to address effectively at sector level without further government resource and sustained commitment.

Future research development

Given the corpus of research that highlights the challenge of achieving absolute academic judgement in higher education, there is a continued need to critically examine our claims for assessment standards. As Bloxham states:

> the academy needs a scholarship of professional judgement in academic grading and its quality assurance that has credibility to both the assessors and the assessed; where the expressions of academic standards presented to students accurately reflect the formulations of standards used by lecturers themselves.
> (Bloxham, 2012, p. 190)

Here we propose a research agenda that should provide the underpinning evidence base for developing policies and practice of standards in use. This first area, concerning assessment judgement on the ground, is very much set within the local (micro) context of individuals. There is then research needed at the (meso) sub-disciplinary and/or programme level. Finally, there is a need to consider the external subject or professional (macro) level.

The authors in this book have argued that the sector and its stakeholders should embrace the notion that assessment judgement is ultimately a social process. It informs and is informed by a range of interacting processes involving codifications of standards as referents, internalised tacit standards, interactions between personal standard frameworks and concrete pieces of student work, and discussions among markers, colleagues and wider stakeholders. These processes need further research, but this is also difficult to achieve. Much of what happens during the judgement process takes place in assessors' minds and behind closed doors, and accessing such things has always been a challenge for empirical researchers. The current dogma in higher education is that more detail within and further emphasis on codifications will solve the academic standards problem. Thus, any practices that appear to contravene this dogma may discredit their actors and are well hidden from public view, and therefore also from researchers. When facilitating the PDC we encountered many academics who were relieved to hear about the limitations of codifications and felt their personal or team practices validated. These are the practices that need further research since so little is known about what really happens on the ground when assessment judgements are made and finalised and how academic standards are attended to in practice.

Chapter 8 notes that evidence for calibration, while promising, is still in its infancy. As such, we posit a need for a wider and more nuanced evidence base of approaches to calibration, its effectiveness and its impact on the standards held by individual academics, disciplinary communities and sector standards more broadly. At the meso and macro levels, this includes systematising dialogue among academic communities regarding standards, and developing more collaborative and inductive ways of building explicit statements of standards, for example by developing them collaboratively among staff and students with reference to concrete exemplars of student work. More work is also needed to evidence whether and where calibration is being embedded into institutional and national policies. It is important to build student confidence in the fairness and consistency of standards judgement, particularly given their lack of satisfaction with assessment. Emphasis should be placed on participatory processes that enable the co-construction and internalisation of meaningful criteria, supporting the assessment literacy of academics and students (O'Donovan et al., 2008).

Further research could deepen our understanding of the role of codification (Chapter 13), used alongside other methods of assessing standards, such as comparative judgement (Chapter 16). Comparative judgement methods are widely used to compare standards across school-level qualifications, but their use in higher education is rare. Existing research has demonstrated, across varied subjects and student ages, that comparative judgement offers great potential for validly and reliably assessing complex, open-ended assessment tasks. The holistic nature of comparative judgement methods means they are sensitive to the socially constructed and tacit nature of academic standards. As such, comparative judgement could be used as part of professional development to stimulate dialogue between higher education assessors about one another's standards, to help them understand the role of holistic and relative judgement in their grading of work, and to move towards more shared understanding and practice. There is unharnessed potential for comparative judgement methods to be used to investigate academic standards in higher education.

Conclusion

Aligning the standards in one higher education institution with those in another, and with those expected by relevant subject or professional accrediting bodies, is both a demanding regulatory goal and an ongoing challenge for the higher education sector internationally (Sadler, 2011; Dill & Beerkens, 2013; Jarvis, 2014). Despite the move in many countries to codify standards in written form as a means of communicating and sharing them, we argue that this is not sufficient due to personalised interpretation of their key terms. If variability of academic standards is due to standards being socially constructed in use, then social processes need to be employed in order to address the issue. As such, the development of calibration within disciplines, fields or professions, using collaboratively developed codifications and supported by government/ learned societies, offers the best method to move towards such an end goal for the sector (O'Connell et al., 2016), contextualised within the localised and socially constructed nature of academic standards (Stowell et al., 2016; Ajjawi et al., 2021). This conclusion is very much shaped by our participation in the UK Degree Standards Project. This was designed to help maintain degree standards and their reasonable comparability across UK higher education by enhancing sector-owned processes for the professional development of external examiners and exploring methods of calibration of standards through disciplinary communities.

It seems the most beneficial university education for students, as well as for society, remains academic programmes designed by, and whose relative academic standards are assured through, the collective actions and shared understanding of knowledgeable academic staff working alongside subject/ professional peers. Calibration forms a strong line of defence against internal or external factors that may operate to encourage grade 'inflation'. Carried out across a range of scales, internal and external to institutions, calibration can help to reassure higher education stakeholders internationally that academic standards are assessed with relative comparability across space and over time, providing substantive evidence for the integrity of student attainment, and helping to assure that 'good' achievement outcomes represent improvements in teaching and student learning.

References

Allen, D. (2020). What can be done about degree algorithm variations? WONKHE blog. Available at: https://wonkhe.com/blogs/what-can-be-done-about-degree-algorithm-variations-2/. Accessed 18 January 2024.

Ajjawi, R., Bearman, M. & Boud, D. (2021). Performing standards: a critical perspective on the contemporary use of standards in assessment. *Teaching in Higher Education*, 26 (5), 728–741. https://doi.org/10.1080/13562517.2019.1678579.

Beutel, D., Adie, L. & Lloyd. M. (2017). Assessment moderation in an Australian context: processes, practices, and challenges. *Teaching in Higher Education*, 22(1), 1–14. https://doi.org/10.1080/13562517.2016.1213232.

Bloxham, S. (2009). Marking and moderation in the UK: false assumptions and wasted resources. *Assessment & Evaluation in Higher Education*, 34(2), 209–220. https://doi.org/10.1080/02602930801955978.

Bloxham, S. (2012). 'You can see the quality in front of your eyes': grounding academic standards between rationality and interpretation. *Quality in Higher Education*, 18(2), 185–204. https://doi.org/10.1080/13538322.2012.711071.

Bloxham, S. & Boyd, P. (2012). Accountability in grading student work: securing academic standards in a twenty-first century quality assurance context. *British Educational Research Journal*, 38(4), 615–634. https://doi.org/10.1080/01411926.2011.569007.

Bloxham, S. & Price, M. (2015). External examining: fit for purpose? *Studies in Higher Education*, 40(2), 195–211. https://doi.org/10.1080/03075079.2013.823931.

Bloxham, S., Hughes, C. & Adie, L. (2016). What's the point of moderation? A discussion of the purposes achieved through contemporary moderation practices. *Assessment & Evaluation in Higher Education*, 41(4), 638–653. https://doi.org/10.1080/02602938.2015.1039932.

Bridges, P., Cooper, A., Evanson, P., Haines, C., Jenkins, D., Scurry, D., Woolf, H. & Yorke, M. (2002). Coursework marks high examination marks low: discuss. *Assessment & Evaluation in Higher Education*, 27(1), 35–48. https://doi.org/10.1080/02602930120105045.

Coates, H. (2010). Defining and monitoring academic standards in Australian higher education. *Higher Education Management and Policy*, 22(1), 41–58. https://doi.org/10.1787/17269822.

Dill, D.D. & Beerkens M. (2013). Designing the framework conditions for assuring academic standards: lessons learned about professional, market, and government regulation of academic quality. *Higher Education*, 65(3), 341–357. https://doi.org/10.1007/s10734-012-9548-x.

Finch Review (2011). *Review of External Examining Arrangements in Universities and Colleges in the UK: Final report and recommendations*. Report commissioned by UniversitiesUK and GuildHE.

Hartley, P. & Whitfield, R. (2011). The case for Programme-Focused Assessment. *Educational Developments*, 12(4), 8–12.

Higher Education Academy (HEA). (2012). Grade Point Average Programme Outline. Accessed 21 September 2023. https://www.advance-he.ac.uk/guidance/teaching-and-learning/transforming-assessment/grade-point-average-gpa

Hudson, J., Bloxham, S., den Outer, B. & Price M. (2016). Conceptual acrobatics: talking about assessment standards in the transparency era. *Studies in Higher Education*, 42(7), 1309–1323. https://doi.org/10.1080/03075079.2015.1092130.

Jarvis, D.S.L. (2014). Regulating higher education: quality assurance and neo-liberal managerialism in higher education – A critical introduction. *Policy and Society*, 33(3), 155–166. https://doi.org/10.1016/j.polsoc.2014.09.005.

Jephcote, C., Medland E. & Lygo-Baker, S. (2021). Grade inflation versus grade improvement: are our students getting more intelligent? *Assessment & Evaluation in Higher Education*, 46(4), 547–571. https://doi.org/10.1080/02602938.2020.1795617.

Lok, B., McNaught, C. & Young, K. (2016). Criterion-referenced and norm-referenced assessments: compatibility and complementarity. *Assessment & Evaluation in Higher Education*, 41(3), 450–465. https://doi.org/10.1080/02602938.2015.1022136.

Mason, J. & Roberts, L.D. (2024). Consensus moderation: the voices of expert academics, *Assessment & Evaluation in Higher Education*, 48(7), 926–937. https://doi.org/10.1080/02602938.2022.2161999.

Medland, E. (2015). Examining the assessment literacy of external examiners. *London Review of Education*, 13(3), 21–33. https://doi.org/10.18546/LRE.13.3.04.

Medland, M. (2019). I'm an assessment illiterate': towards a shared discourse of assessment literacy for external examiners. *Assessment & Evaluation in Higher Education*, 44(4), 556–580. https://doi.org/10.1080/02602938.2018.1523363.

O'Connell, B., De Lange, P., Freeman, M., Hancock, P., Abraham, A., Howieson, B. & Watty, K. (2016). Does calibration reduce variability in the assessment of accounting learning outcomes? *Assessment and Evaluation in Higher Education*, 41(3), 331–349. https://doi.org/10.1080/02602938.2015.1008398.

O'Donovan, B., Price, M. & Rust, C. (2008). Developing student understanding of assessment standards: a nested hierarchy of approaches. *Teaching in Higher Education*, 13(2), 205–217. https://doi.org/10.1080/13562510801923344.

Price, M., Rust, C., O'Donovan, B. & K. Handley, K. 2012. *Assessment Literacy: The Foundation for Improving Student Learning*. Oxford: The Oxford Centre for Staff and Learning Development.

QAA (Quality Assurance Agency). (2007). *The Classification of Degree Awards*. Gloucester: Quality Assurance Agency.

QAA (Quality Assurance Agency). (2022). External Examining Principles. Available at: https://www.qaa.ac.uk/the-quality-code/external-examining-principles. Accessed on 18 January 2024.

Richmond, T. (2018). *A Degree of Uncertainty: An Investigation into Grade Inflation in Universities. Reform Report [online]*. Accessed 19 September 2023. https://reform.uk/publications/degree-uncertainty-investigation-grade-inflation-universities/

Rosovsky, H. and Hartley, M. (2002). *Evaluation and the Academy: Are We Doing the Right Thing? Grade Inflation and Letters of Recommendation*. The American Academy of Arts and Sciences. Cambridge, America.

Rust, C. (2009). Assessment standards: a potential role for subject networks. *Journal of Hospitality, Leisure, Sport, and Tourism Education*, 8(1), 124–128.

Rust, C. (2011). The unscholarly use of numbers in our assessment practices: what will make us change? *International Journal for the scholarship of Teaching and Learning*, 5 (1), Article 4. Available at: https://doi.org/10.20429/ijsotl.2011.050104.

Sadler, D.R. (2009). Indeterminacy in the use of preset criteria for assessment and grading. *Assessment & Evaluation in Higher Education*, 34(2), 159–179. https://doi.org/10.1080/02602930801956059.

Sadler, D.R. (2011). Academic freedom, achievement standards and professional identity. *Quality in Higher Education*, 17(1), 103–118. https://doi.org/10.1080/13538322.2011.554639.

Sadler, D.R. (2013). Assuring academic achievement standards: from moderation to calibration. *Assessment in Education: Principles, Policy & Practice*, 20(1), 5–19. https://doi.org/10.1080/0969594X.2012.714742.

Sadler, D.R. (2014). The futility of attempting to codify academic achievement standards. *Higher Education*, 67, 273–288. https://doi.org/10.1007/s10734-013-9649-1.

Sadler, D.R. (2017). Academic achievement standards and quality assurance. *Quality in Higher Education*, 23(2), 81–99. https://doi.org/10.1080/13538322.2017.1356614.

Simonite, V. (2003). The impact of coursework on degree classifications and the performance of individual students. *Assessment & Evaluation in Higher Education*, 28(5), 459–470. https://doi.org/10.1080/02602930301675.

Stewart, N., Brown, G.D.A. & Chater, N. (2005). Absolute identification by relative judgment. *Psychological Review*, 112(4), 881–911. https://doi.org/10.1037/0033-295X.112.4.881.

Stowell, M. (2004). Equity, justice and standards: assessment decision making in higher education. *Assessment & Evaluation in Higher Education*, 29(4), 495–510. https://doi.org/10.1080/02602930310001689055.

Stowell, M., Falahee, M. & Woolf, H. (2016). Academic standards and regulatory frameworks: necessary compromises? *Assessment & Evaluation in Higher Education*, 41(4), 515–531. https://doi.org/10.1080/02602938.2015.1028331.

UKSCQA (UK Standing Committee for Quality Assessment). (2019). *'Degree Classification: Transparency, Reliability and Fairness – A Statement of Intent'*. London: UKSCQA.

Watson, D. (2006). *Who killed what in the quality wars*. Gloucester: Quality Assurance Agency.

Wyse, S., Page, B., Walkington, H. & Hill, J. (2020). Degree outcomes and national calibration: debating academic standards in UK Geography. *Area*, 52(2), 376–385. https://doi.org/10.1111/area.12571.

Yorke, M., Bridges, P. & Woolf, H. (2000). Mark distributions and marking practices in UK higher education; some challenging issues. *Active Learning in Higher Education*, 1(1), 7–27. https://doi.org/10.1177/1469787400001001002.

Yorke, M., Woolf, H., Stowell, M., Allen, R., Haines, C., Redding, M., Scurry, D., Taylor-Russell, G., Turnbull, W. & Walker, L. (2008). Enigmatic variations: Honours degree assessment regulations in the UK. *Higher Education Quarterly*, 62(3), 157–180. https://doi.org/10.1111/j.1468-2273.2008.00389.x.

Index

Page numbers in *italics* denote figures, those in **bold** denote tables.

AAC&U *see* American Association of Colleges and Universities
academic standards: calibration of *see* calibration; codification of *see* codification; current landscape 227–228; defining 25–27, 40; future directions to protect standards in practice 229–233; future for national and institutional policies 228–229; future research development 233–235; and quality standards, distinction between 58, 126; stability of standards 19; standard setting 95; standardisation 40–41, 228, 229
accountability 12, 27, 29, 38, 41, 43, 76, 121; assessment for 3
accounting education 170; Australia 19, 47, 96, 99, 101, 195
accreditation 57, 58, 59, 80, 157, 214
Adie, L. 61, 98, 138, 206
AdvanceHE (AHE) 58, 111, 120, 123, 147, 204, 207, 232, 233; Degree Standards Project *see* Degree Standards Project; Professional Development Course (PDC) for External Examiners *see* Professional Development Course (PDC) for External Examiners; Professional Standards Framework 112; register of external examiners 133, 146, 232
AHELO project *see* Assessment of Higher Education Learning Outcomes
Ajjawi, R. 25, 26, 30, 32–33, 40, 171, 176, 180, 206, 227, 228, 232, 235
Alcock, L. 220, 221
Alderman, G. 204
Alexiadou, N. 43

algorithms, degree 15, 16, 120, 203, 228
Allahar, A. 13
Allen, D. 15, 228, 229
Alves de Oliveira, B.L.C. 42
American Association of Colleges and Universities (AAC&U), VALUE project 19, 41, 48
American Association of State Colleges and Universities 41
Andrade, H. 169, 170, 171
Arambewela, R. 13
ARC Network 148
artefacts, standardised 26–27, 33
Arthur, W. 149
arts and humanities 227–228
assessment 14–15, 38; for accountability 3; for certification 3; consistency *see* consistency; learning oriented 3; nationalised 229; PDC and learning about 157–158; student self-assessment 169, 170, 172, 180; *see also* formative assessment; summative assessment
assessment criteria 13, 14, 26, 27–28, 62, 63, 97, 123, 205, 230; interpretation of 30; overlap/interference 31; within rubrics 172–174, *175*, *176*; selection of 30; weighting of 174
Assessment of Higher Education Learning Outcomes (AHELO) project (OECD) 42–43, 46
assessment literacy 5, 7, 60, 61, 66–67, 80–92, 123–124, 127, 138, 211–212, 229–230; conceptualisations and challenges 82–88; constituent elements of 84, **85**, *89*; definitions of 83; of external examiners 5, 7, 60, 77, 80–92, 84–85,

123–124, 127, 147, 154, 230, 232, 233; shared language of 83–84, 89, 90, 230; students 234
assessment rubrics 5, 14, 19, 25, 26–27, 30, 97, 123, 169–185, 212, 220, 222, 230; and analytic versus holistic judgement 173–174; assessment criteria within 172–174, 175, 176; benefits of using 170–171; challenges of using 171–172; characteristics of effective 172–174; creating effective 174–176; dialogic implementation of 169, 176–178, 179, 180, 181, 182; effective use of 178–180; using exemplars when developing 175–176, 179; reasons for using 170; students and co-construction of 171, 179–180
Australia 13, 37, 43–48, 121, 221; accounting education 19, 47, 96, 99, 101, 195; 'Achievement Matters' project 19, 96, 101; calibration of standards 19, 46–47, 48, 96, 99, 100, 101, 195; codification of standards 45; Department of Education, Employment and Workplace Relations 44, 45; external referencing 37, 47–48, 98, 99–100; Graduate Skills Assessment (GSA) 45–46; Group of Eight 47; Higher Education Standards Panel 47; learning standards 38, 44–45, 46–47; Learning and Teaching Academic Standards project 45, 47; quality policy 43–44; Quality Verification System 47; social moderation 98–100; Tertiary Education Quality and Standards Agency (TEQSA) 47, 59; Threshold Learning Outcomes 45; *Transforming Australia's Higher Education System* 44; University Accord policy review 48
Australian Learning and Teaching Council 44, 45
Australian Technology Network 46
Australian Universities Quality Agency (AUQA) 43–44
autonomy, institutional 72, 73, 75, 77, 78, 87, 110, 111, 118, 119, 121
average marks 31; Grade Point Average system 229

Bachan, R. 191, 202
Bagues, M. 202
Baird, A.F. 202
Baird, J.A. 62
Baker, S. 2
Baldwin, P. 43
Ball, S.J. 37
Bamberger, A. 38
Barad, K. 178
Barnett, R. 13
Bartholomew, S.R. 220, 221
BASES (British Association for Sport and Exercise Sciences) 116, 186, 187, 188, 192; Undergraduate Endorsement Scheme (BUES) 188, *189*
Baume, D. 2
Bearman, M. 25, 26, 30, 32–33, 171, 176, 180
Beck, M. 58
Bedford, S.B. 47
Bedggood, R.E. 14
Beerkens, M. 43, 231, 235
Bell, A. 169, 170, 171–172
Bell, L. 2
benchmark statements 39, 143, 158, 188, 205
benchmarks 30, 31, 39, 44, 94, 214, 230
Benjamin, R. 46
Berezvai, Z. 203
Beutel, D. 93, 94, 206, 207
Biesta, G. 11
Biggs, J. 81, 170
Biglan, A. 187
Birks, M. 149
Birrell, B. 13
BIS (Department for Business, Innovation and Skills) 74
Bisson, M.-J. 219
Blanco, G.L. 41
Blignaut, S. 149
blind marking 2, 64
Bloxham, S. 1, 12, 14, 25, 26, 27, 28, 31, 40, 60, 61, 62, 72, 75–76, 80, 81, 82, 83, 85, 86, 88, 93, 94, 117, 128, 138, 147, 156, 169, 171, 173, 176, 199, 204, 206, 207, 220–221, 230, 231, 232, 233
Bologna Process 16
Bolton, P. 11
Bond, C. 11, 13, 15, 27, 29
Boud, D. 3, 169, 172
Bourdieu, P. 29
Bouwer, R. 221
Bovill, C. 83
Boyd, P. 12, 14, 26, 27, 28, 61, 82, 86, 93, 147, 171, 176, 206, 220, 230, 232

Bradley, D. 44
Bradley—Terry mathematical model 218, 221, 222
Bramley, T. 218, 219, 222
Brazil 37, 41–42, 48; ENADE 42, 43; ENC 41–42, 43; Provão 41–42; SINAES 42
Brennan, J. 60
Bridges, P. 228
British Association for Sport and Exercise Sciences *see* BASES
British Psychological Society (BPS) 117
Brookhart, S.M. 169, 170, 173, 179, 180
Brooks, V. 81
Brown, J.S. 32
Brown, R. 18, 118
Bryant, A. 149
Buckley, J. 98, 100, 101
business studies 170
Buswell, J. 100

calibration 5, 6, 7, 18–19, 20, 32, 33, 46–47, 48, 66, 77, 78, 93, 94–106, 110, 128, 132–133, 164, 178, 179, 194–195, 204–205, 206, 229, 230–231, 233, 234, 235; benefits of 96–97; case studies *see* geography; sport and exercise science; challenges of implementation 102–103; and Degree Standards project 16, 110, 116–118, 147, 160, 186, 194; implementation 97–102; initiatives with students 104; subject-based 116, 116–118, 117, 155–156, 160, 186, 192–197, **197–198**, 207–214, 229, 231; workshops 116, 117–118, 192–199, 207–212; *see also* social moderation
Canada 13, 43, 80
Carasso, H. 118
Carless, D. 3, 180
Carnegie, G. 38
Carrick Institute 44
Carson, J.T. 172
certification 1, 3, 11, 113, 115, 127, 154
Chan, C.K.Y. 83
Chan, Z. 169, 170, 180
Charmaz, K. 149
Chartered Association of Business Schools 117
Chen, L.-K. 12
China, enrolment in degree programmes 11
Clare, J. 48
Coates, H. 25, 232

codification of standards/criteria 13, 14–15, 20, 26, 27, 28–29, 33, 39–40, 45, 81, 97, 101, 171, 205, 230, 234, 235
Colina, F.E. 41
Collegiate Learning Assessment (CLA) 40, 43, 46
Colley, H. 75
communities of assessment practice 18, 32, 76, 84, 97, 162, 208, 213, 231
comparability of standards 15, 16, 19, 20, 37–38, 81, 110, 119, 121, 132, 147, 148, 153, 161, 163, 202, 205, 227, 230, 235
comparative judgement 6, 217–225, 234–235; application to higher education 223–224; applications to education and standards 219–220; holistic judgement 222, 234; lack of rubrics 220–221; law of 218; measurement model 221–222; origin and rationale of 217–219; paradoxes of 220–222
competition 2, 11, 12, 37, 38, 44, 110
confidence, assessor 96–97, 113, 161, 206
consensus moderation 61, 67, 94, 206; *see also* social moderation
Conservatoires UK 116
consistency 2, 4–5, 16, 17–18, 20, 25, 62–63, 66, 81, 95, 96, 178, 202, 204–205, 206, 230
consumers, students as 12–13, 20
continuing professional development (CPD) 148; *see also* professional development; Professional Development Course (PDC) for External Examiners
Côté, J. 13
Council of Australian University Leaders in Learning 47
COVID-19 pandemic: and learning loss 11–12; 'no detriment' policies introduced during 202; and PDC for External Examiners 138, 148, 152, 161
Crimmins, G. 61, 95, 96, 97, 98, 101, 103, 206
criteria *see* assessment criteria
criterion referencing 27–28, 30, 101, 173, 206, 220, 229
critical friend role of external examiners 60, 75, 87, 126, 133, 143
Crossouard, B. 12, 28
Cui, V. 2

Cumming, J.J. 19
Cuthbert, M. 80, 82

Davies, B. 222, 223
Dawson, P. 28
Dean, A. 13
Dearing Report (1997) 60
Deeley, S.J. 83
degree algorithms 15, 16, 120, 203, 228
degree outcomes statements 120
degree qualification 1; classification system 1, 2, 19, 20, 120, 202–203; first-class 12, 191, 202, 203; upper second-class 191, 202; value of 20, 21, 231
Degree Standards Project 3, 5, 16, 63, 76, 90, 109–122, 136, 147, 192, 204, 207, 230, 231, 232, 235; and calibration of standards 16, 110, 116–118, 147, 160, 186, 194; changes in higher education policy impacting 118–120, 121; funding 145; purpose of 110, 111; *see also* Professional Development Course (PDC) for External Examiners
Delandshere, G. 29
DeLuca, C. 83
Denmark 60, 80, 232
Dennis, I. 76
Denton, P. 83
descriptors, grade and level 14, 25, 26–27, 170, 172, 175, 179, 188
DEWR Ltd 113, 115, 117, 118, 148
dialogue 3, 32, 57, 84–85, 93, 94, 104, 113, 159, 206, 213, 231, 234; consensus-seeking 3, 95, 116, 179, 180, 230; and rubric design and use 169, 176–178, 179, 180, 181, 182
Dietrich, J. 46
Dill, D.D. 231, 235
disability, students with a 137
discriminal dispersion 218, 223
diversification of student body 11, 20
Donovan, J. 14
Drennan, L. 58
Du, Y. 171
Duguid, P. 32
dumbing down 12, 13

Ecclestone, K. 13, 62
education studies 175–176, **176, 177**
EHEA *see* European Higher Education Area
employability 1, 13

ENADE, Brazil 42, 43
engineering 227
epistemology/epistemic assumptions 27, 29, 32, 206; *see also* knowledge
Eraut, M. 88
Europe: Bologna Process 16; external examiners 60
European Higher Education Area (EHEA) 16; Standards and Guidelines for Quality Assurance 59
European Network for Quality Assurance in Higher Education 59
evaluative judgement 25, 27, 28, 29, 170, 172, 178, 182
Evans, C. 162
exemplars 31–32, 94, 95, 102, 230, 234; and calibration in sport and exercise science 195, 196, **198**; and rubric development 175–176, 179
expectations, students 12–13
explicit articulation of standards/criteria 13, 14–15, 16, 27, 28–29, 30–31, 220
explicit knowledge 26, 176, 206
external examiners 59–61, 63, 65, 204; appointments 60, 74, 82, 109, 110, 121; assessment literacy 5, 7, 60, 77, 80–92, 84–85, 123–124, 127, 147, 154, 230, 232, 233; assumptions underpinning role of 81–82; calibration of standards *see* calibration; confidence 113, 171; critical friend role 60, 75, 87, 126, 133, 143; role as guardian of national standards 126, 142; influence of background and experience 86, 87–88, 128; as maintainers of academic standards 143, 163; opportunities for academics to work as 20; personal standards frameworks 86–87, 88, 89, 157, 232; process checker role 126, 142, 143; professionalisation of *see* professional development/ professionalisation; reports 74, 118, 142–143, 145; reward and recognition for 159; role of 60, 74, 75, 123, 126, 133, 142–143, 145, 156–157; role perceptions 87–88, 89
'External Examining Principles' (QAA) 66, 72, 75, 76–77, 85–86, 121
external examining system 3, 5, 71–79, 80, 81, 89–90, 110, 120, 147; apparent problems with 74–76; 'cottage industry' approach 75, 76, 78; downgrading of 81, 88, 89, 120; as peer review process

71, 73, 74, 76, 77–78; pressure on 74; quality of underlying practice 81–82; recent developments in 76–77; stakeholder commitment to 77; strengths of 72–74; transparency 76, 109
external referencing 37, 47–48, 94, 98, 99–100

fairness 2, 12, 29, 62, 66, 71
feedback 14, 28, 32, 58, 62, 98, 127, 137, 144, 160, 170, 179, 180, 182, 211, 233; literacy 211, 233
fees, student 12, 119
Finch Review 80, 109, 110, 232
first-class degrees 12, 191, 202, 203
Fisher, R. 45
Fitzgerald, L. 221
formative assessment 3, 111, 148, 151, 152, 169, 203
Fraile, J. 171, 180
Framework for Higher Education Qualifications (FHEQ) 187, 188, *189*
Freeth, D. 149
Freire, P. 172

Gaens, T. 202
Gaunt, D. 80
geography 206–207; calibration case study 116, 117, 207–214; 'good' degrees awarded in 203; Subject Benchmark Statement 210, 212
Germany 121
Gibbs, G. 14
Gibbs, P. 13
Gillard, J. 44
Gillis, S. 61
Gipps, C.V. 3, 220
globalisation 11, 37–38
Gosling, D. 61
grade descriptors 14, 25, 26–27, 170, 172, 175, 188, *189*
grade inflation 2, 12, 15, 16, 20, 25, 110, 119, 121, 191, 203, 227, 235
Grade Point Average system 229
grade(s) 38, 227; improvement 2; numerical 31, 227
Graduate Skills Assessment (GSA), Australia 45–46
Grainger, P. 206
Greatbatch, D. 58
Grek, S. 38
Grove, J. 13

GuildHE 19, 60, 72, 74, 75, 159

Hall, J. 13
Hammersley-Fletcher, L. 61
Hancock, P. 99, 101, 102, 103
Handley, K. 27, 28, 31, 97
Hanlon, J. 62, 96, 97
Hannan, A. 60
Hardison, C.M. 40
Hartley, J. 63
Hartley, M. 2, 227
Hartley, P. 228
Hartog, P. 62
Harvey, L. 13, 27, 57, 58
Haslam, S.A. 182
Haupt, G. 149
HEA *see* Higher Education Academy
Hefce *See* Higher Education Funding Council for England
Heldsinger, S.A. 221
HEQC *see* Higher Education Quality Council
Hersh, R.H. 15
HESA (Higher Education Statistics Agency) 12
Higgins, R. 14
Higher Education Academy (HEA) 15, 74, 76, 82, 83, 110, 111, 128, 229; *see also* AdvanceHE
Higher Education Funding Council for England (HEFCE) 13, 16, 60, 86, 110, 119, 123, 147, 203; Revised Operating Model for Quality Assessment 109, 118–119
Higher Education in the Learning Society report 39
Higher Education Quality Council (HEQC) 17–18, 44, 74, 75
Higher Education and Research Act (2017) 119, 121
Higher Education Standards Framework, Australia 47
Higher Education Standards Panel, Australia 47
Higher Education Statistics Agency (HESA) 12
Ho, S. 169, 170
Holland, J. 58
Hospitality, Leisure and Tourism 98
Hounsell, D. 171, 190
House of Commons Innovation, Universities, Science and Skills Committee 17
Hudson, J. 13, 14, 27, 29, 76, 86, 232

Hughes, C. 138
Humphry, S.M. 221
Hursh, D. 40

India 80, 232
input measures 26, 66
Institute of British Geographers (IBG) 116, 204, 207, 210, 211
institutions as source of variability 187, 191
inter-rater reliability 219
internal moderation 61
international students 13
interpretation of standards/criteria 27, 30

Jankowski, N. 41
Jarvis, D.S.L. 89, 147, 235
Jephcote, C. 2, 202, 203, 227, 229
Jessop, T. 190
Jones, I. 219, 220, 221, 222, 223
Jones, R. 43
Jones, S.R. 219
Jonsson, A. 169, 170, 179, 180

Kallo, J. 43
Kandlbinder, P. 97
Kelly, A.P. 59
Kemp, D. 43
Kennedy, A. 162
Key Influential Characteristics (KIC) 192, 196, 199
Kilgour, P. 171
Kim, M.J. 38
Kirkpatrick, D.L. 149, 152, 156, 158
Klenowski, V. 98
Knight, P. 39, 40, 45, 47
Knight, P.T. 182
Knight, S. 104
knowledge: explicit 26, 176, 206; tacit 26, 28, 101, 128, 171, 176, 178, 204, 206; *see also* epistemology
Kohoutek, J. 60
Krause, K-L. 47
Kristensen, B. 60

Lambert, H. 12, 15
law assessments 96, 98, 116
league tables 41, 110, 203
learning loss, and COVID-19 pandemic 11–12
learning outcomes 16, 25, 45, 46, 58, 97, 170, 172
learning standards 38, 44–45, 46–47

Learning and Teaching Academic Standards project, Australia 45
Lewis, H.R. 15
Lewis, S. 38
Li, G. 38
Liao, L. 171
Lillis, T. 178
Lingard, B. 37
Lingard, R.L. 38
Linn, R.L. 94
Liu, G. 41
Lok, B. 229
Luo, J. 83
Lygo-Baker, S. 2

Macfarlane, B. 15
MacKay, J.R.D. 14
Maleckar, B. 190
managerialism 6, 13, 14, 20, 29
Marginson, S. 37
Mark, E. 13
markets 12, 13, 16, 38, 203
marks/marking 27–28, 28, 147, 227–228; aggregation 228; average marks 31; blind marking 2, 64; calibration *see* calibration; consistency *see* consistency; criteria *see* assessment criteria; distributions 62; double 64, 66; fairness 62, 66; mark profiles 31; marking guides 26; marking schemes 13; moderation in advance of 63, 65, 66; reliability 2; 'rogue' marks 62; second marking 62, 63, 66, 204, 228; *see also headings under* grade
Marshall, N. 222
Mason, J. 67, 103, 206, 207, 214, 231
massification of higher education 11, 227
master's degrees 12
mathematics 220, 227
Maxwell, G.S. 19
Mayhew, K. 11
McCubbin, A. 48
McCune, V. 32, 171, 190
McIlroy, D. 83
McKinsey 11–12
McKnight, L. 172
medical education 96
Medland, E. 60, 61, 80, 81, 84, 85, 86, 88–89, 138, 159, 229, 232
Mejía Ramos, J.P. 219
Merrow, J. 15
Mills, J. 149
Miranda, G.J. 42

Index   245

moderation 93–94, 138, 204, 220, 221; approaches to implementation in UK 62–63; consensus 61, 67, 94, 206; external 59–61; internal 61; post-marking/assessment 62–63, 94; staff perceptions of 63–66; *see also* external examiners; external examining system; social moderation
Mok, K.H. 11
Müller-Benedict, V. 202
Münch, R. 38
Murphy, R. 81
Myrhaug, D. 60

National Centre for Research Methods 223
National Committee of Inquiry into Higher Education 39
National Student Survey (NSS) 14
National Union of Students (NUS) 14
nationalised assessments 229
neoliberal ideologies 37–38
Netherlands 60
Neumann, R.S. 28, 190
New Zealand 80, 232
Newstead, S.E. 76
Nicol, D. 104, 172, 180
No Child Left Behind Act (USA, 2002) 40
norm-referencing 28, 65, 206, 229
Northedge, A. 32, 178
Northern Ireland 16, 30, 118, 120, 148
Nuckles, M. 32
numerical grades 31, 227
nursing studies 170
NUS (National Union of Students) 14

objectivity 27, 37–38; illusion of 29, 33
O'Byrne, D. 11, 13, 15, 27, 29
O'Connell, B. 96, 97, 99, 101, 206, 214, 220, 235
O'Connor, K.M. 61
O'Donovan, B. 14, 15, 26, 28, 29, 30, 31, 32, 171, 180, 234
OECD *see* Organisation for Economic Co-operation and Development
Office for Students (OfS) 3, 12, 16, 119, 120, 121, 191, 202, 203
Ofqual 221
O'Hagan, S.R. 2
O'Leary, M. 2
Organisation for Economic Co-operation and Development (OECD) 37, 38, 42–43; Assessment of Higher Education Learning Outcomes (AHELO) project 42–43, 46; Programme for International Student Assessment (PISA) 42–43
Orr, S. 28, 29, 62, 85, 94, 204, 220
Orsmond, P. 61
Ozga, J. 43

pairwise judgements *see* comparative judgement
Panadero, E. 169, 170, 179, 180
participation in higher education 11, 20
Partington, J. 63
PDC *see* Professional Development Course (PDC) for External Examiners
peer review 18, 47–48, 61, 63, 98, 172, 179; calibration 19, 99–100, 103, 116, 147; consensus/social moderation 94, 103; external examiners 71, 73, 74, 76, 77–78; students 104, 180, 218, 221; of teaching 58, 61
Pell, G. 95
Pereira, C.A. 42
personal standards frameworks 1, 86–87, 88, 89, 157, 206, 211, 229, 232, 234
PISA (Programme for International Student Assessment) 42, 43
Pitts, J. 96
Pollitt, A. 219, 221
Poole, B. 61, 62
Popham, W.J. 82, 173
positivism 3
power relations 102–103, 176–178, 182, 206, 207, 213
Price, M. 32, 60, 72, 75–76, 76, 80, 81, 82, 83, 84, 85, 88, 128, 170, 204, 206, 229, 230, 232
process checker role of external examiners 126, 142, 143
Professional Development Course (PDC) for External Examiners 5, 57, 63, 123–135, 230, 232–233, 234; and COVID-19 pandemic 152, 161; delivery modes 112, 113, 133–134, 139–141, 148, 152; design of 123–125; Develop the Developer programme for facilitators 111, 113–116, 119, 137–138, 152; evaluation of *see* Professional Development Course (PDC) for External Examiners, evaluation of; geography academics 207, 210–211; impact on participants' home institutions 159–161; impact on practice of external examining

158–159, 161; institutional case study *see* University of Gloucestershire (UoG); institutional roll-out of 153–155; intended learning outcomes for 124–125; learning outcomes 156–158, *157*; participant feedback 134–135, 139, 140, 141, 143, 149, 153; reasons for effectiveness of 161–163; register of course completers 133, 146, 232; staffing issues 145–146, 155; structure of 125–133; support system 146, 155

Professional Development Course (PDC) for External Examiners, evaluation of 113, 147–165; evaluation methodology 148–151; importance of 148; results and learning gained 152–163; strengths and limitations of evaluation approach 151–152

professional development/professionalisation: external examiners 5, 16, 20, 57, 63, 75, 77, 78, 85, 90, 110, 123, 229, 232–233, *see also* Degree Standards project; Professional Development Course (PDC) for External Examiners; higher education staff 3, 47, 97

Programme for International Student Assessment (PISA) 42, 43

Purvis, A. 61

quality assurance 5, 6, 13–15, 16, 27–28, 43–44, 57–59, 61, 65, 66–67, 89–90, 109, 118, 148, 163, 233

Quality Assurance Agency (QAA) 17, 18, 19, 39, 57–58, 59, 60, 63, 74, 76, 80, 81, 83, 110, 128, 159, 186, 190, 202, 212, 230, 232; benchmark statements 39, 143, 158, 188; degree classification descriptors 120; External Examining Principles 66, 72, 75, 76–77, 85–86, 121

Quality Code *see* UK Quality Code for Higher Education

quality standards 81, 110, 228; and academic standards, distinction between 58, 126

Quality Verification System, Australia 47

Ramsden, P. 18
ranking 38, 41–42
Reddy, Y.M. 169, 170
reference points for academic standards 6, 40, 86, 125, 129, 130, 156, 157, 158, 163, 164, 188, *189*, 204, 206, 210, 212, 230

regulation 12, 13, 20, 119
Reimann, N. 97, 117
relative academic standards 26, 28
reliability 2, 3, 29, 81, 94, 119
Review of Australian Higher Education (Bradley Report) 44
Rhodes, E. 62
Richards, K. 203
Richmond, T. 17, 228, 229
Rinne, I. 2
Rizvi, F. 37
Roberts, L.D. 67, 103, 206, 207, 214, 231
Robson, A. 45
Rojstaczer, S. 202
Rosovsky, H. 2, 227
Royal College of Veterinary Surgeons 116
Royal Geographical Society (RGS) 116, 204, 207, 210, 211
Royal Society of Chemistry 116
rubrics *see* assessment rubrics
Rust, C. 14, 18, 28, 31, 39, 40, 117, 170, 176, 180, 227, 231

Sadler, D.R. 2, 16, 18–19, 25, 26, 27, 28, 29–30, 31, 32, 38, 40, 46, 47, 61, 67, 93, 94–95, 147, 170, 171, 172, 174, 199, 204, 205, 206, 207, 214, 220, 228, 230, 231, 232, 235
Salmi, J. 41–42
Sambell, K. 3
Scale Separation Reliability (SSR) 218–219
Schwartzman, S. 41, 42
Scotland 30, 118, 120
Scott, M. 178
Scottish Funding Council (Sfc) 118–119
second marking 62, 63, 66, 204, 228
Sefcik, L. 47, 94, 95, 97, 102, 103
self-assessment, students 169, 170, 172, 180
SET (student evaluation of teaching) scores 203
shared understanding of standards 32, 33, 47, 61, 63, 75, 78, 85, 95, 205, 213, 228, 231; using rubrics plus dialogue to develop 176–178, 182; *see also* communities of assessment practice
sharp academic standards 26, 28
Shay, S. 28, 29, 93, 147
Silver, H. 60, 74, 75, 81, 129
Simonite, V. 228
SINAES, Brazil 42
Snowdon, D. 30

Snowdon, G. 13
social construction of standards 4–5, 6, 37, 61, 66, 77, 123, 128, 147, 171, 206, 228, 232, 234, 235
social moderation 5, 7, 32, 66, 93, 94–106, 132–133, 144, 147, 155, 160–161, 178, 179, 207, 209, 212, 229, 230–232; benefits of 96–97; challenges of implementation 102–103; exemplar pieces of work for, difficulties in selection and distribution 102; group process, power dynamics and relationships 102–103; implementation of 97–102; initiatives with students 104; *see also* calibration; consensus moderation
socio-constructivist perspective 3, 7, 26, 28, 32, 33, 93, 128, 176, 229
sociocultural view 30, 174, 178, 205–206, 220
sociomaterial framing of standards 26, 33
Spellings Commission 40–41
Spender, J. C. 31
sport and exercise science 144; calibration case study 116, 117, 186, 192–197, **197–198**; disciplinary characteristics in 186–191; institutions as source of variation in 187, 191; people as source of variation in 187; tasks as source of variation in 187, 190–191; tools as source of variation in 187–188
stakeholders: commitment to external examiner system 77; global 38
standardisation 228, 229; of testing of standards, USA 40–41
Stella, A. 44
Stewart, N. 230
Stiggins, R.J. 83
Stowell, M. 27, 147, 228, 232, 235
strategic leadership 182
Strathern, M. 13, 29
student(s): assessment literacy 234; calibre of 12; co–construction of rubrics 171, 179–180; co-construction of standards 234; as consumers 12–13, 20; diversification 11, 20; expectations 12–13; fees 12, 119; international 13; with disabilities 137; numbers 11; peer review 104, 180, 218, 221; satisfaction 14, 137; self-assessment 169, 170, 172, 180; social moderation and calibration initiatives with 104; surveys *see* surveys

subject-based calibration 116, 116–118, 117, 155–156, 160, 186, 192–197, **197–198**, 207–214, 229, 231
subject-based teaching quality assessment 57, 58
summative assessment 3, 39, 43, 132, 151, 169, 204, 220, 223
surveys: National Student Survey (NSS) 14; student evaluation of teaching (SET) scores 203
Svingby, G. 179

tacit knowledge 26, 28, 101, 128, 171, 176, 178, 204, 206
tacit standards 86, 87
Tai, J. 172, 178
Tai, P. 97
Tamkin, P. 149
task validity 101
tasks as source of variability 128, 129–130, 190–191, 198–199
Teaching Excellence and Student Outcomes Framework (TEF) 12, 119, 120
techno-rationalism 26, 27, 28, 33, 217, 220, 221, 230
Terry, M.E. 218, 221, 222
Tertiary Education Quality and Standards Agency (TEQSA), Australia 47, 59
A Test of Leadership Charting the Future of US Higher Education (Spellings Commission) 40
Textor, M. 11
Thomson, K. 61
Thornes, J.E. 203
Thurstone, L.L. 217–218, 222
To, J. 104
tools as source of variability 128, 129–130, 187–188, 198–199
Torrance, H. 171, 172
transparency 29, 37, 170, 171–172; external examining system 76, 109
Trounson, A. 46
Trowler, P.R. 73, 182
true-score-plus-measurement-error 221
trustworthiness of standards 16–18, 25
Tsoukas, H. 13–14
Tuning Educational Structures in Europe 16
Turner, J.C. 182

UK Quality Code for Higher Education 20, 58–59, 65, 72, 109, 120, 121, 126;

Advice and Guidance on External Expertise 112, 142
UK Standing Committee for Quality Assessment (UKSCQA) 19–20, 119; Statement of Intent 119–120, 228–229
United States of America (USA) 37, 43; Collegiate Learning Assessment (CLA) 40, 43, 46; Department of Education 13, 40; Grade Point Average system 229; quality oversight (accreditation) 59, 80; standardised testing of standards 40–41
Universities UK (UUK) 12, 19, 60, 72, 74, 75, 120, 159, 203
University of Gloucestershire (UoG), Professional Development Course (PDC) for External Examiners case study 136–146; impact of PDC for institution 141–145; institutional context 136–137; modes of delivery 139–141; timeline of PDC development 138–139

validity 3, 94
VALUE project (AAC&U) 19, 41, 48
van Daal, T. 220, 221
variability 2, 5, 127–128, 133, 193–195, 211–212, 235; common approaches aiming to reduce **205**; institutions as sources of 187, 191; people as source of 128–129, 133, 187, 198–199; tasks as source of 128, 129–130, 190–191, 198–199; tools as source of 128, 129–130, 187–188, 198–199

verbal descriptions of standards 29–30
Vidovich, L. 43
Vilamovska, A-M. 40
Vincent, D. 83
Voluntary System of Accountability (VSA) 41
Vygotsky, L. 128, 176

Wales 30, 118, 120
Warren Piper, D. 60, 76
Watson, D. 232
Watty, K. 96, 97, 99, 195, 206, 207, 214
'ways of thinking and practising' (WTPs) 190, 199
Wegner, E. 32
Welsman, S. 45
Wenger, E. 182
Wheadon, C. 219, 221, 223
Whitfield, R. 228
Wieczorek, O. 38
Wigglesworth, G. 2
Williams, S. 74
Willis, J. 83
Wilson, G. 47
Wittgenstein, L. 33
Woodhouse, D. 44
Wyse, S. 203, 231

Yiqi, L. 104
Ylonen, A. 187
Yorke, M. 30, 40, 227, 228

Zajda, J. 38
Zhao, H. 171, 176
Zimmerman, B.J. 172

Milton Keynes UK
Ingram Content Group UK Ltd.
UKHW021705041224
451949UK00018B/318